The Role of Transportation in the Supply Chain

J. Kenneth Hazen
and
Clifford F. Lynch

Editor: Cheryl McMains
Cover by Lamar Caldwell

ISBN-13 978-0-9744167-4-8
ISBN-10 0-9744167-4-6

Library of Congress Control Number: 2008932795

Copyright CFL Publishing
5100 Poplar Avenue, Suite 1500
Memphis, TN 38137
www.ctsi-global.com
www.cflynch.com

This book is dedicated to those millions of transportation professionals, past and present, who have made the U.S. transportation system the best in the world.

The Role of Transportation in the Supply Chain

J. Kenneth Hazen
and
Clifford F. Lynch

The Role of Transportation in the Supply Chain

Table of Contents

General Characteristics
    Private Carriers
    For-Hire Carriers
General Industry Overview
Operating Characteristics
    Equipment
    Terminals
    Hub and Spoke
    Air Traffic Control
Cost Structure
    Fuel
    Labor
    Pricing
Current Issues

The Early Years
The Industry Today
Operations
Cost Structure
Competition
Pricing
Service Characteristics
Safety and Environmental Concerns
Trans-Alaska Pipeline System
Mardi Gras Project

The Early Years
The Equipment
The Inland Waterway System
The Significance of the Industry
Characteristics of the Industry
Cost Structure
Competition

Global Intermediaries
    Customs Brokers
    NVOCC
    International Freight Forwarders
    Ship Agent
    Ship Broker
Managing the Process
    Terms of Sale
    Documentation
    Pricing
Foreign Trade Zones
Land Bridges
North American Free Trade Agreement
Inland Ports
Security
The Future

    Sample Contract for Motor Carriage
    Trade Publications
    Trade Associations
    In-house vs. Contract Carrier Costs
    Sample Checklist for Freight Bill Audit and Payment
    Sample Checklist for FBA&P – International Invoices
    Sample Freight Bill Payment Service Agreement

Acknowledgements

As is the case with most books written about the supply chain, we have relied on the writings, ideas, and actions of the thousands of transportation and logistics professionals we have encountered during our years in this industry. To all those who added to our base of knowledge, either knowingly or unknowingly, we express our sincerest appreciation.

To Cheryl McMains whose patience, editing, and word processing skills turned hundreds of handwritten pages and notes into a real book, thank you.

Finally, we would never have completed this task without the assistance and cooperation of AAA Cooper Transportation, Alliance Texas, American Trucking Associations, American Waterways Operators, Rick Blasgen, Janet Bonkowski, Con-way Trucking, Larry Cox, Mike Crum, Pat Daugherty, Reid Dove, Bill Fredrick, Ingram Barge Company, Scott Keller, John Langley, Mitch Macdonald, John Mascaritolo, Memphis-Shelby County Airport Authority, Tom Nightingale, Don Piper, Schneider National, Ted Stank, and Union Pacific Railroad.

To all of you, we are deeply indebted.

Disclaimer

It is not the intent or purpose of this book to summarize all the information that might be available on the subject of transportation. It is such a vast and important topic that millions of pages have been written about all aspects of the industry. Every effort has been made, however, to ensure that what has been included in this book is as accurate as possible.

The reader is urged to seek out other material that might be of particular interest and tailor it to individual needs and curiosities.

In some instances, names of transportation companies, logistics service providers and publications are cited. These citations are intended as examples only and should not be considered recommendations of particular companies, directories, or journals.

The contractual suggestions included are intended only as suggestions and are not to be construed as legal advice. Before entering into any contract for transportation services, competent legal counsel should be sought and the resultant advice followed.

- J. Kenneth Hazen
- Clifford F. Lynch

About the Authors

Ken Hazen is President and CEO of CTSI, a supply chain information firm. He is a graduate of the University of Memphis and has over 25 years of experience in the supply chain industry. CTSI provides services to a variety of firms, including many of the Fortune 500.

Cliff Lynch is Executive Vice President of CTSI and has been in the logistics industry since 1958. A graduate of the University of Tennessee and the University of Chicago, he has a broad range of supply chain experience.

Hazen and Lynch are also co-authors of *The Role of Freight Bill Payment in the Supply Chain Industry.*

The Role of Transportation in the Supply Chain

Introduction: Why a Book on Transportation?

Why not?

Transportation is the most fascinating and the most critical element of the supply chain. What young boy or girl has not fantasized about flying an airplane, sitting at the throttle of a diesel locomotive, driving a powerful 18-wheeler looking down on the rest of the world, or standing on the windswept deck of a huge oceangoing ship?

Transportation is steeped in history and invention. Where would we be today if the ancient Romans had not perfected the design for a wheeled cart, George Stephenson hadn't built the first viable steam powered locomotive in 1814, or the Wright brothers hadn't invented a flying aircraft in 1903? [1]

The early railroads, such as the Union Pacific and the Atchison, Topeka & Santa Fe, were largely responsible for settling the western United States, and today oceangoing ships and jet liners have joined the entire world into one large commercial market.

For the past several years, the sophisticated firms have come to better understand and manage their supply chains. They have recognized that starting with the inbound flow of raw materials and ending with the delivery of goods to the consumer, all the activities in between, along with the associated information flows, make up a comprehensive and interrelated process. While technology, manufacturing innovations, and new storage and handling techniques all contribute to the efficient management of this cradle-to-grave concept, the glue that holds it all together is transportation.

In some circles (even at some colleges and universities) there has been a tendency to concentrate more on such subjects as technology, information flows, and handling techniques. It is important to remember, however, the basic underlying transportation systems without which all the other techniques would be meaningless. They are not theoretical. They are real.

Logistics costs in the United States total $1.4 trillion, 10 percent of the Gross Domestic Product. According to the CSCMP State of Logistics Report, transportation costs account for 60 percent of that expenditure. [2] One should not lose sight of which is the dog and which is the tail in this equation.

The burgeoning global economy has reminded us also of the importance of transportation, and to some practitioners this has been a wakeup call. After years of discussing and writing about globalization, we finally have begun to see significantly more true global transportation. Up until a few years ago, while there were any number of firms that had operations in foreign countries, in many cases their logistics activities were confined to the countries in which they were located and those in close proximity. Today, we routinely move products back and forth throughout the world. To some firms, transportation has become as important internationally as it has been in the United States. This represents a learning opportunity for many supply chain managers who have little or no international experience.

The early 2000's reminded us that transportation management is not always as simple as calling a carrier and having them pick up and deliver a shipment at a reasonable cost. An improved economy, increased carrier costs, driver shortages and carrier capacity constraints all aligned at the same time, making it extremely difficult for many shippers to manage their transportation function effectively. To some, it was a stark reminder of how little they knew about carrier economics and relationships.

2

Finally, as we have moved through the organizational continuum, an increasing number of responsibilities have been added to more traditional logistics positions. We have progressed from the days of the Traffic Manager who had a focused, relatively narrow responsibility to the Supply Chain Manager whose primary experience may be in any number of areas. A large number of them have no transportation background whatsoever.

For the practitioner, it is hoped that this book will help fill a void or be a reminder that transportation has been, is, and always will be a critical link in the supply chain.

For the student, a sound knowledge of transportation and its role in both the supply chain and the economy will be an important foundation upon which to build a supply chain capability and career.

Chapter 1: Transportation and the Supply Chain

Transportation is the link that keeps the supply chain intact.

The Significance of Transportation

As far back as one can remember the basic needs of man have been food, shelter, and the ability to communicate. Only slightly less important, however, has been the need for mobility – the ability to move from place to place. In 3500 BC, carts with wheels were invented, and later developed into the chariots used by the early Romans. [1]

In the U.S. the Indian tribes moved from place to place to follow the buffalo and the weather, using crude "trailers" pulled behind their horses; and in 1841, the first wagon train left Independence, Missouri for California. Forty-seven people made this six-month journey in the famed Conestoga wagons. [2]

Courtesy: Union Pacific Railroad

The railroads have been immortalized in song and folklore and were, to a large extent, responsible for the settlement of the United States. With over 3,000 miles separating the Atlantic and Pacific Oceans and 3.5 million square miles in between, commerce within the country would be impossible, and commerce with the rest of the world unthinkable, without an efficient transportation system.

Transportation affects every man, woman, and child in the country – indeed, the world; but it is so pervasive in our lives that we give it little thought unless something goes wrong.

Transportation and Supply Chain Management

Over the years, the definition of supply chain management has been elusive, and the term has meant different things to different people, depending on their individual organizations, responsibilities, and contexts. It often has been confused with logistics and, sometimes, even transportation management. In an effort to clarify the issue, in 2003, the Council of Supply Chain Management Professionals defined both supply chain and logistics management; and to understand the true role of transportation in the supply chain, it is important to understand these definitions.

According to CSCMP,

> *Supply Chain Management encompasses the planning and management of all activities involved in sourcing and procurement, conversion, and all Logistics Management activities. Importantly, it also includes coordination and collaboration with channel partners, which can be suppliers, intermediaries, third-party service providers, and customers. In essence, Supply Chain Management integrates supply and demand management within and across companies.*

> *Supply Chain Management is an integrating function with primary responsibility for linking major business functions and business processes within and across companies into a cohesive and high-performing business model. It includes all of the Logistics Management activities noted above, as well as manufacturing operations, and it drives coordination of processes and activities with and across marketing, sales, product design, finance and information technology.*

6

While this has become the "official" definition of supply chain management, Handfield and Nichols stated it much more succinctly, suggesting that

> *Supply Chain encompasses all activities associated with the flow and transformation of goods from the raw material stages (extraction) through to the end user, as well as the associated information flows. Material and information flow both up and down the supply chain.*

> *Supply Chain Management (SCM) is the integration of these activities through improved supply chain relationships, to achieve a sustainable, competitive advantage.* [3]

In discussing logistics management, CSCMP stated

> *Logistics Management is that part of Supply Chain Management that plans, implements, and controls the efficient, effective forward and reverse flow and storage of goods, services and related information between the point of origin and the point of consumption in order to meet customers' requirements.*

> *Logistics Management activities typically include inbound and outbound transportation management, fleet management, warehousing, materials handling, order fulfillment, logistics network design, inventory management, supply/demand planning, and management of third-party logistics services providers. To varying degrees, the logistics function also includes sourcing and procurement, production planning and scheduling, packaging and assembly, and customer service. It is involved in all levels of planning and execution – strategic, operational and tactical. Logistics Management is an integrating function, which coordinates and optimizes all logistics activities, as well as integrates logistics activities with other functions including marketing, sales, manufacturing, finance and information technology.*

Supply chain, then, includes most of the functions in the manufacture and distribution of goods; i.e.,

- Purchasing
- Transportation
- Inventory Control and Management
- Materials Handling
- Manufacturing
- Warehousing
- Related Systems and Technology

Figure 1-a shows a typical cereal manufacturer's supply chain stretching from the crops in the fields to the consumer's pantry shelf – sometimes called the "farm-to-pantry" chain.

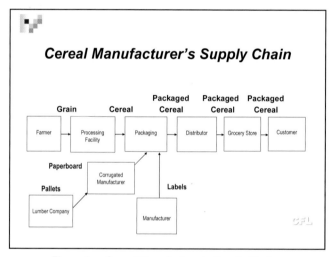

Figure 1-a. Cereal Manufacturer's Supply Chain

Logistics consists of these functions that impact on the movement and storage of goods, along with the related information flows. One can readily see the importance of transportation in this process. Indeed, it is the link that holds the entire supply chain together.

Coyle, Bardi, and Novak define transportation as the "creation of time and place utility." [4] This means that products can be moved to a place where they have a higher value than their origin point at the time when they are needed. Stated another way, transportation is the process of moving people or goods from place to place. In the

8

supply chain context, this would include the movement of raw materials, supplies, and finished products.

Goods and people can be transported in a number of different ways and in subsequent chapters, six modes will be discussed – air, motor carriers, railroads, pipelines, domestic water carriers, and ocean carriers.

Transportation and the Economy

It is important to remember that the demand for transportation is a derived demand. In other words, in order for there to be a demand for transportation, there must be a demand for the products that will be transported. For example, if suddenly, everyone in the country stopped eating oranges, there would be no demand for truck transportation to move oranges out of the state of Florida. If there is no place utility requirement, time utility becomes unnecessary; and there is no need for transportation.

Notwithstanding this possibility, there are strong national and world economies, and transportation plays an important role in them. In the United States, freight costs represent about 6 percent of Gross Distribution Product. In 2007, the total cost of transportation in the country was over $840 billion, or almost 61 percent of the total cost of logistics. See Figure 1-b.

Costs	2006	2007	% Increase
Inventory Carrying	$345	$376	8.9
Warehousing	101	111	9.9
Transportation	801	848	5.8
Administration	58	62	6.8
Total	**$1,305**	**$1,397**	**7.0**

Source: CSCMP State of Logistics, 2008

Figure 1-b. U.S. Logistics Costs (Billions of $)

9

Broken down by mode, transportation expenditures were

- Motor $671 billion
- Rail   58
- Air   41
- Water   38
- Freight Forwarders   30
- Oil Pipelines   10

These amounts are significant, and transportation costs are a major consideration when introducing new products, entering new markets, or designing distribution networks.

For example, the landed cost of a product at a particular destination is directly impacted by transportation costs. Figure 1-c is an example of how transportation costs can shift demands in various markets.

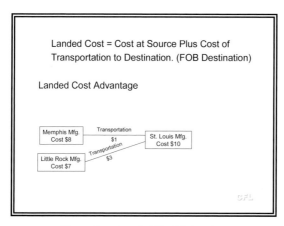

Figure 1-c. Landed Cost Advantage

Suppose a popular DVD can be purchased for $10 in St. Louis, but supplies are short. The same DVD is available in Little Rock for $7, but the cost to get it to St. Louis is $3. There is no price advantage, but if the DVD is available in Little Rock, the St. Louis market would open up for the Little Rock distributor as long as the St. Louis shortage existed.

The same DVD is available in Memphis for $8, but the Memphis distributor has a favorable contract with UPS that enables him to deliver the DVD to St. Louis for $9. He will have the advantage in the St. Louis market, even if the St. Louis distributor has an ample inventory.

The (derived) demand for the UPS transportation from Memphis to St. Louis would continue as long as there was underlying demand for the DVD.

Transportation facilitates lower prices for the consumer by affording a means for various manufacturers to enter a given market. Increased competition can mean lower prices for the consumer; and regardless of where the goods originate, if the landed costs are competitive, a manufacturer can serve an unlimited number of markets.

Transportation also affects land values. If a potential manufacturing or distribution site lies at the junction of two major interstate highways, the value of the land will be considerably more than that of a comparable tract located on a state road in a rural area of Kansas. Depending on the products involved, the same is true for proximity to rail, water, or air transportation. Property close to the FedEx hub in Memphis or the UPS hub in Louisville, for example, is more valuable to a small parcel shipper than similar tracts located on a major railroad.

To over 10.5 million people in the U.S. transportation is particularly important. According to the Bureau of Labor Statistics, this was the total employment in transportation-related industries in 2006. This amounted to 7.7 percent of the non-farm employment in the country.

Possibly the most important impact of all is the geographic equalization that transportation facilitates. Most agricultural products in the country are grown in a specific geographic region. Whether it be citrus from Florida and Texas, artichokes from California, apples from Washington, or grain from the Midwest, our consumption would be boring indeed if it were not for the transportation system that allows agricultural products to move freely and economically to all parts of the country.

The same equalization allows producers of all goods to locate near the source of their raw materials, yet serve markets all over the U.S.

Service Components of Transportation

While cost is to most shippers the most important transportation consideration, the service components can be critical, as well. Under certain circumstances, service can be far more important than the cost of moving the product.

Availability. Obviously, the type service a firm needs must be available to it. Whether a company ships by truck, rail, barge, air, or in an ocean container, it is important to be located where the mode used and the equipment needed are available. It also is important for a shipper to have relationships with the carriers that facilitate this availability, particularly in times of short capacity. During the motor carrier capacity shortage of 2003 – 2004, those shippers who had maintained good relationships with their core carriers fared far better than those who had not.

For some shippers, however, the nature of their products makes it more difficult to obtain reliable and economic service. More advance planning is required to guarantee availability. Take for example, Trinity Industries located in Dallas, Texas. One of their products is a wind tower now being used quite extensively in California, Arizona and other states to generate electricity. These towers are moved by highway in 80-foot sections, requiring extra long, extendable flatbed trailers, escort services, and other precautions.

Transit time, simply stated, is the elapsed time from the pickup of a shipment to its final destination. This can vary from weeks for an ocean carrier to hours for air shipments. Typically, the shorter the transit time, the higher the cost. Air shipments are more expensive than truck, truck is more expensive than rail, etc.

Reliability, or consistency, is an important service component, as well. This is particularly true when transit times are included in inventory models. If a truck shipment from a manufacturing plant in Chicago to a distributor in Los Angeles consistently takes three days, the distributor will provide a three-day supply of stock to compensate for the transit time. If, however, 30 percent of the inbound shipments take four days, he must increase his inventory levels by one day even though he won't need it 70 percent of the time.

Several years ago, inventory managers did not really care (within certain limits, of course) how long transit times were as long as they were consistent. This is no longer true however. With the more recent emphasis on speed and reliability, the preferred transit time will be both short and reliable.

Figure 1-d illustrates the "score" of the various domestic modes in each of these categories.

Characteristic	Air	Motor	Rail	Pipeline	Water
Availability	3	1	2	5	4
Transit Time					
• Speed	1	2	3	5	4
• Reliability	5	2	3	1	4

1 = Best, 5 = Worst

Figure 1-d. Service Characteristics [5]

Conclusion

With the growth in the global economy, transportation has become an even more critical link in the supply chain; and there is every reason to conclude that it will continue to be so. There will be modal shifts, infrastructure problems, personnel shortages, and rising costs; but these issues will be dealt with as they arise, just as they have been in the past. There is no other option. Without transportation, there is no economy.

Questions for Understanding

1. Explain the difference between supply chain and logistics.

2. Transportation has been defined as the "creation of time and place utility." What does this mean?

3. Explain the term "derived demand" and its relationship to transportation.

4. Transportation facilitates geographic equalization. What impact does this have on the consumer?

5. Discuss the service components of transportation and their relationship to supply chain costs.

Chapter 2: Transportation Regulation

> *"That government is best which governs least"*
> - Thomas Paine

The Early Years

It was not always so easy, however. In the early days of transportation development, our first major transportation companies, the railroads, enjoyed a virtual monopoly in most areas of the country in which they operated. At first, they were left to battle it out with the canals, riverboats, and wagons; but it quickly became apparent that the then existing common law would be insufficient to control abuses.

While transportation by its very nature has always leaned in the monopolistic direction, during the development years, it was particularly egregious. Some of the highly abusive tactics of the rail carriers are discussed in more detail in Chapter 3, but suffice it to say here, the common law method of regulation failed. More and more, the rail carriers as they developed westward were, in the opinion of many, out of control.

(While to the modern supply chain manager much of this may be interesting but irrelevant history, an understanding of the developmental and regulated years is important to the understanding of carrier strategies and operations as they exist today.)

Beginning in the 1830's various types of governmental control were attempted, but it was not until the end of the War Between the States that control over monopolies and their abuses was attempted in any meaningful way. [1]

The war brought with it a number of changes. The southern states in most cases were devastated, and the movement of settlers to the West was about to begin. In 1863, President Lincoln signed the Homestead Act, opening up public lands to those brave enough to move west. Many of these settlers were immigrant farmers, and agricultural surpluses quickly developed. [2] Industrialization was gaining headway, inflation was rampant, and business ethics were at an all time low. Significant fortunes were being made by some at the expense of others. [3]

The agricultural issue was particularly significant in that the farmers in the Midwest found themselves at a competitive disadvantage to those new farming areas in the West. Rail rates were high, service was poor, and discrimination was commonplace, making it difficult to compete. The railroads and the grain elevators were controlling the market. As a result, the farmers banded together into the National Grange; and largely through their efforts, in 1871, the state of Illinois set the regulatory stage by establishing the maximum rates that could be charged for storing and transporting agricultural products. Munn and Scott, a Chicago grain storage firm, was found guilty of violating this law, but appealed it.

In 1877, the Supreme Court heard the appeal in the groundbreaking case of *Munn vs. Illinois* (94 U.S. 113, 1877). Speaking for the majority, Justice Waite stated that "state power to regulate extends to private industries that affect the public interest." [4] The decision also affected similar laws regulating railroad rates, and other Grange states quickly passed similar laws.

The national government was keeping a close eye on these developments and was starting to explore the notion of federal regulation. Commissions were appointed to study the question, and in spite of the political power of the railroads and their owners, the idea of federal regulation was gaining support.

Finally in 1886, the straw that broke the state regulatory back was the October, 1886, Supreme Court decision in the case of *Wabash, St. Louis and Pacific Railroad Company v. State of Illinois* (118 U.S. 557). In this case, the same statute that was upheld in *Munn v. Illinois* was attacked again, but this time the Court said

> "Notwithstanding what is there said, this court holds now, and has never consciously held otherwise, that a statute of a state, intended to regulate or to tax or to impose any other restriction upon the transmission of persons or property or telegraphic messages from one state to another, is not within that class of legislation which the states may enact in the absence of legislation by congress; and that such statutes are void, even as to that part of such transmission which may be within the state.

> "It follows that the statute of Illinois, as construed by the supreme court of the state, and as applied to the transaction under consideration, is forbidden by the constitution of the United States, and the judgment of that court is reversed."

Bolstered by this decision, as well as the older 1824 decision in *Gibbons v. Ogden* (22 U.S. 1.1824), on April 5, 1887, the Act to Regulate Commerce, commonly known as the Interstate Commerce Act, was passed. [5] This legislation made the railroads the first industry in the country to be subject to any form of federal regulation. Its purpose was to neutralize the monopolistic power of the rail carriers.

Courtesy: Union Pacific Railroad

The act (Pub. L. No. 49-104, 24 Stat. 379) applied to interstate transportation only, specifically stating that it did not apply to "the transportation of passengers or property, or to the receiving, delivering, storage, or handling of property, wholly within one State, and not shipped to or from a foreign country from or to any State or Territory..."

The act specifically outlawed

1. unjust and unreasonable charges.
2. rebates, drawbacks, or other forms of kickbacks.
3. any unreasonable preference or advantage to any person or firm.
4. refusal to interchange traffic between and among different railroads.
5. higher rates for short hauls than for longer hauls over the same routes, under the same conditions, etc. (This Section 4 of the act is often referred to as the Long and Short Haul Clause.)
6. the pooling of freight charges or earnings among various railroads.

What evolved into the most tedious and, some say, most bureaucratic provision of all, was the requirement that all carriers subject to the act print and publish all rates and charges on all commodities hauled from and to all points served. While this was necessary to ensure equal treatment, the Interstate Commerce Commission in later years had literally trillions of the rates on record (without computers).

Only those published rates could be charged, and ten days notice was required for any changes.

The act went on to outline the redresses for violations, and established a five-person Interstate Commerce Commission to manage the entire process.

The Interstate Commerce Act by no means solved all the problems and had to be strengthened as the industry progressed. Rebates continued to be a problem – so much so that even the railroads sought relief from the pressure of their large customers.

In 1903, the Elkins Act made the receiving of a rebate unlawful, along with departure from the published rates. It made both shippers and carriers liable for violations. [6]

The Hepburn Act of 1906 continued to strengthen regulation in a number of ways, including:

1. Giving the ICC power to prescribe maximum rates.
2. Bringing pipelines, ferries, etc. under ICC jurisdiction.
3. Requiring the adoption of uniform accounting practices for all carriers.
4. Placing the burden of proof in appeals situations on the shipper rather than the ICC.

Finally it increased the size of the Interstate Commerce Commission from five to seven members.

The Mann-Elkins Act of 1910 strengthened the long- and short-haul clause of the original act and provided that the ICC could suspend a proposed rate increase for 120 days while it determined the reasonableness of the proposed charges. [7]

The Panama Canal Act of 1912, the main purpose of which was to authorize the construction of the Panama Canal, also provided that the ICC would have control over rail-owned water operations. The 1887 act had provided for control only over joint rail-water moves. [8]

By now, most were comfortable that the monopolistic power of the rail carriers had been contained, and for several years there was little significant legislation passed.

On April 6, 1917, the United States entered World War I, and the country's railroads quickly proved their inadequacy to serve the war effort. Costs were up, revenues were down, and a number of carriers were in bankruptcy. In order to ensure efficient rail operations during these trying times, President Woodrow Wilson nationalized the majority of the U.S. railroads. [9]

The Transportation Act of 1920 returned the rails to private ownership and authorized extensive financial assistance. It also directed the ICC to develop a plan to consolidate the nation's railroads into a limited number of systems.

One important provision of this act was the often quoted "Rule of Rate Making." In this paragraph, the ICC was instructed to guarantee that in determining reasonableness of a rate, the railroads would earn "a fair return on a fair value."

While this legislation did not meet expectations of many, it did set a tone for more positive control and the ability of carriers to earn a fair return on their investment.

Sampson and Farris summarized this entire monopoly era well, categorizing the regulation as shown in Figure 2-a.

The Arrival of the Motor Carriers

By the mid-1930's, the trucking industry had made some significant technological breakthroughs. Pneumatic tires, hydraulic brakes, and paved highways were commonplace. The Federal Aid Road Act and the Federal Highway Act of 1921 had provided for government investment in roads, and significant construction was underway.

The discussions prior to the regulation of motor carriers were not too unlike those regarding the railroads several years earlier. Nor was the legislation. The Motor Carrier Act of 1935 (49 U.S.C. 31502), which was enacted as Part II of the Interstate Commerce Act, carried forward the anti-monopoly thinking of the original legislation. The act was supported by shippers, truckers, and railroads alike.

One major difference, however, was the classification of carriers. While all railroads were subject to the original Interstate Commerce Act, the Motor Carrier Act recognized that all motor carriers were not "common carriers."

The new law classified carriers into five different groups; i.e.,

1. Common carriers holding themselves out to the general public.
2. Contract carriers which operate under contract for a limited number of shippers.
3. Private carriers that own the products they haul.
4. Brokers who arrange for, but do not provide, transportation.

5. Exempt carriers – free from all but safety, hours-of-service, and equipment standards.

It also provided the following:

1. All new common carriers would require a "certificate of public convenience and necessity." To obtain that certificate it was necessary to prove that the carrier was fit, willing, and able to provide the service and that future public convenience and necessity required its presence in the marketplace. Contract carriers were required to get permits, as well.

    Carriers in existence at the time the law was enacted were "grandfathered" and did not have to obtain new certificates or permits.

2. Rates were required to be just and reasonable, published thirty days in advance, and strictly adhered to. If rates were found to be unlawful, the ICC had the power to prescribe maximum, minimum and/or actual rates.

3. All mergers and consolidations were to be approved by the ICC.

4. The ICC had control over the issuance of securities above a certain amount.

Agricultural commodities were exempt from regulation. Some of the other rail provisions – i.e., long and short hauls, joint rates, etc. – did not apply to the motor carriers due to the more competitive and diversified marketplace. [11]

Most informed supply chain managers believe that regulation made the motor carriers less efficient and shipper costs higher. It was almost impossible to secure new or expanded authority unless there were no objections by other carriers, and there almost always were. Classifications and rates were often ambiguous and many times shippers paid vastly different rates on similar commodities. The rates on cooked poultry were higher than those on uncooked poultry, charges for cornmeal were higher than those for corn, etc.

ELEMENTS OF TRANSPORTATION MONOPOLY CONTROL [10]
RATES AND DISCRIMINATION ELEMENTS

1. All rates must be just and reasonable; all unjust and unreasonable rates are illegal. The ICC has power to determine reasonableness and prescribe maximum and minimum rates.
2. All shippers must be treated equally if they have similar transportation circumstances and conditions (no personal discrimination).
3. All undue preference and prejudice to any person, locality, or type of traffic is illegal (broad discrimination prohibition).
4. A carrier may not charge more for a short haul than for a long haul where the short haul is included in the long haul over the same line and in the same direction. Exceptions allowed by petition.
5. Rates must be published and available to all. No deviation from the published rate is allowed under penalty of law. Rebates and passes illegal (except for certain exceptions relative to passes).
6. The general level of rates for carriers as a group are to be so established as to allow the carrier to earn a fair rate of return on a fair value. Excessive individual carrier earnings are to be recaptured in part and made available as loans to carriers earning less than the determined fair level.
7. Rates may be suspended for a limited time while they are being investigated.
8. A carrier may not carry its own products in competition with other shippers (except lumber).
9. Commodity classification procedures may be controlled by the ICC.
10. Intrastate rates may be raised so as not to discriminate against interstate commerce.

SERVICE ELEMENTS
1. Car service rules must be formulated, filed, and approved by the ICC. The commission may control car movement in emergencies.
2. The ICC may establish through routes and joint rates.
3. The commission may order joint use of terminals.
4. All abandonments and extensions must be approved by the ICC
5. All pooling or combination must be approved by the ICC (after both were illegal per se for some time).
6. Labor disputes must progress through a complicated series of time-consuming administrative procedures in an effort to effect settlement of industrial conflict without work stoppage.

SECURITY AND FINANCIAL ELEMENTS
1. All accounts must be uniform and open for inspection.
2. Periodic and detailed financial reports must be rendered.
3. The ICC may divide revenues from joint rates with the needs of carriers as a standard.
4. All changes in capital structure and the issuance of securities must be approved by the commission.
5. All reorganization and bankruptcy must be approved by the ICC. A special procedure is established to facilitate restoration of the carrier to sound financial health.
6. All consolidations and mergers must fit a master plan and have ICC sanction (after being absolutely illegal for a period of time).

Figure 2-a

Congress and the ICC felt, however, at least at that time, that the "protection" for the public against unfair and unreasonable rates outweighed the perceived disadvantages – a view not necessarily shared by the shipping public.

Air Carriers

In 1938, the Civil Aeronautics Act brought airlines under the same types of controls exerted earlier over the motor carriers. Control of entry, rates and charges, earnings, safety, and other elements were brought under a governing body. [12] Although President Franklin D. Roosevelt had wanted to place airlines under the control of the ICC, in this case better judgment prevailed, and a five-member Civil Aeronautics Board was prescribed by the act.

Water Carriers

Not surprisingly, the railroads, which often competed with the increasing number of barges on U.S. rivers, lobbied long and hard for the regulation of domestic water carriers. Finally, in 1940 they got their wish when the Transportation Act of 1940 was enacted as Part III of the Interstate Commerce Act. This regulation was quite similar to that for the other carriers, although there were a number of exemptions; i.e., bulk liquid, other bulk commodities when not more than three are in a vessel, etc.

Probably the most important section of the Transportation Act of 1940, however, was Congress' attempt to establish a national transportation policy. This stated policy was as follows:

> "It is hereby declared to be the national transportation policy of the Congress to provide for fair and impartial regulation of all modes of transportation subject to the provisions of the act, so administered as to recognize and preserve the inherent advantage of each; to promote safe, adequate, economical and efficient service and foster sound economic conditions in transportation and among the several carriers; to encourage the establishment and maintenance of reasonable charges for transportation services, without unjust discriminations, undue preferences, or advantages, or unfair

or destructive competitive practices; to cooperate with the several States, and the duly authorized officials thereof; and to encourage fair wages and equitable working conditions – all to the end of developing, coordinating, and preserving a national transportation system by water, highway, and rail as well as other means, adequate to meet the needs of the commerce of the United States, of the Postal Service, and of the national defense. All of the provisions of this act shall be administered and enforced with a view to carrying out the above declaration of policy." [13]

The Post-War Years

A number of enhancements were made to the regulatory framework after 1940. Freight forwarders, which will be discussed in Chapter 8, were brought under ICC control through the 1942 Freight Forwarder Act, designated as Part IV of the Interstate Commerce Act. * The by then customary controls were put into place with one unusual feature. A freight forwarder could not control a carrier subject to Parts I, II, or III, although those carriers could control a freight forwarder.

The Reed-Bulwinkle Act of 1948 allowed carriers to establish rate bureaus for the purpose of joint rate making. This legislation specifically exempted them from antitrust regulation. (This practice actually continued until 2007.)

The Transportation Act of 1958 was generally considered to be the last major piece of legislation prior to the trend toward deregulation. There were some exceptions – i.e., the establishment of Amtrak and Conrail – but the 1958 legislation was the last piece of full regulatory refinement.

The act

1. Provided financial aid to railroads.

---

* Freight forwarders can be defined as firms that consolidate the shipments of several shippers, often small-to-medium-sized firms, into larger shipments for which they negotiate lower rates with carriers.

2. Clarified the distinction between private and for-hire carriers.
3. Clarified the motor carrier agricultural exemption.
4. Eliminated "umbrella" rate making. Probably the most significant statement in the entire piece of legislation was, "Rates of a carrier shall not be held up to a particular level to protect the traffic of any other mode."

The Era of Deregulation

There have been proponents of deregulation since long before the day the Interstate Commerce Act was enacted, but they received very little support until the 1960's. More and more transportation

Courtesy: Schneider National

practitioners and experts were becoming convinced that economic regulation had become obsolete and was, in fact, resulting in higher transportation costs and therefore higher prices to the consumer than would have been experienced if the regulatory provisions did not exist. But it was not until April 5, 1962, that any significant attention was given to the subject.

It was on that date that President John F. Kennedy set a tone that would reverberate throughout the offices of shippers and carriers throughout the country. [14] In a special message to Congress on transportation, he called for a new national transportation policy. In this address he made a comment which became the call to arms for deregulation proponents everywhere. After outlining the strengths of the U.S. transportation system, he said:

> "But pressing problems are burdening our national transportation system, jeopardizing the progress and security on which we depend. A chaotic patchwork of inconsistent and often obsolete legislation and regulation has evolved from a history of specific actions addressed to specific problems of specific industries at specific times. This patchwork does not fully reflect either the dramatic changes in technology of the past half-century or the parallel changes in the structure of competition."

25

He then went on to say:

> "For some seventy-five years, common carriage was
> developed by the intention of Congress and the requirements
> of the public as the core of our transport system. This
> pattern of commerce is changing – the common carrier is
> declining in status and stature with the consequent growth of
> the private and exempt carrier. To a large extent this change
> is attributable to the failure of federal policies and regulation
> to adjust to the needs of the shipping and consuming public;
> to a large extent it is attributable to the fact that the burdens
> of regulation are handicapping the certificated common
> carrier in his efforts to meet his unregulated competition.
> Whatever the cause, the common carrier with its obligation to
> serve all shippers – large or small – on certain routes at
> known tariffs and without any discrimination performs an
> essential function that should not be extinguished."

The stage was set once again. In 1975, President Gerald Ford
advocated legislation to reduce trucking regulation and appointed
commissioners to the ICC who were in favor of increased
competition. [15] These commissioners began to speak out in favor
of a more competitive environment – something that had seldom, if
ever, been done by their predecessors.

In 1976, Congress passed the Railroad Revitalization and Regulatory
Reform Act (Pub. L. 94-210, Feb. 5, 1976, 90 Stat. 31), frequently
referred to as the 4R Act. This legislation was enacted primarily as a
response to rail bankruptcies, particularly in the eastern United
States, but in retrospect was probably the first major step toward
deregulation. [16]

In addition to the financial relief provisions, the bill contained several
regulatory reform sections. The most important of these were:

1. Establishment of a "zone of reasonableness." Section 202
    provided that rail rates would not be considered "unjust and
    unreasonable" if they exceeded long-run marginal costs (on
    the low side) and (as to the high side) applied to traffic as to
    which the railroads did not have "market dominance" (a term

related to concepts of monopoly power). The railroads were to be allowed to explore this "zone of reasonableness," with presumptions against suspension or challenge of proposed rates, at a rate of 7% per year. [17]

2. A provision allowing the ICC to exempt from regulation entire categories of traffic if they found regulation was unnecessary.
3. Refinement of the law on mergers and abandonments.
4. Direction to the carriers to revise car service rules (per diem, etc.) *

While President Ford and his newly appointed chairman of the ICC were very sympathetic toward deregulation, it was President Jimmy Carter who became its true champion.

In 1978, the Airline Deregulation Act (Pub. L. 95-504) was signed into law. Supported by President Carter and Alfred Kahn, the Carter-appointed, pro-deregulation chairman of the Civil Aeronautics Board, this legislation, in effect, deregulated the airline industry. Important safety and air traffic control activities remained in the hands of the FAA.

Among the act's many provisions were:

1. Elimination of the CAB's authority to set fares.
2. Liberalization of standards for starting new airlines.
3. Authorization for the offering of domestic service by international carriers.
4. Authorization for the CAB to grant antitrust immunity to carriers.
5. Authorization for airlines to take over routes underutilized by competitors.
6. Dissolution of the CAB and the transfer of the remaining regulatory authority to the Department of Transportation.

While not everyone agreed that the deregulation was a success, air fares did drop dramatically. Some carriers went out of business

---

* These are the rules under which rail carriers interchange equipment among themselves.

when they simply were unable to compete (Braniff, Eastern, and Pan Am, for example) and/or control their costs and labor.

On balance, however, the airline experience encouraged the government to move ahead; and on July 1, 1980, the Motor Carrier Act of 1980 (S. 2245) was signed into law. In signing the bill, President Carter said:

> "The heart of the Motor Carrier Act of 1980 is its call for prompt and sweeping change of the regulations that have insulated the trucking industry from competition since 1935. No longer will trucks travel empty because of rules absurdly limiting the kinds of goods a truck may carry. No longer will trucks be forced to travel hundreds of miles out of their way for no reason or prohibited senselessly from stopping to pick up and deliver goods at points along their routes.

> "The Motor Carrier Act of 1980 will bring the trucking industry into the free enterprise system, where it belongs. It will create a strong presumption in favor of entry by new truckers and expanded service by existing firms. It will build upon progress the Interstate Commerce Commission has begun to make in opening opportunities for minorities, for women, and for all truckers who are eager to provide good service at a competitive price.

> "It will phase out most of the antitrust immunity that has allowed rate bureaus to fix prices. It will eliminate red tape and encourage price competition by allowing trucking companies to price their goods within a zone of reasonableness not subject to ICC review, and it immediately ends antitrust immunity for all rates set through that zone. The premise of the rate-zone provision is that increased competition between truckers will prevent abuses of this pricing freedom. I expect the ICC to implement this legislation effectively and promptly to ensure the vigorous competition needed to make greater pricing freedom work in the interest of shippers and consumers."

While the act did not totally decontrol the motor carriers, it made it a much more open environment. The law provided for:

1. Ease of entry into the business (certificates of public convenience and necessity).
2. Broadening of the list of agricultural commodities that were exempt from regulation.
3. Improvements in service to smaller communities.
4. Phasing out of antitrust immunity that allowed rate bureaus to fix prices.
5. Freedom to assume new routes.

Probably the most important provision of all, however, was the ability to price freely within a "zone of reasonableness." Within that zone of plus or minus 15 percent carriers could increase or decrease rates without interference.

Three months later on October 14, 1980, the Staggers Rail Act (Pub. L. 96-448) was signed into law. It removed many rail regulatory restraints and gave to the rail carriers the same kind of pricing freedom that had been provided to the motor carriers. The new legislation

1. Legalized railroad-shipper contracts.
2. Removed ICC authority over minimum rates as long as they covered variable costs.
3. Removed ICC authority over maximum rail rates unless market dominance existed, the rate was 180 percent of variable cost, or both.
4. Made it easier for carriers to abandon unprofitable routes.
5. Allowed ICC to exempt railroads from all regulation in markets where they had no dominance.
6. Allowed for quarterly general rate increases to offset inflation.

Several other laws were enacted in the 1990's. The Negotiated Rates Act of 1993 provided for settlement of undercharge claims which had been subject to a considerable amount of abuse by agencies trying to collect charges for bankrupt carriers. *

The Trucking Industry Regulatory Reform Act of 1994 eliminated the need for motor carriers to file individual tariffs, and the ICC was given the authority to deregulate certain categories of freight. [18]

In 1995, the ICC Termination Act (Pub. L. 104-88) eliminated the Interstate Commerce Commission and transferred its remaining responsibilities to the newly formed Surface Transportation Board within the U.S. Department of Transportation.

One important provision of this law was the restatement of a National Transportation Policy for the various modes of transportation.

For the nation's railroads the law stated

> "In regulating the railroad industry, it is the policy of the United States Government –

---

* Before deregulation, carriers were required to publish all rates and charge only those rates. This was called the "filed rate doctrine" and was designed to prevent discrimination among shippers. In 1980, when the rules of entry were relaxed, there was an influx of new carriers, and in the competitive frenzy and confusion many times carriers never got around to filing new rates when they were established. The 1980 law did not eliminate this requirement, however; and as the increased competition led to bankruptcy for many carriers, bankruptcy trustees filed claims against shippers for undercharges or the difference between the newer, negotiated (but unpublished) rates and the original published rates. (At one time the Interstate Commerce Commission estimated that the total amount of these claims outstanding was $27 billion.)

Thanks largely to the efforts of the late Bill Augello, a prominent transportation attorney, the 1993 legislation exempted small shippers, eased the burden for large shippers, and succeeded in having the bankruptcy trustees' actions declared "unreasonable practices."

30

"(1) to allow, to the maximum extent possible, competition and the demand for services to establish reasonable rates for transportation by rail;

"(2) to minimize the need for Federal regulatory control over the rail transportation system and to require fair and expeditious regulatory decisions when regulation is required;

"(3) to promote a safe and efficient rail transportation system by allowing rail carriers to earn adequate revenues, as determined by the Board;

"(4) to ensure the development and continuation of a sound rail transportation system with effective competition among rail carriers and with other modes, to meet the needs of the public and the national defense;

"(5) to foster sound economic conditions in transportation and to ensure effective competition and coordination between rail carriers and other modes;

"(6) to maintain reasonable rates where there is an absence of effective competition and where rail rates provide revenues which exceed the amount necessary to maintain the rail system and to attract capital;

"(7) to reduce regulatory barriers to entry into and exit from the industry;

"(8) to operate transportation facilities and equipment without detriment to the public health and safety;

"(9) to encourage honest and efficient management of railroads;

"(10) to require rail carriers, to the maximum extent practicable, to rely on individual rate increases, and to limit the use of increases of general applicability;

"(11) to encourage fair wages and safe and suitable working conditions in the railroad industry;

"(12) to prohibit predatory pricing and practices, to avoid undue concentrations of market power, and to prohibit unlawful discrimination;

"(13) to ensure the availability of accurate cost information in regulatory proceedings, while minimizing the burden on rail carriers of developing and maintaining the capability of providing such information;

"(14) to encourage and promote energy conservation; and

"(15) to provide for the expeditious handling and resolution of all proceedings required or permitted to be brought under this part.

The policy for motor carriers, water carriers, brokers, and freight forwarders was as follows.

"(a) In General. – To ensure the development, coordination, and preservation of a transportation system that meets the transportation needs of the United States, including the United States Postal Service and national defense, it is the policy of the United States Government to oversee the modes of transportation and –

"(1) in overseeing those modes –

"(A) to recognize and preserve the inherent advantage of each mode of transportation;

"(B) to promote safe, adequate, economical, and efficient transportation;

"(C) to encourage sound economic conditions in transportation, including sound economic conditions among carriers;

"(D) to encourage the establishment and maintenance of reasonable rates for transportation, without unreasonable discrimination or unfair or destructive competitive practices;

"(E) to cooperate with each State and the officials of each State on transportation matters; and

"(F) to encourage fair wages and working conditions in the transportation industry;

"(2) in overseeing transportation by motor carrier, to promote competitive and efficient transportation services in order to –

"(A) encourage fair competition and reasonable rates for transportation by motor carriers of property;

"(B) promote efficiency in the motor carrier transportation system and to require fair and expeditious decisions when required;

"(C) meet the needs of shippers, receivers, passengers, and consumers;

"(D) allow a variety of quality and price options to meet changing market demands and the diverse requirements of the shipping and traveling public;

"(E) allow the most productive use of equipment and energy resources;

"(F) enable efficient and well-managed carriers to earn adequate profits, attract capital, and maintain fair wages and working conditions;

"(G) provide and maintain service to small communities and small shippers and intrastate bus services;

"(H) provide and maintain commuter bus operations;

"(I) improve and maintain a sound, safe, and competitive privately owned motor carrier system;

"(J) promote greater participation by minorities in the motor carrier system;

"(K) promote intermodal transportation;

"(3) in overseeing transportation by motor carrier of passengers –

"(A) to cooperate with the States on transportation matters for the purpose of encouraging the States to exercise intrastate regulatory jurisdiction in accordance with the objectives of this part;

"(B) to provide Federal procedures which ensure that intrastate regulation is exercised in accordance with this part; and

"(C) to ensure that Federal reform initiatives enacted by section 31138 and the Bus Regulatory Reform Act of 1982 are not nullified by State regulatory actions; and

"(4) in overseeing transportation by water carrier, to encourage and promote service and price competition in the noncontiguous domestic trade."

Finally, the pipeline policy in the act was:

"(a) In General. – To ensure the development, coordination, and preservation of a transportation system that meets the transportation needs of the United States, including the national defense, it is the policy of the United States Government to oversee of the modes of transportation and in overseeing those modes –

"(1) to recognize and preserve the inherent advantage of each mode of transportation;

"(2) to promote safe, adequate, economical, and efficient transportation;

"(3) to encourage sound economic conditions in transportation, including sound economic conditions among carriers;

"(4) to encourage the establishment and maintenance of reasonable rates for transportation without unreasonable discrimination or unfair or destructive competitive practices;

"(5) to cooperate with each State and the officials of each State on transportation matters; and

"(6) to encourage fair wages and working conditions in the transportation industry.

"(b) Administration To Carry Out Policy. – This part shall be administered and enforced to carry out the policy of this section."

Following the passage of the ICCTA, railroads were regulated solely by the STB. The act also lifted the remaining restrictions on trucking rates with three exceptions: Rates for household-goods moves, rates for certain joint motor-water movements, and rates set collectively by motor carrier bureaus. But in drafting the law, Congress also made provisions for the collective ratemaking issue to be revisited in the future. The law mandated a periodic review of existing motor carrier bureau agreements under a "public interest" standard – a task that would fall to the STB.

Finally, 108 years after the passage of the Interstate Commerce Act, the nation's carriers were to operate in an open, competitive economy (almost).

There was still one major loose thread, and on May 7, 2007, the STB snipped it off. In a ruling many shippers had awaited for over a quarter of a century, the board terminated its approval of the agreements among 11 motor carrier bureaus to collectively determine and set truck rates.

When Congress passed the Reed-Bulwinkle Act in 1948, it allowed motor carrier rate bureaus to set rates collectively and granted them antitrust immunity for doing so. And that's exactly what the carriers did for the next 30-plus years. Rates were set via a two-part procedure: First, the National Classification Committee (one of the 11 bureaus that were a part of this proceeding) established ratings for all products based on their transportation characteristics. Then, the bureaus established the rates. Those rates were what most shippers paid.

When Congress passed the Motor Carrier Act of 1980, it did not lift *all* pricing restrictions. Nor did it rescind antitrust immunity for the collective ratemaking process. The practice was allowed to continue, although after 1980, many carriers chose not to participate.

In the 2007 review, the STB concentrated, as it should have, on whether its continued approval of collective ratemaking agreements would be consistent with the public interest – specifically to fostering such national transportation policy goals as encouraging fair competition (with reasonable rates); allowing a variety of quality and price options to meet changing market demands and the diverse requirements of the shipping public; and maintaining a sound, safe, and competitive privately-owned motor carrier system. After more than two years of deliberation, the STB concluded, among other things, that the current system put certain shippers at a disadvantage in bargaining and that collective rate increases had probably artificially inflated rates. From there, it wasn't much of a stretch to decide that the current arrangements fell short of meeting the national transportation policy's requirements.

Most practitioners agree that the deregulation of transportation was a necessary and overdue step. Rates have reflected market conditions rather than being held at artificial levels, and for the most part, service is better. Shippers and carriers alike are free to be creative and innovative in establishing rate and service parameters. Intermodal carriage, as we know it today, would not have been possible under the regulatory framework.

Many carriers did not survive due to an inability, for whatever reason, to compete in a free marketplace; but the system is no doubt better off without them.

Twenty-five years after the enactment of the Staggers Act, the *Association of American Railroads Insider* newsletter of October 24, 2005, contained the following article.

"October 14, 1980, one of the most successful pieces of transportation legislation ever passed by Congress became law when President Jimmy Carter signed the Staggers Rail Act of 1980. The bill was named for Chairman Harley O. Staggers (D-WV) of the House Energy and Commerce Committee, where the legislation was drafted.

"Before Staggers became law, the nation's rail freight network was at a crossroads. More than 20 percent of the industry had gone into bankruptcy over the previous decade. Earnings averaged less than two percent on investment. Rates were rising faster than inflation.

"Deferred maintenance was mounting as accident rates soared. Market share was in what seemed to be a never-ending downward spiral.

"With the Staggers Act, Congress chose to tackle the root problem: an unresponsive regulatory system that made it virtually impossible for railroads to respond to the disciplines and opportunities of the marketplace. The act was passed and the rail industry has rebounded amazingly:

- Productivity has tripled.
- Intermodal traffic has almost quadrupled.
- Market share has increased.
- Rates have declined by more than half, yet earnings have improved sharply.
- A third of a trillion dollars in private capital has been invested to maintain and improve tracks, signals, communications systems, freight cars and locomotives.

- Accidents are down to two-thirds.
- And rail service is good enough to meet the just-in-time demands of the 21st Century economy.

"U.S. freight railroads move more freight than any other rail system in the world; more, in fact, than all of Europe's railroads combined, and they do it at lower rates as well.

"As a recent study by Clifford Winston of the AEI Brookings Joint Center on Regulatory Studies put it, 'The inefficiencies created by rail regulation put a stranglehold on the industry that prevented it from competing effectively.' He called Staggers 'a rare win-win for consumers and industry.'"

Certainly, in the early years, regulation was necessary to protect the public from abuse, and there are some that, even today, would feel more comfortable under a protected environment. There appears to be little doubt, however, that the deregulation of transportation has had a significant positive impact on carriers, shippers, and consumers.

Figure 2-b is a chronology of important events in the regulatory history of transportation.

Photography by Greg Thorpe
Courtesy: Ingram Barge Company

Date	Event	Major Impact
1824	Gibbons v. Ogden	Empowered Congress to regulate commerce.
1877	Munn v. Illinois	Allowed state regulation of transportation.
1886	Wabash, St. Louis and Pacific Railroad Company v. State of Illinois	Prohibited regulation of interstate commerce by the states.
1887	Act to Regulate Commerce	Regulated railroads. Established ICC.
1903	Elkins Act	Outlawed receipt of rebates.
1906	Hepburn Act	Gave ICC power to set maximum rates. Increased size of ICC.
1910	Mann-Elkins Act	Provided for ICC suspension of rates.
1912	Panama Canal Act	Gave ICC control over rail-owned water operations.
1917	Nationalization of Railroads	Federal government took control of railroads.
1920	Transportation Act	Returned railroads to private ownership. Established Rule of Rate Making.
1935	Motor Carrier Act	Regulated trucking.
1938	Civil Aeronautics Act	Regulated airlines. Established CAB.
1940	Transportation Act	Regulated water carriers. Established National Transportation Policy.
1942	Freight Forwarder Act	Regulated freight forwarders.
1948	Reed-Bulwinkle Act	Antitrust immunity for collective rate making.
1958	Transportation Act	Eliminated umbrella rate making. Provided rail financial aid.
1962	Special Message on Transportation to Congress by John F. Kennedy	Advocated competition in transportation industry.
1976	Railroad Revitalization and Regulatory Reform Act (4R Act)	Established "zone of reasonableness." Granted more rate freedom.
1978	Airline Deregulation Act	Deregulated air transportation.
1980	Motor Carrier Act	Major stride toward deregulation. Increased ease of entry.
1980	Staggers Rail Act	Freedom to negotiate rates and contracts. Ease of abandonment.
1995	ICC Termination Act	Abolished ICC. Established new transportation policy. Established STB.
2007	Surface Transportation Board	Rescinded antitrust immunity for collective rate making.

Table 2-b. Key Dates in Transportation Regulation/Deregulation

Questions for Understanding

1. What were the major influences on passage of the Act to Regulate Commerce in 1887?

2. What restrictions did the Motor Carrier Act of 1935 place on motor carriers?

3. Discuss the impact of the Motor Carrier Act of 1980 on entry into the trucking business.

4. Discuss the pros and cons of the Staggers Rail Act.

5. Should transportation be regulated by the federal government? Why or why not?

Chapter 3: Rail Carriers

Do you hear the whistle down the line?
I figure it's engine number forty-nine.
She's the only one that'll sound that way,
On the Atchison, Topeka, and Santa Fe [1]

Notwithstanding Mark Twain's love affair with the Mississippi River, for the majority of us, the railroads have been the most fascinating mode of transportation. Almost since the first mile of track was laid, they have been memorialized in music, literature, toys, and movies. What young boy has not fantasized about holding the throttle of a powerful steam (or later diesel) locomotive laboring up the eastern slope of the Rockies or speeding through the prairies of Kansas or the buffalo herds in Wyoming?

Thoreau said, "...when I hear the iron horse make the hills echo with a snort like thunder... it seems as if the earth has got a race now worthy to inhabit it." [2]

Photography by Clifford Lynch

The railroads are America, and most historians will agree that if it were not for their development in the 1800's, the development and population dispersion of the entire United States might have been quite different.

History and Development

It all began in England in the late 1700's when the steam engine was invented. In 1753, the first steam engine found its way to the colonies, but it was used to pump water from a mine. [3] While there were several iterations of steam engines over the next 75 years, George Stephenson is generally considered to have invented the first steam locomotive engine for a railroad. This was in 1814 – 1815. While a tramway locomotive had been built several years earlier, it was designed for use on a roadway rather than a track. [4]

On May 24, 1828, the Baltimore & Ohio Railroad opened the first regular service railroad in the country. The 13-mile line ran from Baltimore to Erlicott Mill, Maryland, and was powered by horses until 1830 when its first steam engine, the Tom Thumb, made its initial run. [5] On that day, the chief engineer for the B&O said:

> "Today's experiment must, I think, establish beyond a doubt the practicality of using locomotive steam power on the Baltimore and Ohio Railroad for the conveyance of passengers and goods at such speeds and with such safety as will be perfectly satisfactory to all parties concerned and with such economy as must be highly flattering to the interest of the company." [6]

Several weeks later, in a famous race between the Tom Thumb and a horse-drawn carriage, the locomotive broke a belt and lost the race; but, in spite of that ill-timed mishap, had proven the advantage of steam over horse.

From that point on, railroads developed rapidly, particularly in the East. In the 1830's lines were built that later would become the Pennsylvania Railroad, New York Central System, Boston & Maine, New York, New Haven & Hartford, and others that will be familiar to the railroad buff. [7]

Expansion continued up until the War Between the States when construction was curtailed in the East, and virtually ceased in the West and the South. [8] After the war, construction resumed rapidly, and in 1869, the Central Pacific and the Union Pacific met at

Promontory Point, Utah, becoming the nation's first transcontinental railroad. By the 1880's, extensive trackage had been constructed by carriers such as the Southern Pacific, Texas & Pacific, and the Atchison, Topeka & Santa Fe. By 1900, there were 240,300 miles of track in the country, and construction finally peaked in 1929 when there were 381,400 miles of rail in the U.S. [9]

No discussion of this era of railroading would be complete without mention of the so-called railroad (sometimes referred to as robber) "barons." Many of the personal fortunes in the country were built on the backs of the railroads, and in several cases resulted from stock manipulation, predatory pricing, discrimination, and other unsavory acts. The predatory management style of some of the railroad owners was largely responsible for the regulation discussed in the previous chapter. Cornelius Vanderbilt, the founder of the New York Central System, was the richest man in the country when he died in 1877. [10] That same year Jay Gould and Jim Fisk manipulated gold and Erie Railroad stocks, amassing large fortunes. [11] Not all of the rail builders were crooks, of course, but because of their significant net worth, they were called robber barons by many less fortunate. At the same time, however, they had proven that "rags to riches" was possible. Some of the familiar industrialists who made their fortunes in railroading were Andrew Carnegie, Charles Crocker, Henry Flagler, Jay Gould, Edward H. Harriman, Collis P. Huntington, Mark Hopkins, Leland Stanford, Cornelius Vanderbilt, and James J. Hill. [12]

After 1920, regulation and financial difficulties began to take a toll on the railroads. Mergers and abandonments rather than expansion became the primary business model, and the country began to see a consolidation of the industry. From 381,417 miles of track in 1929, by 2005, the Class I system had decreased to 164,291 miles. See Figure 3a.

Photography by Clifford Lynch

Year	Miles of Track
1830	22
1870	52,900
1910	240,293
1920	252,845
1930	381,417
1960	340,779
1970	319,092
1980	270,623
1990	200,074
2000	168,535
2005	164,291

Source: Association of American Railroads, *Railroad Facts – 2006* and D. Philip Locklin, *Economics of Transportation*

Figure 3-a. Miles of Track Operated by U.S. Class I Railroads

The number of individual railroads declined as well. In 1944 there were 131 Class I carriers. In 2007 there were seven. Railroads are classified according to revenues. See Figure 3b.

Railroad Classification	Revenue Threshold
Class I	> $319.2M
Regional/Class II	$25.2M - $319.2M
Local/Class III	< $25.5M

Note: Based on 2005 dollars; revenue thresholds are adjusted annually for inflation.

Source: Association of American Railroads: Bear, Stearns & Co. Inc.

Figure 3-b. Surface Transportation Board – Railroad Classifications

Courtesy: Union Pacific Railroad

The Class I carriers represent approximately 68 percent of rail mileage, 89 percent of the employees, 93 percent of the revenue, and handle 90 to 95 percent of all rail traffic with the short line and regional carriers hauling the remainder. In 2007 the Class I railroads operating in North America were

	Miles of Track
Burlington Northern Santa Fe	32,000
Canadian National	20,300
Canadian Pacific	14,000
CSX Transportation	21,000
Kansas City Southern	5,800*
Norfolk Southern	21,000
Union Pacific	32,000

* includes 2,600 miles in Mexico

To illustrate the magnitude of the merger and acquisition activity, consider the Union Pacific. The current system is composed of the following carriers (in order of merger): [13]

Union Pacific (original company)
Spokane International
Missouri Pacific
Western Pacific
Missouri Kansas Texas
Chicago & Northwestern
St. Louis Southwestern
Denver & Rio Grande
Southern Pacific

Other Class I carriers show a similar genealogy.

Some industry insiders believe further merger activity is inevitable, possibly resulting in as few as two systems.

Characteristics and Utilization

Equipment

There are nine basic pieces of equipment (rolling stock) utilized by the railroads.

- Locomotives: The power that keeps it all going. Most locomotives today are diesel electric and generate about 3500 horsepower.

- Boxcar – plain: Conventional "box" with floor, sides, and roof with no internal modifications.

- Boxcar – equipped: A "box" with interior equipment (i.e., moveable bulkheads, racks, extendable side walls, etc.) often used for autos, auto parts, some consumer goods.

- Covered hoppers: Closed hopper car with hatches on top, sloping floors, hatches on the bottom for discharge, used for grain, flour, etc.

- Hopper: Similar, but without a top such as a coal car.

- Flat cars: No sides or top. May be used for large equipment, containers, etc.

- Refrigerator cars: An insulated boxcar with a refrigeration unit.

- Gondola: An open, low-sided car, often used for junk and other hard-to-load, bulk commodities.

- Tank car: A tubular shaped tank for chemicals, various types of oils and other liquids.

Total ownership of the various types of equipment is shown in Figure 3-c.

Type	Total All Owners	Class I Railroads	Other Railroads	Car Companies and Shippers *
Box cars:				
Plain box	20,002	1,260	5,543	13,199
Equipped box	113,828	75,342	35,773	2,713
Covered hoppers	382,145	111,797	21,674	248,674
Flat cars	168,131	92,828	21,645	53,658
Refrigerator cars	24,321	18,250	3,635	2,436
Gondolas	200,713	102,371	20,636	77,706
Hoppers	150,131	70,757	10,311	69,063
Tank cars	247,893	723	29	247,141
Others	5,081	1,511	949	2,621
Total	**1,312,245**	**474,839**	**120,195**	**717,211**

Locomotives   22,779

* It is interesting to note that, other than locomotives, the rail carriers own less than half the equipment they utilize.

Source: *AAR Railroad Facts – 2006*

Figure 3-c. Freight Cars in Service 2005

Figure 3-d illustrates the 2006 equipment distribution for one Class I carrier, the BNSF.

Box cars	
Plain	8,937
Equipped	641
Covered Hoppers	33,488
Flat Cars	11,382
Refrigerated Cars	4,631
Gondolas	13,998
Hoppers	11,277
Tank Cars	426
Other	341
Total	**85,121**

Locomotives   6,330

Source: BNSF Annual Report – 2006

Figure 3-d. BNSF Equipment Distribution – 2006

Conventional Operations

Railroads are utilized for any number of products, but the majority of the tonnage hauled today, excluding intermodal, consists of bulk commodities, with coal the largest percentage by far. Figure 3-e shows the distribution of significant commodities hauled in 2005.

Commodity	Tons Originated 000's	% of Total
Coal	804,139	42.4
Chemicals/Allied Products	167,199	8.8
Non-metallic Minerals	145,697	7.7
Farm Products	140,441	7.4
Others Ranging from 1.1% to 6.3%		33.7
Total		**100.0**

Adapted from: *AAR Railroad Facts – 2006 Edition*

Figure 3-e. % of Tonnage by Commodity

Rail carriage is also popular for long hauls. According to the AAR, the average length of haul for the Class I railroads in 2005 was 894 miles.

Rail carriers have large capacity and are able to handle large quantities of products over long distances. While they obviously have competition, often rail is the only reasonable option for shippers. Bulk commodities such as coal, ore, sand, gravel, etc. can move by barge but barge traffic is limited by the paths of the waterways. Pipelines may offer an option for oil and gas but only via somewhat inflexible routes.

Rail competition with motor carriers is for the most part limited to intermodal traffic, but for distances beyond 1,000 miles, they are usually the carrier of choice for other traffic, as well.

One interesting innovation for bulk commodities, particularly coal, has been the unit train. In the regulatory environment which prevailed prior to 1980, carriers were prohibited from publishing rates in quantities larger than a carload. While some exceptions were made for five- and ten-car quantities of grain, it was not until after 1980 that carriers were allowed to further innovate.

Probably the best example of a unit train involves the shipment of coal. Usually under relatively long-term contracts, carriers agree to assign locomotives and hopper cars to a specific movement from the mines to a power plant, for example. These through trains, combined with rapid loading and unloading facilities, have resulted in greatly improved service and reduced costs. After the train is made empty at its destination, it goes directly back to its origin.

Intermodal *

Certainly the most exciting development for the railroads in recent years has been the growth of intermodal traffic. Although the Chicago Great Western Railway put the first trailer on a flat car in 1936, it was not until 1952 that the Canadian Pacific Railway became the first major carrier to introduce the service. [14] Since 1993, however, there has been a significant growth in intermodal traffic, particularly containers. This has resulted primarily from the dramatic increase in imports, primarily from Asia, arriving at U.S. ports in containers, and the diversion of freight from the highways to the rails. In 2007, approximately 50 percent of the rail intermodal shipments involved containers from ocean-going container ships.

Photography by Clifford Lynch

Motor carriers, faced with rising fuel costs and driver shortages as well as improved rail intermodal service, have diverted highway traffic to intermodal service. J. B. Hunt, for example, one of the nation's leading motor carriers, in

---

* Intermodal involves the shipping of freight using multiple modes of transport at the same time. While this definition may describe several different configurations, the most common usage is trailer or container on flat car – TOFC or COFC.

2007 owned more containers than trailers. Figure 3-f illustrates the dramatic growth in intermodal traffic between 1993 and 2005. While the amount of trailer traffic has varied with conditions in the industry, the growth in container movements has been consistent.

Year	Trailers*	Containers*	Total*
1993	3.5	7.2	10.7
1994	3.8	8.1	11.9
1995	3.5	7.9	11.4
1996	3.3	8.1	11.4
1997	3.5	8.7	12.2
1998	3.4	8.8	12.2
1999	3.2	8.9	12.1
2000	2.8	9.2	12.0
2001	2.6	8.9	11.5
2002	2.5	9.3	11.8
2003	2.6	10.0	12.6
2004	2.9	11.0	13.9
2005	3.0	11.7	14.7

* in millions
Adapted from *AAR Railroad Facts – 2006 Edition*

Figure 3-f. Class I Rail Intermodal Traffic 1993 – 2005

If the nation's railroads continue their trends toward improved service, intermodal traffic should continue to be a significant factor in their revenues and growth. Consumer goods manufacturers and distributors that formerly would not think of building a distribution center without a rail siding no longer consider that important. In fact, most that did have interior rail sidings have filled them in to obtain more warehouse storage space. As long as the center has access to motor carrier service and is within a reasonable distance of an intermodal yard, that is all that is necessary.

Intermodal service is provided primarily through *intermodal marketing companies* (IMC) that act as intermediaries between carriers and shippers. These companies, such as Hub Group and Pacer and motor carrier-owned agents of firms like J. B. Hunt and

Schneider, solicit intermodal freight from shippers, then offer it to the carriers in a significant combined volume. Both the shipper and the IMC benefit from the lower rates that are offered for the larger amounts of tonnage. (As an aside, none of these innovative arrangements would have been possible prior to the 1980 elimination of regulation.)

There are several hundred such entities in the country; and they offer a valuable service, particularly to the smaller shipper. The major risk is that they assume no liability. The "contract for carriage" remains between the shipper and the railroad; and if, for example, the IMC does not pay the freight charges previously collected from the shippers, the shippers are still liable to the carriers.

Although not as significant as they were before the entry of the IMC's into the business, another form of discount, high volume shipper is the *Shippers' Association*. These associations are non-profit entities that consolidate the intermodal freight of their member companies and, like the IMC's, offer it to the rail carriers in the larger quantities. Savings accrue to the member companies after administrative costs are deducted.

Rail Infrastructure

Rail carriers have a heavy investment in infrastructure and an ongoing major maintenance expense. Rolling stock, tracks, terminals, yard equipment, cranes, and rights-of-way all require significant capital and maintenance expenditures. According to the BNSF, to lay a mile of track costs between $3 million and $5 million, depending on location. In 2005, 478,401 tons of rail and 14,260,000 crossties were laid by the Class I railroads. [15] In 2006, the BNSF and UP alone laid over 1,800 miles of rail and 7,626,000 crossties.

Locomotives are very expensive, as well. In 2003, the BNSF purchased 281 new locomotives for $270 million, or a whopping $960,854 each. [16] The good news is that they have a relatively long life. The average age of a locomotive in service on the Norfolk Southern system in 2006 was 17.7 years. Freight cars averaged 30 years. [17]

For that year, capital expenditures in total were $6.4 billion, $5.4 billion for roadway and structures, and $1.0 billion for equipment. [18]

The significant right-of-way expenses lend credence to the argument that rail carriers are penalized vis-a-vis motor carriers since the latter operate over government-provided rights-of-way. With the increasing importance of rail transportation in the country, it seems probable that at some point the government must step in and provide some form of financial assistance; i.e., loan guarantees, tax concessions, investment tax credits, or outright grants.

Another major part of the rail infrastructure is the terminal or yard. There are two basic types of yard utilized by the carriers – the *classification yard* and the *intermodal transloading yard*.

The classification yard is used for conventional shipments of boxcars, tank cars, hoppers, etc., and it is here that outbound cars are assembled into blocks for inclusion in outbound trains.

When inbound trains arrive at these yards, the process is reversed, and cars are pulled out of trains for switching or delivery to other carriers.

There are three types of classification yard. A *flat* yard is a relatively level yard in which cars are moved to and from various tracks using a switch engine.

Photography by Clifford Lynch

A *hump* yard utilizes a manmade hill. In these operations cars are pushed to the top of the hump where they are uncoupled and roll down into the classification tracks. The cars are automatically switched into the right track, and retarders on the rails control the speed at which the car enters the designated track.

A *gravity* yard operates on the same principle as a hump yard, but here the entire yard is sloped in one direction.

A typical classification yard can handle between 1,000 and 3,000 cars daily.

Photography by Clifford Lynch

The intermodal (transloading) yard is quite a different operation. Here outbound trains of containers, double-stacked, are assembled. Motor carriers drop the containers on their chassis at the rail yard; and from here, they are transported by yard tractors or hostlers and parked alongside long sidings on which flat cars are waiting. Overhead cranes, which span the track(s) and the trailers, lift the containers off the chassis and place them on the flat cars where they are locked into place.

For inbound container trains the process is reversed.

While the process sounds tedious, the rail carriers have become quite efficient at it. A large intermodal facility, such as the BNSF Hobart Yard in California, can handle well over a million lifts annually. (A lift designates either the placement of

Photography by Clifford Lynch

a container on a flat car or the placement on a chassis.)

Financial Structure

In 2005, the rate of return on net investment for all Class I carriers was 8.5 percent, the highest it has been since 1996. Most years have been lower. [19]

As described above, the required investment in rail equipment and rights-of-way gives the carriers high fixed costs. These are the costs that remain the same regardless of how much freight is hauled.

53

Maintenance costs can be categorized as semi-variable since they are not directly proportionate to the amount of traffic hauled, yet are somewhat influenced by volume. In times of financial stress, some carriers have deferred maintenance expenses; and while they may get some short-term benefit, long-term they are forced to catch up or risk serious operating difficulties and accidents.

Variable costs are those expenses that vary with the volume of freight hauled. The major variable costs for a railroad are fuel and labor which have been of particular concern during the early 2000's.

In the past, railroad labor was a more significant factor than it is today. Over the years the rail carriers have been successful in eliminating some of the work crews such as unnecessary brakemen and firemen. In 1982, for example, after several years of negotiation, the railroads eliminated cabooses on trains, saving approximately $400 million annually. The standard crew is now two employees – both riding in the locomotive. [20]

Notwithstanding this, labor costs are a major expense. In 2005, Class I carriers spent $10.9 billion on 162, 000 employees. This amounted to almost 23 percent of total revenue. [21]

Fuel costs are the second most important variable cost and by far the most volatile. In 2005, the rail carriers consumed 4.1 billion gallons of diesel fuel at a cost of $6.2 billion. [22] The cost per gallon has risen consistently every year and shows no signs of modifying that pattern.

Figure 3-g shows diesel fuel costs as a percentage of total operating expenses for three Class I carriers for the years 2004 – 2006.

| | | % of OE | |
Carrier	2004	2005	2006
BNSF	14	19	24
NS	11	12	14
UP	17	22	24

Source: BNSF, NS, and UP Annual Reports - 2006

Figure 3-g. Diesel Fuel Costs as a % of Total Operating Expenses

 This cost structure provides the railroads with economies of scale, however. While one could argue that all costs are variable over the long run, as new investment is required, at least over the short run, rail costs are largely fixed. This structure results in a low incremental cost for adding additional volume while increasing revenues and profits. For example, the cost of adding one more car of coal to a 100-car train is small, yet the revenue for that car is the same as the first one that went into the train.

Future of Rail Freight Transportation

The future for the rail carriers looks better in the year 2007 than it has looked in many years. Figure 3-h shows the expected growth from the year 2002 to 2035.

Year	Millions of Tons	Billions of $
2002	1,879	382
2035	3,525	702
% Increase	87.5	83.7

Adapted from U.S. Department of Transportation, Federal Highway Administration, Office of Freight Management and Operations, Freight Analysis Framework, 2006

Figure 3-h. Expected Rail Growth 2002 – 2035

In 2007, Bear Stearns projected that railroads would make back marketshare over the next ten years, "abetted by 1) offshore manufacturing, which lends itself to railroads at the ports; 2) the rails' significant fuel-efficiency edge over trucks; and 3) the public's growing frustration with highway congestion." [23]

Passenger Transportation

No discussion of railroads would be complete without some mention of passenger transportation. From 1867 when George Pullman came up with the idea of a sleeper car until the 1950's, train travel was exciting, comfortable, and less expensive than the other options. In 1943, one could ride in a Pullman car with a bedroom and private bath for 3.3 cents per mile. A coach seat would cost you 2.2 cents. [24] And there was nothing like being lulled to sleep by the "clackety clack" of the wheels as the train made its way toward your destination. A businessman could board the train at dinner in Chicago, enjoy an excellent meal, have a good night's sleep, and get off the train in New York right after breakfast.

Two major developments changed that. Air transportation became more available and reliable, and people simply became unwilling to spend the time it took to travel by train. There were other reasons such as improved highways, but suffice it to say, passenger transportation began to decline, equipment became dated and poorly maintained, and the carriers were losing huge amounts of money. Bankruptcies and service terminations followed; and finally, it became clear that for rail passenger transportation to survive, government intervention would be absolutely critical.

Finally, in 1971, the National Railroad Passenger Corporation doing business as Amtrak was formed. This government-owned carrier assumed the passenger operations of 20 railroads and began to operate over their tracks for a fee. The carriers contributed rolling stock, equipment and capital, and in return they were allowed to discontinue their own passenger service. [25]

Amtrak continues to operate and provide at least some passenger service, but it has yet to become self-sufficient. It serves 500 destinations in 46 states over 21,000 miles of routes and has 19,000 employees. [26] The bad news is that service can be erratic, and it continues to lose approximately $1 billion annually.

The one bright spot in the Amtrak operations has been in the so-called Northeast Corridor running from Boston to Washington, DC. Amtrak has introduced high speed trains offering a popular service from and to cities such as Boston, New York, Philadelphia, and Washington. In 2000, Amtrak began the Acela Express, offering 150 mph service on a modern train using existing tracks. These trains offer a very comfortable ride and shorter travel times; i.e.,

Boston to New York in three hours 23 minutes and New York to Washington in two hours 45 minutes. [27]

Even so, the U.S. still lags behind other countries in the development of high speed trains, and it is not clear that passenger transportation will ever be a profitable venture in this country. However, in spite of frequent threats to eliminate Amtrak funding, the government seems to be willing, at this point, to guarantee at least some passenger service for most of the country. [28]

Questions for Understanding

1. Discuss the reasons for the growth of intermodal movements between 1995 and 2005.

2. Briefly explain the cost structure of the rail carriers.

3. What actions by the rail carriers led to their regulation?

4. Explain economies of scale as they relate to rail carriers.

5. Should the government subsidize rail passenger service? Why?

Chapter 4: Motor Carriers

> *"If you've got it, a truck brought it."*
> — American Trucking Associations

The above former marketing slogan of the American Trucking Associations, in only eight words, for the most part summarizes the motor carrier industry. Whether products move by rail, air, water, or over the highway, somewhere in the process a truck is involved. In 2007, truck transportation costs of 635 billion dollars accounted for 75 percent of all freight transportation costs, and 61 percent of *total logistics costs*. This was 6.2 percent of 2007 Gross Distribution Product. [1]

History and Development

As will be discussed in Chapter 7, the early colonial development of water transportation was brought about primarily by the lack of any good overland method of moving people and goods. It was not until the 1770's that significant road construction began. Called *post roads*, these early thoroughfares were built between major cities, and for the most part, along the coastlines. One of the first types of highway transportation was the movement of mail, hence the name post roads. [2] Even during the rail expansion years numerous highways also were being built, although most were local.

The first truck using the internal combustion engine was built in 1895 by Karl Benz; and in the U.S. the Winston Company built a single-cylinder, six horsepower gasoline engine vehicle in 1898. [3] (Although invented in 1890, the diesel engine was not commonly used in trucking in the U.S. until the 1970's.) [4] By 1900, truck transportation had begun in earnest, limited only by the absence of good, paved roads. In 1900, there were 700 trucks in use in the country.

In the late 1890's the expansion and improvement of the highway system was championed by three unlikely bedfellows. The farmers wanted to "get out of the mud" and get to markets easier; the railroads needed good, reliable transportation from the production points to the railheads; and the cyclists wanted a place to ride (a desire strongly supported by the bicycle manufacturers.) [5]

As automobiles became more affordable and available, their owners became more vocal, as well. This pressure continued; and by 1915, forty-five states had enacted some form of law to encourage highway construction. Twenty-four actually had designated state highway systems. Growth was slow, however, due primarily to lack of funds.

Finally in 1916, Congress passed the Federal Aid Road Act in which 75 million dollars were designated for highway improvement. The states were to design, construct, and maintain their highway systems with the government providing funds based on a formula which considered population, mileage, etc. [6]

The Highway Act of 1921 provided for the concentration of funds in a few road systems rather than trying to pave the entire country. A system of primary highways, not to exceed 7 percent of each state's mileage, was designated for construction and/or improvement. [7] It was also at about this time that states began to adopt a gasoline tax to aid in financing the highway system.

The industry expanded significantly after World War I. By then, there were enough highways and a broad enough acceptance of the automobile that the business of truck transportation began to flourish. Also the depression of 1929 – 1930 left millions unemployed, and the government saw highway improvement as a convenient method of providing jobs as well as stimulating the economy. * The WPA (Works Progress Administration), founded for this purpose, is said to have built 650,000 miles of new roads, 78,000 bridges, and assorted other structures.

Since there was no control over entry into the trucking business, more and more new carriers set up shop; and finally, the extreme competition resulted in some of the same abuses seen in the railroad industry some forty years earlier. As discussed in Chapter 2, the Motor Carrier Act of 1935 sought to put an end to abuses, unfair competitive practices, and to control the number of carriers allowed to operate in the country. After 1935, while the industry continued to expand, it did so at a much slower rate than before.

The regulation brought with it even more bureaucracy than that created by rail and other transport regulation, and it became extremely difficult to enter the business. Applications to do so were met with strong, often vocal, and sometimes ridiculous resistance by competing carriers and modes. One of the most entertaining stories of the regulated era was the account of the great "yak fat caper." (See next page.)

In 1954, the current system of interstate highways was conceived, and on June 29, 1956, the Federal-Aid Highway Act was signed into law by President Eisenhower. In doing so, he stated, "Our unity as a nation is sustained by free communication of thoughts, and by easy transportation of people and goods." This system, which envisioned 46,000 miles of multi-lane, limited-access highways, took its position as one of history's major highway transportation developments, along with the diesel engine, pneumatic tires, and hydraulic brakes.

The controlled entry into the industry and the strict regulation of rates continued until the Motor Carrier Act of 1980 was signed into law by President Carter. Although the trucking industry had already

---

* The WPA was part of President Franklin D. Roosevelt's "New Deal." At that time most economists subscribed to the Keynesian economic theory that during times of depression, deficit spending by a government could accelerate recovery. In this case, it at least helped.

become a vital part of our economy, it was not until this new legislation that the industry was at last free to operate in a truly competitive environment, allowing innovation and creativity on the part of shippers and carriers alike.

In 1980, there were approximately 20,000 registered motor carriers in the United States. By 1990, this number had doubled.

"The Yak Fat Caper"

For sure, economic regulation is well-intentioned, but bureaucracies don't always operate as intended. The 20th century had its share of bizarre regulatory events.

In November 1970, the Interstate Commerce Commission's 11 commissioners and 1,800 employees invested weeks seeking to determine an appropriate rate for scratch pads. Trucking companies argued a higher rate should be applied to scratch pads with advertising printed upon them than those without advertising. This proceeding followed one in which attorneys argued as to the appropriate rate for hauling powdered lime – whether shippers should pay more when it is used for industrial purposes rather than on farms.

It took 17,000 pages of testimony during the early 1960s and a trip to the Supreme Court for the Southern Railway to gain permission to put a larger covered hopper car – the Big John – into service. The railroad complained that trucks operating with a regulatory exemption were hauling 6 million tons of poultry feed annually from the Midwest to the Southeast. The Southern wanted to compete by using a new car with twice the capacity of a boxcar, but barge operators complained the Big John would spell revenue losses for water carriers. The ICC initially sided with the barge lines; but after the Supreme Court told the ICC to try again, it gave the railroad a green light for the 100-ton capacity Big John, and the Southern increased its annual haul of grain from 700,000 tons to 72 million.

But the case that will cause the ICC to live in infamy was argued over a commodity that didn't even move in domestic transportation – yak fat. Robert Hilt, president of Hilt Truck Line of Omaha, Neb., was furious that whenever he filed a new rate proposal with the ICC, railroads protested that the rate didn't cover costs and should be suspended.

To prove his point, in 1965 Hilt proposed to transport fat derived from the longhaired ox of Tibet and Central Asia. He filed a tariff item on 80,000-pound truckload lots of yak fat from Omaha to Chicago at a rate of 45 cents per 100 pounds. Immediately railroads operating in the West filed a seven-page protest that the rate was not compensatory in light of available cost data and demanded suspension of the rate pending investigation.

Former *Traffic World* Associate Editor Stan Chapman sensed something curious and called Hilt, who confessed: "The yak fat rate was published in our tariff to determine if the numerous rate protests we have been receiving from the railroads were to protect railroad traffic or just a form of harassment. Our research showed that there is not a single yak within 10,000 miles of Omaha – even in zoos," said Hilt. The complaint was dismissed. But *Railway Age* magazine quoted a rail official; "I don't care if somebody tries to put in a rate on distilled moonbeams – if the stated rate looks to be unrealistic and noncompensatory, we'll protest."

- by Frank N. Wilner
(Reprinted from *Traffic World*)

Significance of the Industry

As stated at the beginning of this chapter, in 2006 motor carriage accounted for 78 percent of all transportation costs or 61 percent of total logistics costs.

Number of Carriers

As of August, 2006, there were 579,588 motor carriers in the country, including for-hire and private entities. (See Figure 4-a.)

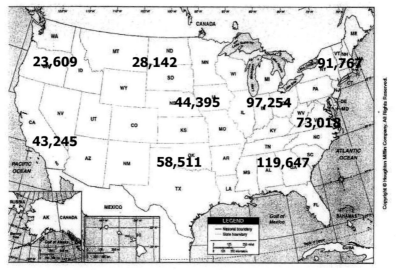

Source: Federal Motor Carrier Safety Administration, U.S. Department of Transportation

Figure 4-a

Private carriage accounts for about 48 percent of this number, making proprietary transportation an important and significant segment of the trucking industry. Eighty-seven percent of the carriers operate six or fewer power units, 8.7 percent operate seven to 20, and only 4.2 percent have more than 20. [8] In spite of their perceived size, no one carrier has over a 2 to 3 percent market share.

Number of Employees

In 2004, there were about 3.3 million drivers in the country, making the industry a significant employer. (See Figure 4-b.)

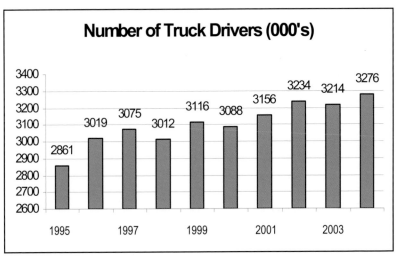

Source: *Employment and Earnings – Household Data*, Bureau of Labor Statistics, U.S. Department of Labor

Figure 4-b

Intercity Tonnage and Miles

Motor carrier tonnage increased by almost 40 percent between the years 1993 and 2003 as evidenced by Figure 4-c.

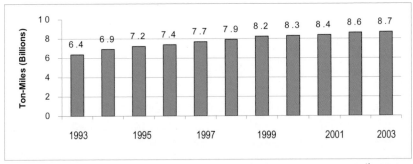

Source: Eno Transportation Foundation, *Transportation in America*, 20th Edition.

Figure 4-c. Domestic Intercity Truck Tonnage

Motor carrier ton miles increased by over 44 percent during the same period. (See Figure 4-d.)

Source: Eno Transportation Foundation, *Transportation in America*, 20th Edition.

Figure 4-d. Intercity Truck Ton Miles

Motor carriers haul almost every type commodity including those handled in packages, bulk or liquid form, or refrigerated. Meanwhile in ton-miles, they account for about 31 percent of all products shipped.

General Characteristics

Types of Carriers

There are a number of differentiations among the various carriers. First of all, a carrier can be either *for-hire* or *private*. A for-hire carrier holds itself out to the general public to provide transportation for a fee. A private carrier hauls products that are transported in furtherance of its owner's core business. Private trucks can be used for hauling supplies and raw materials, distribution of finished goods, or both.

A *local* for-hire carrier operates within a particular commercial zone. An *intercity* or *over-the-road* carrier hauls freight between cities.

A for-hire carrier may be designated as *common* or *contract*. A common carrier holds itself out to the general public to provide transportation without discrimination and at a reasonable cost. A contract carrier is just what the name implies – one that hauls products for specific shippers under specific contract.

Finally, a for-hire carrier may be either truckload (TL) or less-than-truckload (LTL). An LTL carrier hauls shipments of approximately 10,000 pounds or less, while a TL carrier hauls shipments that are large enough to fill a trailer. In some cases, when shipments do not quite fill a trailer, the shipper may be willing to pay for the excess space to facilitate the faster movement of the shipment in truckload service.

Examples of truckload carriers are

> J. B. Hunt
> Schneider National
> Swift Transportation
> Werner

Courtesy: Schneider National

Examples of less-than-truckload carriers are

> AAA Cooper
> ABF Freight Systems
> YRC
> FedEx Freight
> UPS Freight

Courtesy: AAA Cooper

Some carriers like Con-way Freight offer both truckload and less-than-truckload services.

One of the major trucking decisions for many firms will be whether to use for-hire carriers or operate a private fleet. There is no correct answer to this question, and the route chosen will depend on the individual needs and characteristics of the firm. Some will see private trucks as marketing assets – essentially as fleets of moving billboards that fan out across the country each day. It's hard to argue with that. If you spend any time at all on the nation's highways, you're bound to receive constant reminders of the existence of Wal-Mart, Steelcase Furniture and Corona Beer.

Others see their private fleets as bargaining chips. For them, that fleet is an important source of leverage when they negotiate rates with for-hire carriers. Even in today's seller's market, they'd rather go into a negotiating session with this leverage than without it. And many companies operate their private fleets as profit centers, making money by hiring out their excess capacity. Today, more than 50 percent of the nation's private fleets operate with for-hire authority.

But the most common reason for maintaining a private fleet is service. Almost every company that operates its own trucks does so because it has unique service requirements that only a private fleet can reliably meet.

Private carriers will have the same cost and labor pressures as for-hire carriers, possibly even more so depending on their size, and a careful cost analysis should be made before making the decision to buy or lease tractors and trailers rather than use for-hire service.

Operating Characteristics

Equipment

There are a number of different types of equipment in use by the various motor carriers. (See Figure 4-e.)

Line haul vehicles are usually those with three or more axles. [9] In most states, carriers are allowed to haul a gross weight (vehicle and cargo) of 80,000 pounds in rigs with five axles. Since each state sets its own length and weight requirements, carriers must pay particular attention to the regulations of those states the tractors and trailers will be traveling through.

Straight trucks are used primarily for intercity movements. Shorter 28-foot trailers are often utilized by LTL carriers to pick up freight within a local service area before it is consolidated for over-the-road movement.

U.S. COMMERCIAL TRUCK CONFIGURATIONS

Source: American Trucking Associations

Figure 4-e

Other types of trailers not shown, such as tanks and flatbeds, are used for special situations and cargo. Flatbeds are used for steel and heavy, often oversized, equipment, and a tank trailer may be used for anything from milk to chemicals.

Tractors used in over-the-road service are manufactured by a number of firms, with the most popular being Freightliner, International, Peterbilt, Kenworth, Mack, and Volvo. Engines are usually provided by suppliers such as Caterpillar, Cummins, Detroit Diesel, and Mercedes. Mack and Volvo provide their own. [10]

Terminals

The terminal operations for truckload and less-than-truckload carriers are quite different. When a truckload carrier has a pickup request, it sends a driver and a tractor and trailer to the designated pickup point where it is loaded. The driver then proceeds directly to the destination of the load and spots the trailer for unloading. As a result, truckload carriers have very few terminals. Those they do have are used primarily for maintenance of equipment, provision of driver services, and other administrative activity.

An LTL carrier, on the other hand, will pick up several small shipments from shippers within its pickup area and take them to a terminal where they are consolidated into truckloads for transportation to terminals in other cities.

At the destination city, the truck will proceed to a company terminal where it will be unloaded and the shipment "deconsolidated;" i.e., the smaller shipments which made up the truckload will be separated and delivered to their final destination within that city's commercial zone. These terminals often are referred to as Pickup and Delivery Terminals (PUD). (See Figure 4-f.)

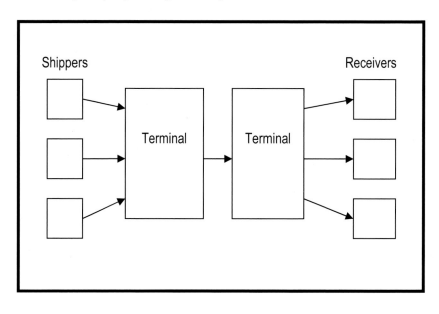

Figure 4-f. Typical LTL Freight Flow

Depending on traffic flow, there also may be a break-bulk terminal within the system where freight is partially deconsolidated at an intermediate point for shipment to multiple destination terminals. (See Figure 4-g.) These terminals also sometimes serve as domiciles for drivers.

69

Depending on the size of the carrier, an LTL carrier could have several hundred terminals.

A relay terminal, also used by LTL carriers, is one that involves no handling of the freight. Driver hours-of-service rules (which will be

Courtesy: AAA Cooper

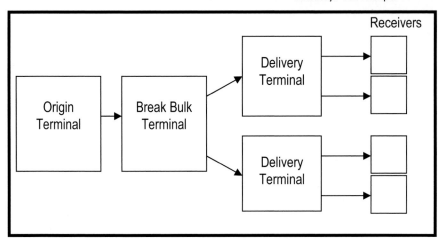

Figure 4-g. LTL Break Bulk Terminal Flow

discussed later in this chapter) sometimes will make it impossible for a driver to make an entire trip (legally). In this case, drivers may exchange entire rigs or trailers at an intermediate point and return to their home terminal. For example, a driver can leave Memphis with a load of Atlanta freight at roughly the same time an Atlanta driver leaves there with Memphis shipments. They will meet at a truck stop in Birmingham, exchange trailers or entire rigs, and return home.

Not only will the drivers be within legal driving limits, they will be back at home that night, sleeping in their own beds. This has become particularly important as carriers have attempted to provide a better lifestyle for their drivers. This relay process is sometimes referred to as a slip seat operation.

70

Labor

Clearly, the most significant cost for motor carriers is labor. As indicated in Figure 4-h, labor accounts for 55 cents per mile, or almost 20 percent of total expenses. According to the American Trucking Associations, in 2004, 1.3 million of the 3.3 million drivers in the industry were in over-the-road, long-haul service. [11]

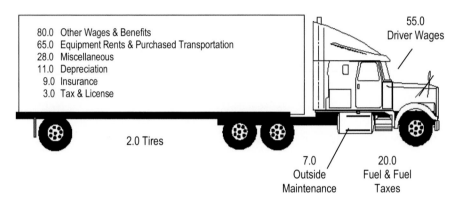

80.0 Other Wages & Benefits	55.0 Driver Wages
65.0 Equipment Rents & Purchased Transportation	
28.0 Miscellaneous	
11.0 Depreciation	
9.0 Insurance	
3.0 Tax & License	

2.0 Tires

7.0 Outside Maintenance

20.0 Fuel & Fuel Taxes

Source: *Motor Carrier Annual Reports, 2003*, ATA

Note: Figures are derived from reports filed with t he U. S. Department of Transportation (DOT) by carriers with $3 million or more in annual revenue. Figures include all types of carriers that filed with the DOT , except household goods carriers. Carriers with annual revenue below $3 million do not file. A different mix of carriers prevents direct comparisons from the 2002 figure reported in the 200 4 edition of *American Trucking Trends*.
Source: *Motor Carrier An nual Reports, 2003*, ATA

Figure 4-h

Prior to 1980, when one thought of a truck driver, he or she almost always thought of the Teamsters; and indeed, during the early, formative days of the industry, the union was a significant force. Founded in 1903, the International Brotherhood of Teamsters was instrumental in getting fair wages and reasonable working conditions for its members and, without a doubt, was responsible for many positive changes in the industry. Unfortunately, some of the IBT locals engaged in heavy-handed, often violent, organizational tactics and work stoppages; and for years the union was suspected, and its officers in some cases convicted, of illegal uses of funds or racketeering.

James Hoffa was elected president in 1957 and brought a new energy to the union's 1.5 million members. Part of this energy, however, was spent on loans of pension fund assets to individuals of questionable character. A significant portion of Las Vegas development in the 1950's and 1960's was accomplished with Teamster funds. While popular with the membership, during his tenure Hoffa was plagued with government investigations, legal problems, and even imprisonment. In spite of that, membership continued to expand; but in 1975, Hoffa mysteriously disappeared. (He was presumed murdered, but his body has never been found.)

After the deregulation of the industry in 1980, there was an abrupt decline in Teamsters membership. There were no longer barriers to entering the business, and virtually all of the new carriers that began to enter the market utilized non-union drivers.

Today, the union has 1.4 million members, but this includes airline employees, warehousemen, some magazine and newspaper employees, and motion picture workers. There are approximately 120,000 drivers covered under a National Master Freight Agreement (primarily LTL carriers) and several hundred thousand others under individual agreements. The largest single employer of Teamsters in the United States is United Parcel Services with about 200,000 union members. [12] However, considering the total number of drivers in the system, the union is no longer a significant overall factor.

In addition to being the largest cost factor for a carrier, labor is also one of the most difficult operating components with which a carrier must deal.

In recent years, there have been several issues of concern with the motor carrier labor force. The first, and most significant overall, is a shortage of qualified individuals who want to be long-haul truckers. According to *Global Insight*, the average annual wage of a driver is $37,400. [13] Combine this with some 200 to 250 nights away from home, and one can see why this occupation might not be too attractive. Some drivers make more, of course, but they are often away from home more, as well.

Courtesy: Schneider National

In 2004, there was a shortage of about 20,000 drivers, projected to increase to 111,000 by 2014. (See Figure 4-i.)

Figure 4-j shows the projected shortage compared to the truckload tonnage growth forecast. This shortage, of course, could be greater or less, depending on the economy and the demand for motor carrier transportation.

Motor carriers have attacked this problem in several different ways. Schneider National, for example, in 2007 increased the pay of their over-the-road drivers (who are paid by the mile) by as much as

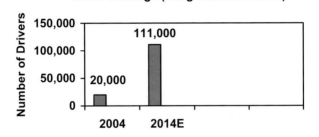

Driver Shortage (Long-haul TL Drivers)

Source: *Global Insight*

Figure 4-i. Truck Driver Shortage Projections

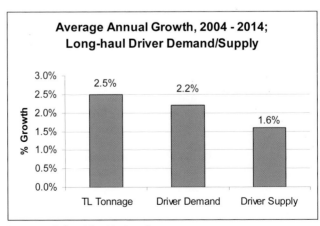

Source: Schneider National

Figure 4-j. 10-Year Avg. Annual Growth, Long Haul Driver Demand/Supply

73

$4,500 annually. Their highest paid drivers now can make as much as $60,000. They also, along with other carriers, have changed their dispatching system to provide more "at-home" nights for their drivers. While this is an advantage to the drivers, it reduces overall productivity. Figure 4-k shows the impact of increased nights at home on the productivity per driver.

Time-at-Home Productivity Impact

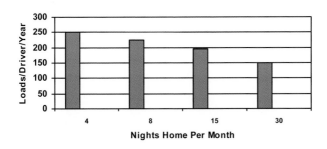

Source: Schneider National

Figure 4-k

Schneider National also has solicited husband/wife driver teams through the American Association of Retired Persons. According to the 2004 U.S. Census update, the total population between the ages of 44 and 64 is growing rapidly, but recruiting in this age bracket will not be a long-term solution to the problem.

Courtesy: Schneider National

Stated simply, motor carriers will continue to have a significant challenge in attracting new employees into what many believe to be a less-than-satisfactory work environment.

The second major labor issue facing the motor carriers is the revision of the driver hours-of-service rules. In 2004 the Federal Motor Carrier Safety Administration issued the first significant revision to the hours-of-service rules since 1962. These changes were made due to a growing concern over increased accident fatalities involving large trucks and driver fatigue. Since 2004 these rules have been overturned twice and stayed by two courts.

The new rules provided for an increase from ten to eleven maximum hours of driving time after ten consecutive hours off duty. Offsetting this, however, was a provision that when resting, the drivers using the sleeper berth must take at least eight consecutive hours in the berth, plus two consecutive hours off duty, in the berth, or a combination of the two. The rules also provided that on-duty time includes all time spent loading, unloading, waiting, or having meals. Figure 4-I summarizes the old and new rules.

HOURS-OF-SERVICE RULES	
2003 Rule Property-Carrying CMV Drivers Compliance Through 9/30/05	2005 Rule Property-Carrying CMV Drivers Compliance On & After 10/1/05
May drive a maximum of 11 hours after 10 consecutive hours off duty.	No change.
May not drive beyond the 14th hour after coming on duty, following 10 consecutive hours off duty. *	No change.
May not drive after 60/70 hours on duty in 7/8 consecutive days. A driver may restart a 7/8 consecutive day period after taking 34 or more consecutive hours off duty.	No change.
Commercial Motor Vehicle (CMV) drivers using a sleeper berth must take 10 hours off duty, but may split sleeper-berth time into two periods provided neither is less than 2 hours.	CMV drivers using the sleeper-berth provision must take at least 8 consecutive hours in the sleeper berth, plus 2 consecutive hours either in the sleeper berth, off duty, or any combination of the two.

* Formerly eight consecutive hours off duty.
Source: Federal Motor Carrier Safety Administration

Figure 4-I

While the rules may seem somewhat complicated to the uninitiated, the net effect was to make drivers less productive since they spent less time driving. It is interesting to note, however, that there was only one fatigue-related fatal crash in 2003, none in 2004, and one in 2005. Obviously, the changes have been quite controversial, and everyone, from sleep experts to drivers, has weighed in on the subject. The ideal situation, of course, is to establish rules that make drivers as safe and productive as possible.

Suffice it to say that labor is and will continue to be a major cost and a significant concern for the motor carrier industry.

Fuel

Another significant cost for the motor carriers is fuel. As shown in Figure 4-h, in 2003 fuel amounted to 20 cents per mile. These comparisons can be misleading, however. This table was based on a per gallon diesel fuel cost of $1.81. By 2005, diesel fuel had reached $2.40. In October of that year, prices actually went over $3.15 per gallon. Early 2008 brought a record price of $4.75.

Fuel costs have increased dramatically since 2007, and have created hardships for both shippers and carriers, alike. Because of their unpredictability, in May, 2000 a fuel surcharge program was established whereby fuel cost increases would be compensated for outside the general increases in rates. This program continues in effect today. These charges are based on an index published every Monday by the Department of Energy. Theoretically, if prices go up, the shipper pays more; if prices go down, the shipper pays less.

Under this program, when a carrier raises its line-haul rates, it (again theoretically) does not consider fuel costs since they are covered by the surcharges. While intuitively the program sounds very logical, as a practical matter it has not been a rousing success. Shippers suspect some carriers (and rightly so) of profiting from fuel surcharges, and at best the program is confusing. In the face of rising fuel costs, in 2006, one LTL carrier even reduced its fuel surcharge by 25 percent.

In spite of the surcharges, unquestionably, the higher costs have had a negative impact on the industry. Figure 4-m illustrates the effect of higher fuel costs on the carriers' ability to remain in business. According to the American Trucking Associations, during the first quarter of 2008, 935 carriers with at least five trucks went out of business. This compared with 385 during the comparable period in 2007, an increase of 142.9 percent. [14]

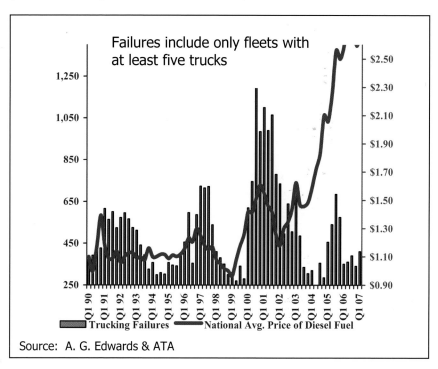

Figure 4-m. Trucking Failures vs. Price of Diesel Fuel

In 2008, fuel costs seemed to be spiraling out of control, and carriers began in earnest to find ways to reduce fuel consumption. Con-way Freight, for example, turned speed governors on its 8,400 tractors back to a maximum of 62 miles per hour.

Down three miles per hour from previous settings, this move was expected to reduce consumption of diesel fuel by 3.2 million gallons annually (over $13 million at $4.25 per gallon). In addition,

72 million pounds of carbon emissions would be eliminated from the environment.

Hardest hit were the 350,000 independent owner-operators in the country. Many of these drivers have thin profit margins in the best of times and, in 2007 – 2008, were forced to park their tractors because of the cost of fuel.

Fuel, no doubt, will continue to be a problem for all modes of transport, but especially for the motor carriers.

Cost Structure

Variable vs. Fixed Costs

The motor carrier industry is characterized by a high variable cost structure, with the largest components being fuel and labor. As a percentage of total costs, variable costs average 70 to 75 percent, with 25 to 30 percent being fixed. Most of the costs shown in Figure 4-h are variable. Drivers are paid by the mile, and if the equipment does not move, there is no fuel used, no tire wear, decreased maintenance, etc.

Fixed costs are low since so little investment is required. Truckload carriers have minimal terminal expense, and all types of motor carriers operate over a publicly provided highway system. While there is some contribution through a federal highway user fee included in the price of diesel fuel, at 24.4 cents per gallon, it is low compared to other modes, and for the carriers, it is a variable cost. States also have a fuel tax which is used for the maintenance of state highways, but these taxes also fall short of the total expense of maintaining a viable highway system.

Operating Ratio

Motor carriers measure their operating efficiencies through a benchmark called an operating ratio. This measures the percent of operating expenses against operating revenue. The formula is

$$OR = (Operating\ Expense/Operating\ Revenue) \times 100$$

This can be illustrated by reviewing the J. B. Hunt Consolidated Statement of Earnings in the 2006 Annual Report.

	2006
Operating revenues, excluding fuel surcharge revenues	$2,897,816
Fuel surcharge revenues	430,171
Total operating revenues	**3,327,987**
Operating expenses	
Rents and purchased transportation	1,124,734
Salaries, wages and employee benefits	892,066
Fuel and fuel taxes	447,309
Depreciation and amortization	183, 604
Operating supplies and expenses	145,794
Insurance and claims	71,582
Operating taxes and licenses	34,447
General and administrative expenses, net of gains on asset dispositions	33,232
Communication and utilities	22,566
Total operating expenses	**2,955,334**

Figure 4-n. J. B. Hunt Operating Revenue/Expenses – 2006

Using the formula above, the J. B. Hunt operating ratio can be calculated as follows:

$$OR = (2,955,344/3,327,987) \times 100$$
$$OR = (.888) \times 100$$
$$OR = 88.8$$

This indicates that 88.8 cents of every dollar of revenue is spent on operations. An OR below 100 is desirable since anything over 100 would suggest there is not enough revenue to cover the expenses.

The operating ratio does not necessarily indicate profitability of a carrier since there are other non-operating expenses, such as interest charges. However, it is a good measure or yardstick with which to measure internal operations as well as those among various other motor carriers.

Issues

In addition to the labor and fuel issues, there are others facing the motor carrier industry, as well.

Safety

Safety is always an issue for carriers of any mode but especially so for the motor carriers. Every day they operate within yards of other trucks or cars and are subject not only to their own drivers' habits and skills, but those of others, as well.

Although fatalities in carrier accidents have decreased, they are and will continue to be a concern of responsible motor carriers.

While the federal government has a number of requirements and inspection programs in place, the carriers themselves are the best policemen. Through rigid equipment inspection and maintenance processes, management of driver hours of service and periodic drug testing, they have made significant strides in improving the safety of their equipment, cargo, and employees, as well as the general public. With rapidly rising insurance premiums, they are finding that their bottom lines are enhanced, as well. Many carriers have increased their deductibles significantly in an effort to offset spiraling insurance costs.

Technology

Motor carriers are becoming more technologically advanced every year. One of the major innovations was the use of satellite technology beginning in 1988. Schneider National, using Qualcomm technology, was the first carrier to establish a major tracking program, and today most large carriers have some kind of positioning system. Basically, they are satellite-based communications and tracking systems that provide real-time communication and position reporting between tractors and their dispatch centers. These systems have proven invaluable in giving

80

customers visibility to their orders, managing drivers and fleets, and increasing reaction times in the case of emergencies.

More recent is the technology providing a tracking system for untethered trailers. Every year thousands of trailers are "misplaced," and this system provides position reporting on those that are not connected to tractors. Not only has this increased the inventory of available trailers, but also has improved personnel productivity by dramatically reducing the number of "trailer hunts" necessary.

Environment

As with other industries, environment is a concern for the motor carriers. New engine requirements, first mandated in 2002, have reduced emissions but have increased the initial price of the engine, as well as the ongoing operating costs.

A new requirement went into effect in January, 2007, and still another will take effect in 2010. Each change will result in progressively lower emissions and, presumably, higher costs and decreased efficiency. [15] Post-2002 engines have been judged to be 4 to 5 percent less fuel efficient and about 5 percent more maintenance intensive. [16]

Highway Infrastructure

Possibly the most serious issue, but the least concerning to many (other than the carriers), is the highway infrastructure.

According to the Federal Highway Administration, freight volumes will grow by 70 percent by 2020, and truck miles will nearly double. By 2043, according to the U.S. Census Bureau, population will have reached 400 million. Based on current construction levels, highway capacity will have expanded by nine percent by that time. But traffic will have surged by 135 percent. As a result, said Pete Ruane, president of the American Road and Transportation Builders Association, by 2043, the average motorist can expect to spend four weeks a year stuck in traffic. "It is a recipe for a gridlocked nation," he said, "unless major steps are taken soon to add new highway and transit capacity." [17]

Even if this opinion is overstated, the infrastructure is a serious problem and will continue to be so unless dramatic action is taken.

Photography by Clifford Lynch

Figure 4-o shows highway congestion in 1998, and 4-p illustrates how it will look in 2020.

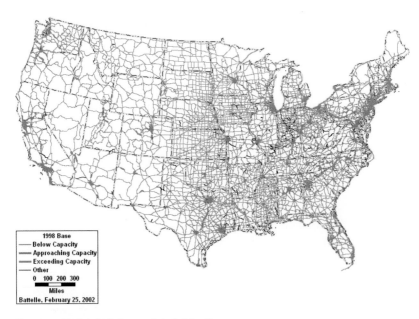

Source: Federal Highway Administration

Figure 4-o. Highway Congestion 1998 – All Vehicles

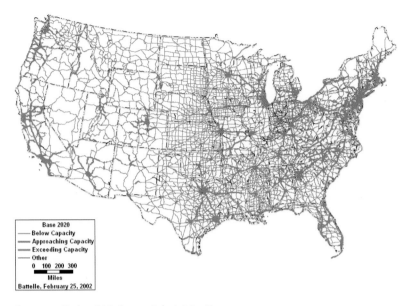

Source: Federal Highway Administration

Figure 4-p. Highway Congestion 2020 – All Vehicles

According to a survey by the American Transportation Research Institute, a division of ATA, the largest U.S. trucking firms ranked their concerns as follows.

1. Hours of Service
2. Driver Shortage
3. Fuel Issues
4. Congestion
5. Regulations
6. Tolls/Highway Funding
7. Tort Reform/Legal Issues
8. Truck Driver Training
9. Environmental Issues
10. On-board Truck Technology

Since so many of these issues are impossible for the carriers to resolve themselves, the public and the government must take an increasing role in their resolution. This industry is simply too important to the U.S. economy to do otherwise.

Questions for Understanding

1. Why are the fixed costs of an LTL carrier higher than those of a truckload carrier?

2. Discuss the merits of operating a private fleet versus the use of common or contract service.

3. What is an Operating Ratio?

4. Discuss the major issues facing the motor carrier industry.

5. Should the government regulate driver hours-of-service rules? Why or why not?

Chapter 5: Air Carriers

"The Wright Brothers created the single greatest cultural force since the invention of writing. The airplane became the first World Wide Web bringing people, languages, ideas, and values together."

- Bill Gates, CEO Microsoft Corporation

History and Development

Although the Wright Brothers are generally credited with inventing and flying the world's first successful airplane in 1903, man has attempted to fly since as far back as one can research. In 877, Abbas Ibn Firnas built what is now called a hang glider, and by some accounts, flew for as long as ten minutes from a small hill in Islamic Spain. [1] Later Leonardo De Vinci would design several aircraft that were not built. Finally, in 1783, the first manned balloon flight was made in Paris. [2] This balloon was not steerable, however; and it was not until 1884 that the first fully controllable airship was flown successfully. While airships (then called dirigibles) received a considerable amount of attention in the 1800's, they were frail, slow, and dangerous. It was the heavier-than-air aircraft of the 1900's that actually initiated manned flight.

Once the Wright Brothers had introduced a controllable heavier-than-air plane, aircraft development expanded dramatically, and the airplane rapidly became popular as an instrument of war. By the end of World War I the U.S. had built 17,000 planes and trained

10,000 aviators. [3] The government began airmail service in 1918, and the beginning of World War II saw a dramatic increase in aircraft production. During the years 1940 through 1945, a total of 160,000 fighters, bombers, and transports were built by the United States alone. [4]

By 1949, the first jetliner had flown, and in 1952, the DeHavilland Comet, a two-engine jet was introduced into scheduled service.

In 2006, over 76,000 commercial aircraft carried 745 million passengers in scheduled service. [5]

General Characteristics

As with motor carriers, airlines can be classified as either private or for-hire.

Private Carriers

Private aircraft for the most part are used to move company personnel (or private individuals) around the country, and in some cases, the world. While they no doubt can be valuable business tools, in more than a few instances, they are utilized  more for comfort and image. Whatever the reason, according to the National Business Aviation Association, approximately 11,000 companies operate about 16,000 private aircraft. These can range from a small two-seat, propeller-driven plane to a lavishly equipped large jet. Most, however, seat about six passengers and are used for trips of less than 1,000 miles.

For-Hire Carriers

The government classifies U.S. airlines by their annual operating revenue into three major categories – major, national, and regional. All carriers are required to have two certificates from the federal government – a fitness certificate issued by the Department of Transportation and an operating certificate issued by the Federal Aviation Administration.

The fitness certificate provides that the airline must be fit, willing, and able to provide the service and can authorize the carrier to offer both cargo and passenger service. The operating certificate spells out such things as the requirements for maintenance of equipment and flight crew training.

The *major airlines* have annual operating revenues in excess of $1 billion. They provide nationwide and, in some cases, worldwide service. Examples are American Airlines, Delta Airlines, FedEx Express, Northwest Airlines, and Southwest Airlines.

The *national airlines* have annual operating revenues between $100 million and $1 billion. Many of these airlines are large regional carriers but may be international as well. Examples include Aloha Airlines, Hawaiian Airlines, Mesaba Airlines, and Pinnacle Airlines.

The *regional airlines* generate less that $100 million annually and generally operate as feeder airlines. According to the Air Transport Association, there are over 80 of these, and this category has been one of the fastest growing segments since the airlines were deregulated in 1978. [6]

Cargo carriers can include any of the above. Cargo can be carried either in the bellies of passenger jets or by all-cargo aircraft such as those operated by UPS Airlines or FedEx Express.

A *commuter carrier* is technically a regional carrier and is used primarily to carry passengers from small airports to larger hubs.

Finally, a *charter carrier* is one that does not operate on a fixed schedule or over a designated route. They are utilized for the movement of large groups of people between specific points and are used frequently by travel groups, sports teams, casinos, and the government. Charters can be used for cargo, as well.

Courtesy: Northwest Airlines

Airlines also can be classified as either a *legacy* or a *low-cost* carrier. In the United States, the term legacy refers to those carriers that existed prior to the Airline Deregulation Act of 1978. They are

American Airlines
Continental Airlines
Delta Airlines
Northwest Airlines
United Airlines
U.S. Airways

These larger airlines are characterized by such things as frequent flyer programs, first and business classes, lounges, and other frills and perks.

The *low-cost carriers*, however, usually fly smaller aircraft such as a Boeing 737 or DC-9, have one class of service, do not reserve seats, have faster turn-around times, and use secondary airports. This business model has been quite successful for airlines such as JetBlue, AirTran Airways, and Southwest Airlines which has been profitable every year since 1973. [7]

General Industry Overview

As suggested by the earlier figures, the airline industry is a vital component of our transportation economy.

Figure 5-a shows the financial highlights for U.S. carriers during the year 2006.

(Millions of $)	
Operating Revenues	$163,824
Passenger	101,208
Cargo	22,544
Charter	5,562
Other	34,510
Operating Expenses	156,279
Operating Profit	7,545
Net Profit	$3,045

Source: Air Transport Association – 2007 Economic Report

Figure 5-a. Financial Highlight – Scheduled U.S. Airlines - 2006

Operational highlights for the same period are shown in Table 5-b.

(In Millions)	
Passengers Emplaned	744,600
Revenue Passenger Miles	797,422
Cargo Revenue Ton Miles	29,283
Aircraft Departures (Thousands)	11,268
Aircraft Miles	7,912
Average Flight Stage Length (Miles)	702

Source: Air Transport Association – 2007 Economic Report

Figure 5-b. Operational Highlights – Scheduled U.S. Airlines – 2006

In Figure 5-c important passenger and cargo statistics are shown for the top 20 airlines.

Over 544,000 people are directly employed in the industry, and the total U.S. airline fleet at the end of 2006 totaled 7,626 aircraft of 21 different types, produced by three different manufacturers. [8]

89

Aircraft Departures – All Services	
Southwest	1,093,090
American	789,342
Delta	573,181
United	563,994
SkyWest	556,426
American Eagle	555,911
US Airways	550,028
ExpressJet	491,740
Northwest	489,678
Continental	393,968
FedEx Express	376,968
Mesa	301,204
Atlantic Southeast	291,304
Comair	285,282
Pinnacle	249,644
AirTran	237,114
Chautauqua	201,675
Alaska	181,330
Horizon	179,300
Air Wisconsin	168,159
Revenue Passenger Miles (Millions) - Scheduled Services Only	
American	139,392
United	117,247
Delta	98,769
Continental	76,251
Northwest	72,588
Southwest	67,691
US Airways	69,895
JetBlue	23,310
Alaska	17,814
AirTran	13,798
ExpressJet	10,296
SkyWest	9,497
American Eagle	8,420
Frontier	8,317
Hawaiian	6,832
Atlantic Southeast	6,276
Mesa	6,078
Comair	5,287
Spirit	4,569
Pinnacle	4,304

Cargo Revenue Ton Miles (Millions) – All Services	
FedEx Express	10,543
UPS	6,270
Atlas/Polar	5,342
Northwest	2,269
American	2,241
United	2,048
Delta	1,239
Kalitta	1.190
Continental	1,006
Evergreen Int'l	840
Southern	784
Gemini	761
World	745
ABX	571
Tradewinds	412
US Airways	356
Focus	343
Omni	328
Cargo 360	312
ASTAR	289

Operating Revenues (Millions) – All Services	
American	22,493
FedEx Express	22,068
United	19,334
Delta	17,339
Continental	13,010
Northwest	12,555
US Airways	11,845
Southwest	9,086
UPS	4,571
Alaska	2,693
JetBlue	2,363
American Eagle	1,911
AirTran	1,893
SkyWest	1,849
ExpressJet	1,674
Atlas/Polar	1,360
Atlantic Southeast	1,266
ABX	1,260
Comair	1,201
Mesa	1,146

Source: Air Transport Association – 2007 Economic Report

Figure 5-c. The Top 20 Airlines

91

Operating Characteristics

As can be seen from Figure 5-a, the majority of total carrier operating revenues come from passenger traffic. Whether for cargo or passengers, business or pleasure, the major advantage to air transportation is *speed*. Whether moving an overnight letter via FedEx Express or taking a family vacation, to many, the additional cost is offset by the expedited service.

With an average length of trip of 1,071 miles, airlines are the travel vehicle of choice for most trips of over 1,000 miles. [9] In the case of emergency business or personal travel, speed will be the determining factor, and airlines offer the preferred solution. When shipping extremely high value or perishable products that require almost immediate delivery, once again, air transportation stands above its competition. What would Valentine's Day or Mother's Day be without air transportation of millions of bouquets of flowers around the country?

Other than cost, the main disadvantages to air transportation involve *reliability* and *accessibility*. [10] Weather can be a major factor in air carrier service, and often what seems to be a minor problem at one airport can result in backups all over the country. Once planes are in the air, however, sophisticated air traffic control systems make it possible to enjoy safe flights in most weather.

Accessibility can be an issue for those individuals and businesses located away from a major airport. Depending on the distances involved, it may, in some cases, be faster and/or more economical to use ground transportation.

Equipment

The type of equipment used by the scheduled airlines varies, but the Boeing 737 and 757 were the most widely used in 2006, followed by the MD-80 and Airbus 320.

Examples are the 737 fleet of Southwest Airlines, the MD-80's used by American, the Airbus 300 and 310 and Boeing 727's used by

FedEx Express and Boeing 757's utilized by UPS.

To illustrate, the Northwest passenger fleet consists of the following types of aircraft:

Aircraft	# of Passengers	Cruising Speed
747-400	403	565
747-200	349 – 430	558
A330-200/-300	243 – 298	545
DC10-30	273	550
757-200/-300	182 – 224	530
A319/A320	124 – 148	525
DC9-30/-40/-50	100 – 125	505
RJ-85	69	460
CRJ	44 – 50	510
Saab 340	33 -34	290

Source: *NWA World Traveler*

Figure 5-d. Northwest Airlines Passenger Fleet - 2007

Generally speaking, the smaller aircraft are used for the shorter distances and the lower density routes.

The industry continues to develop new aircraft such as the Airbus 380 and the Boeing 787 "Dreamliner." Both wide-bodied aircraft can hold 600 passengers, although early indicators are that the purchasing airlines will not use such a dense configuration. In any event, the A380 is the largest passenger jetliner ever built.

While on the surface it appears more economical to move passengers in larger planes, there are serious infrastructure problems at many airports that will make it difficult, if not impossible, to handle the larger aircraft.

The secret to a successful air operation is keeping the plane as full as possible. For the years 1996 through 2006, load factors steadily increased, ranging from 69.3 percent in 1996 to 79.2 percent in 2006. *(The load factor equals the number of passengers/total number of seats X 100.)*

93

Terminals

The United States has 3,431 airports that are designated as part of the national airport system. They are categorized as follows. [11]

- Commercial Service Airports (517 airports) – publicly owned airports that have at least 2,500 passenger boardings each calendar year and receive scheduled passenger service:
  - 382 primary airports designated as large, medium, small or non-hub (more than 10,000 passenger boardings each year)
  - 135 nonprimary airports (between 2,500 and 9,000 passenger boardings each year)

- Reliever Airports (274 airports) – those designated by the FAA to relieve congestion at Commercial Service Airports and to provide improved general aviation access.

- General Aviation Airports (2,573 airports) – the remaining airports including privately-owned, public-use airports that enplane more than 2,500 or more passengers annually and receive scheduled airline service.

Courtesy: Memphis-Shelby County Airport Authority

Almost all airports are publicly owned and are funded primarily by revenues generated by the airline activities, concessionaires, vendors, etc. Airlines pay landing fees and rents for gate space, ticket counters, and baggage areas, while vendors and concessionaires pay rent for the space they use. Many airports also charge a passenger facility fee which is added to each passenger's ticket.

More than 95 percent of all airport debt issued in the past 15 years has been through general airport revenue bonds. For the period

2001 – 2005 airports issued $30.1 billion in new debt and refinanced an additional $1.9 billion through this method. [12]

Typically, airports are managed by local airport authorities but, of course, are subject to federal guidelines and regulations.

Courtesy: Memphis-Shelby County Airport Authority

The ten busiest U.S. passenger airports in 2006 are shown in Figure 5-e.

City	Millions of Passengers
Atlanta	84
Chicago	77
Los Angeles	61
Dallas/Fort Worth	60
Denver	47
Las Vegas	46
New York (JFK)	44
Houston	43
Phoenix	41
Newark	37

Figure 5-e. Busiest Passenger Airports - 2006

Hub and Spoke

Most airlines use the hub and spoke approach whereby traffic from smaller airports is fed into larger hubs and from there on to major cities. For example, Delta utilizes Atlanta as a hub, the American hub is in Dallas, and Northwest has hubs at Detroit, Minneapolis, and Memphis. (See Figure 5-f.)

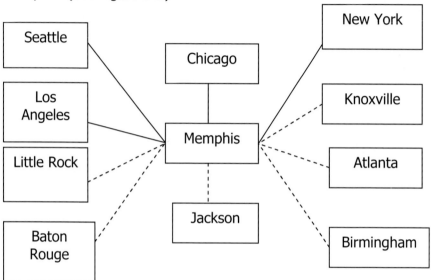

Figure 5-f. Northwest Airlines Hub & Spoke Example

Air Traffic Control

The one major enabler that is provided by the federal government is the air traffic control system. This intricate series of air highways is managed by air traffic controllers located throughout the United States. Air traffic tower controllers at the airport control the aircraft from the time it pulls away from the gate until it is airborne, and from touchdown to the gate. The description of "a typical flight" shown on the following page is taken from the Air Transport Association Airline Handbook and explains the process in detail.

Cost Structure

As is the case with motor carriers, the majority of airline costs are variable and the fixed costs are relatively low. [13] Since airports are funded by the government and the airlines pay only landing fees, if

96

A Typical Flight

From the standpoint of ATC, all airline flights begin with the flight plan, which spells out the route the flight crew plans to follow, alternative airports the crew would use in the event of an aircraft emergency or a problem at the intended destination, as well as the amount of fuel on board the aircraft. The aircraft dispatcher submits the flight plan to ATC prior to the departure of the flight. Many airlines that fly the same routes every day keep flight plans stored in the FAA host computer and merely activate them through their dispatch systems prior to flight. In any event, a flight plan provides crucial information to ATC about what a particular crew intends to do.

Once the pilots have completed their preflight planning, aircraft inspections, and have settled into the cockpit, they make their first call to ATC. Typically this call is made to clearance delivery, which reads back to the crew the filed ATC flight plan and instructions the crew can expect from takeoff to landing. Ideally, but not always, this information matches the route filed in the flight plan. ATC sometimes has system constraints or traffic-management initiatives in place that the flight crew may not be aware of, at which point ATC would give pilots new instructions before or during the flight.

When the flight crew is ready to depart, it contacts ground control for permission to leave the gate. Once an aircraft leaves the gate area and begins to taxi, it comes under the jurisdiction of FAA ground control.

The tower controller assumes full control of the aircraft as soon as it reaches the end of the runway it will use for takeoff. When the runway is clear, the tower grants permission for takeoff. It also instructs the crew on the heading, or direction, it should follow immediately after takeoff.

When safely airborne, tower control hands off the aircraft to departure control, which oversees the flight as it climbs away from the airport and enters the en route airspace. Given the speed and climb capabilities of modern jets, this may only take a few minutes. Departure control then turns over the flight to an en route center.

All of these and subsequent handoffs are accomplished by radio. The controller handling off the flight instructs the crew to contact the next level of ATC surveillance, and gives the crew the necessary radio frequency. Once contacted, a receiving controller acknowledges radar contact with the flight crew and issues instructions for heading and altitude.

Depending on where the plane is going, it may be handed off many times during the course of its flight, from one en route controller to another. En route controllers are assigned to specific sectors or areas in which they work to maintain safe separation of aircraft.

Aircraft separation standards vary according to circumstances. When aircraft are cruising at high speeds in en route airspace, the standard is five miles of horizontal radar separation or 1,000 feet of vertical separation. When aircraft are moving at much slower speeds as they depart or approach the airport terminal area, the standard is three miles of horizontal radar separation.

As an aircraft approaches its destination airport and begins its descent, the flight crew is instructed to contact approach control. An approach controller will issue instructions to the crew to blend the aircraft into the flow of other aircraft arriving at the airport. As soon as the crew is on its final, straight-in approach, the approach controller hands the aircraft off to the airport tower, which grants final clearance to land and monitors the aircraft until it completes its landing and exits the runway. A ground controller then directs the aircraft to its gate.

Source: Air Transport Association Airline Handbook

they don't fly, they don't pay. Figure 5-g shows the operating expenses for U.S.-scheduled airlines in 2005 – 2006.

Operating Expenses	2005	2006	% Change	Share (%)
Flying Operations	54,977	59,179	7.6	37.9
Maintenance	15,460	15,669	1.4	10.0
Passenger Service	9,323	8,679	(6.9)	5.6
Aircraft and Traffic Servicing	21,287	21,151	(0.6)	13.5
Promotion and Sales	8,649	8,391	(3.0)	5.4
General and Administrative	9,114	9,781	7.3	6.3
Depreciation and Amortization	6,772	6,915	2.1	4.4
Transport Related	25,249	26,515	5.0	17.0
Total Operating Expenses	150,828	156,279	3.6	100.0

Source: Air Transport Association – 2007 Economic Report

Figure 5-g. Operating Expenses – U.S.-Scheduled Airlines

Fuel

As with other modes of transport, fuel costs are the most troublesome and unpredictable expense factor. The price per gallon of jet fuel in 2002 was $.77, and by 2006, it was $3.73. [14] [15]

When considering the operating costs of the typical aircraft, this increase is significant. (See Figure 5-h.)

Aircraft	Fuel gallons per hour of operation	Increase per hour 2002 - 2006
747	3,411	$4,093
DC-10	2,405	2,886
727	1,289	1,546

Figure 5-h. Effect of 2002 – 2006 Fuel Increase on Operating Costs Per Hour

The airlines must continue to look for ways to increase fuel efficiency and improve load factors. In 2008, at the height of the fuel cost crisis, Northwest Airlines found that by reducing the speed of aircraft on trans-Atlantic flights by ten miles per hour 162 gallons of fuel would be saved.

Southwest Airlines anticipated a reduction in fuel costs of $42 million annually by adding one to three minutes to its flights.

Other airlines have not survived fuel cost increases, however. In 2008, after fuel costs had surged by 60 percent, five smaller carriers went out of business and one sought Chapter 11 bankruptcy court protection.

Labor

Airlines are very labor-intensive, and in early 2007, labor costs accounted for 24.5 percent of operating expenses. Airline labor costs are 11.1 percent higher than in 2000 in spite of efforts to reduce them through cutbacks and improved productivity. The average compensation for an airline employee in 2006 was $73,197 or 1.1 percent higher than in 2005. [16]

Pricing

Airline pricing is subject to significant discounting depending on restrictions, schedules, timing, and traffic lanes. It is clear that the business traveler usually pays the higher fares since it is not always convenient to plan as far ahead or adhere to less expensive schedules. It would not be uncommon for two people sitting in adjoining seats on the same flight to have paid vastly different fares.

For example, a roundtrip coach ticket from Memphis, Tennessee to New York's LaGuardia Airport booked on September 13, 2006, for departure on September 17 and return on September 18 would have cost $1,215.91. The same trip booked on the same day for an October 13 departure and October 23 return would have cost $245.91.

Where there is little if any competition between cities, fares generally are higher.

Where there is route density – i.e., a major roundtrip lane – fares can be lower. The top ten city pairs are shown in Figure 5-i.

Rank	City Pair	1000's of Passengers
1	Fort Lauderdale-New York	3,783
2	New York-Orlando	3,576
3	Chicago-New York	3,292
4	Atlanta-New York	2,654
5	Los Angeles-New York	2,642
6	New York-West Palm Beach	1,980
7	Boston-New York	1,867
8	Las Vegas-New York	1,786
9	New York-Tampa	1,776
10	New York-San Francisco	1,767

Source: Air Transport Association – 2007 Economic Report

Figure 5-i. Top 10 City Pairs - 2006

Current Issues

Besides the cost of fuel, the major issue facing the airline industry is security. While tremendous strides have been made, there is a need for continued vigilance. In the environment in which we live, we will always be subject to careful scrutiny of both passengers and cargo.

After the tragic events of September 11, 2001, the newly created Transportation Security Administration hired 45,000 full time screeners at 420 commercial airports to screen passengers and luggage. While this has been a source of irritation to many travelers, there should be no doubt that it has increased our safety.

In addition airlines continue to improve their safety records through careful self-policing and care to equipment and employees. In 2005, both accidents and fatalities were low compared to other modes of transport. (See Figure 5-j.)

Scheduled Air Carriers	22
Highway	43,443
Pipeline	19
Railroad	888
Water	0

Source: Bureau of Transportation Statistics

Figure 5-j. Transportation Fatalities by Mode - 2005

Since 2001, air statistics have been similar. [17]

Year	**Accidents**	**Fatalities**
2002	35	0
2003	51	2
2004	24	1
2005	34	3

In 2007, legislation was passed requiring that a procedure be put into place to provide for the screening of 100 percent of cargo placed on passenger aircraft by 2010. While this no doubt will increase costs, this screening will make both passengers and cargo less susceptible to terrorism and carelessness.

Underlying the fuel, security, and labor issues, however, is the basic fight for survival on the part of many U.S. airlines. With both a slow economy and spiraling fuel costs in 2008, some airlines called for re-regulation. Legendary former American Airlines CEO, Robert Crandall, was in favor of a return to regulation, stating in 2008, "It is time to acknowledge that airlines look and are more like utilities than ordinary businesses."

On the other hand, Delta Airline President, Edward Bastian, believed deregulation "has been a great success. Air travel today has never been more affordable and significantly lower in real dollar costs." [18]

In any event, airlines continue to struggle financially. In 2008, Northwest, for example, began to charge for all checked baggage; i.e.,

101

$15 for the first, $25 for the second, and $100 for the third.

Whatever the regulatory answer eventually turns out to be, it is clear that some governmental action will be necessary to ensure an air network that supports our national transportation policy.

Questions for Understanding

1. Discuss the differences between legacy and low-cost air carriers.

2. What are the primary advantages of air transportation? Disadvantages?

3. Describe the hub and spoke operating approach.

4. Discuss the cost structure of an airline.

Chapter 6: Pipelines

> "In 1902, Spindletop, one of the earliest oil fields in the U.S.,
> produced 17 million barrels of oil.
>
> - Pipeline 101

The Early Years

The first crude oil pipeline was laid in Pennsylvania in 1865. The line was modest, only two inches in diameter, four miles in length, and ran directly from the wellhead to a railroad loading station. [1] This was a significant development since prior to that, oil had been transported in wooden kegs loaded on horse drawn wagons. The success of this new line led to others; and by 1920, pipeline mileage had tripled. For the next twenty years development was moderate, but during the early stages of World War II, 48 U.S. oil tankers were sunk by the German submarine fleet. This vulnerability quickly led to a rapid expansion of land-based lines moving oil from Texas and Oklahoma to the eastern seaboard, and by 1946, there were 144,000 miles of pipelines in the country.

During the formative years of the industry, the pipelines were owned by the oil companies. The success of Standard Oil in the early days of the oil industry, for example, was due in large part to their control of pipelines. This less expensive, company-owned, form of transportation gave Standard a significant advantage over the refiners that were forced to use rail transportation. The environment at the time was not too unlike the early days of the rail industry.

Standard Oil was founded by John D. Rockefeller who might justifiably be included in the list of "Robber Barons" in Chapter 3. He became the world's richest man and the first U.S. dollar billionaire.

When other refiners attempted to construct pipelines of their own, they were met with major objections by Standard Oil, who in turn exerted overwhelming influence over the railroads. As a result, some railroads refused to let the pipeline developers cross their rights of way, effectively blocking any significant construction. [2] (By this time, the rapid construction of rail lines in the East made it impossible to travel more than a few miles without encountering a railroad track.)

Because of this and other continuing abuses and discrimination, just as had happened with the early railroads, there was a growing demand for government intervention. In 1906, Congress passed the Hepburn Act which brought oil and refined product pipelines under the control of the Interstate Commerce Commission. They were declared to be common carriers and could be forced to carry oil for independent refiners or producers without discrimination at just and reasonable rates. Many pipeline companies refused to recognize their new status, however, and refused to file tariffs with the ICC. They simply purchased any oil that was offered to them for transportation and maintained they were hauling their own products. It was not until 1912 that this was finally resolved, and the ICC was able to enforce its jurisdiction.

While the Standard Oil monopoly became so insidious that it was finally broken up by the government, most pipelines today are still owned and operated by the oil companies. They are much more "user friendly," however, and provide an economical method of transporting oil, natural gas, and refined products. The only current regulation to which they are subjected is that of the U.S. Department of Transportation Pipeline and Hazardous Materials Safety Administration, whose primary focus is the "safe and secure movement of hazardous materials to industry and consumers by all modes of transportation, including pipelines." [3]

The Industry Today

There are approximately 200,000 miles of oil pipeline in the U.S. today, and this 31 billion dollar system moves about two-thirds of the oil transported in the country. Water carriers handle about 28 percent, with rail and motor carriers sharing the other 6 percent. (See Figure 6-a.)

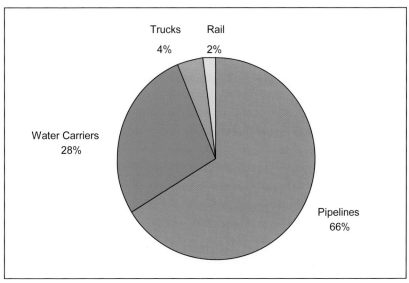

Source: Association of Oil Pipelines

Figure 6-a. Oil Transport in the U.S.

To fully appreciate the volume of oil handled through the pipeline system of the country, consider the following. A modest-sized pipeline will transport about 150,000 barrels daily. To move this volume by motor carrier would require 750 tanker truckloads daily, delivering a load every two minutes around the clock.

Opting for rail would require a 75-car train, with each tank car carrying 2,000 barrels, arriving and unloaded every day. [4]

While there are some pipelines that handle such commodities as water and chemicals, most of the pipeline mileage is devoted to oil, refined products and natural gas, with the primary usage being for oil and oil products.

Some examples of products moved through pipelines follow. [5]

For Vehicles
- Gasoline
- Diesel Fuel
- Kerosene
- Aviation Gas
- Jet Fuel

For Heating
- Natural Gas
- Propane

For Agriculture
- Anhydrous Ammonia
- Diesel Fuel

For Consumer Products
- Crude Oil
- Propylene
- Ethane
- Ethylene
- Carbon Dioxide

Interstate pipelines deliver over 12.9 billion (42-gallon) barrels of petroleum annually. About 7.6 million barrels are crude oil with the remaining 41 percent in refined products.

There are three operations-types of pipeline used in the transportation of oil or natural gas.

The *gathering lines* transport the oil or gas from the wellhead* to the transmission line. These lines are usually small in diameter and relatively short. In some cases, they are above ground rather than buried. In addition, the lines that transport oil from offshore

---

* Wellhead refers to that point at which the product is extracted from the ground.

platforms to the mainland are considered gathering lines.

The *transmission* or *trunk lines* are used to transport large volumes of product from a gathering or storage facility to a processing or storage facility, distribution system, or large volume customer. These lines are larger in diameter, usually 30 to 48 inches, and are buried three to six feet under the ground. They crisscross the U.S. and in some cases connect U.S. facilities with those on other continents.

A *distribution line* runs from the transmission line storage or terminal facility to the final consumer. Gas lines to individual homes fall into this category as do lines transporting oil to its final destination.

The average haul for a crude oil shipment is about 800 miles and for products, approximately 400 miles per shipment. [6]

Although natural gas moves through a similar profile of lines, when one considers the gas lines to individual homes and businesses, there are almost two million miles of gas pipelines in the U.S. About 278,000 miles of these are transmission lines. [7]

Obviously, one doesn't put the oil in one end and have it miraculously appear at the other. A fairly elaborate configuration of equipment is necessary to keep the product moving smoothly.

The *supply* or *inlet station* is the beginning point, or the point at which the product is introduced into the system. The storage facilities will have pumps or compressors to push the oil into the line.

Compressor or *pumping stations* are located all along the line to keep the product flowing. These will be from 20 to 100 miles apart, depending on the terrain and the pressure at which the line is operated.

The *intermediate stations* are located at strategic points on the line allow for part of the product to be released from the line for delivery.

A *block valve station* is located every 20 to 30 miles. These are the points at which the line can be blocked for maintenance or because

107

of damage or a leak. These are critical points of protection for the line. A hunter with a bad aim can cause a small hole that will result in a 75-foot spray of oil being released at 525 pounds per square inch if it is not controlled.

A *regulator station* is used to release pressure and is usually located on the downhill side of a peak in the line.

Finally, the *outlet station* is the point from which the product will be distributed. Oil will move through the total system at the rate of two to five miles per hour.

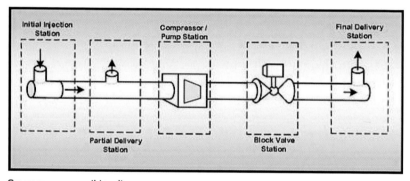

Source: www.wikipedia.com

Figure 6-b. Pipeline Stations

One of the most important pieces of equipment is the pipeline inspection gauge or *pig*. During the process of pigging, this tool, the diameter of which matches the diameter of the line, is propelled by the pressure of the product in the pipeline. It is used for several different operations; i.e.,

1. physical separation of different types of liquids,
2. recording geometric information,
3. inspection of the pipeline wells (It can detect flaws or weaknesses in the pipe.),
4. cleaning of the walls.

The original pigs were made of straw wrapped in wire and squealed when they moved through the pipe. The term "pipeline inspection gauge" was later created as a backronym (the acronym is picked *before* the words it describes) to accommodate the squealing pig analogy. [8]

A pig has been used as a plot device in three James Bond films: *Diamonds Are Forever*, where Bond disabled a pig to escape a pipeline, *The Living Daylights*, where a pig was modified to secretly transport a person through the Iron Curtain, and *The World Is Not Enough*, where a pig was used to move a nuclear weapon through a pipeline. [9]

Cost Structure

Because of the significant cost of pipeline infrastructure, like the railroads, pipeline companies have a high fixed cost. The firms themselves must acquire land and construct the line and all the ancillary equipment, plus maintain them. The Trans-Alaska Pipeline System, for example, was built at a cost of $8 billion.

The level of variable costs is extremely low compared to other modes and consists, for the most part, of fuel and labor. Very little fuel is required to operate pumps and terminals, and the pipelines employ only about 8,000 people for every 10,000,000 employees motor carriers would need to move comparable ton-miles. [10]

Competition

Due to the high cost of entry into the business, the industry is conspicuous by its small number of operators. There is limited price competition that, when combined with the limited number of pipeline companies, results in a minimum of *intramodal* competition.

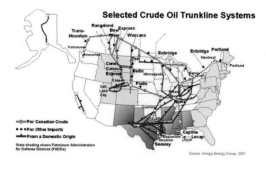

Selected Crude Oil Trunkline Systems

Intermodal competition is somewhat more intense. As indicated above, products transported by pipeline can be moved by water, truck or rail, with water carriers, particularly tankers, being the most competitive. Even so, once a pipeline is in place, it is difficult for other carriers to compete on price and reliability.

Service Characteristics

Obviously, a pipeline has some inherent disadvantages. It has limited accessibility, for example. Not every firm that may want to transport oil or gas is located near a pipeline. The pipeline route is fixed.

The transportation is slow, and in the event of inventory shortages, there is little that can be done to speed it up. The pipelines are somewhat inflexible providing only one way service for a limited number of products.

On the other hand, rates are low, and loss and/or damage almost nonexistent. While pipelines provide slow transportation, product moves continuously and service is reliable. The slow movement can even work to the users' advantage, depending on planned inventory levels and when title passes.

Pricing

There is virtually no differential pricing in the pipeline industry. The nature of the operations provides little opportunity to do so, and rates are typically quoted on a point-to-point or zone-to-zone basis. Minimum shipment tenders range from 500 to 10,000 barrels.

Rates are low. The cost to transport a barrel of petroleum products from Houston to New York Harbor is about one dollar. [11]

Safety and Environmental Concerns

While pipelines are a very safe mode of transportation, they can be targets of vandalism or sabotage. One of the major challenges, however, is the damage from excavations. According to the Office of Pipeline Safety, 43 percent of the oil lost from pipelines

results from people digging into them. To aid in eliminating this, the operators have established "One Call" centers that can provide accurate location information to those planning to excavate. [12]

Next to excavation, corrosion is the second most common cause of spills, and the pipeline companies have developed technologies, including the pigs, to aid in the elimination of or reduction in corrosion.

These tools must be utilized, however, to be effective. On August 6, 2006, BP announced the closing of 22 miles of Alaska pipeline, affecting 200,000 barrels a day. The pipeline had been the site of a major oil spill in March, 2006, and "subsequent inspections revealed severe corrosion." [13] BP acknowledged that it had not had a pig inspection since 1992. [14]

Although many pipelines are 40 to 50 years old, there is no evidence to support a significant problem, assuming proper maintenance. Accidents dropped from 245 in 1994 to 136 in 2005.

While in today's environment, pipeline planning and construction is performed by highly skilled and trained engineers, it would probably be impossible to construct a transcontinental pipeline today. The environmental obstacles to digging a trench across the United States would no doubt be insurmountable.

Trans-Alaska Pipeline System

Probably the most famous pipeline in North America is the Trans-Alaska Pipeline System (TAPS) called the Alyeska Pipeline in Alaska and the Alaska Pipeline in the lower 48 states. TAPS runs 800 miles from Prudhoe Bay, Alaska on the Arctic Ocean to the Gulf of Alaska at Valdez.

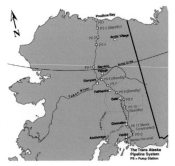

Source: www.alyeska_pipe.com

Figure 6-c. TAPS Pipeline

111

The 48-inch line was built between March 27, 1974, and May 31, 1977, at a cost of $8 billion. At the peak of the work, 21,000 people were employed in the construction. Thirty-one were killed in accidents. [15]

Source: www.alyeska_pipe.com

Figure 6-d. Trans-Alaska Pipeline System

Due to the harsh terrain of fault lines, mountain ranges, and bogs, construction was a significant challenge. Much of the line was built above ground because of the permafrost, making it necessary in 554 instances to bridge the migration paths of caribou and moose.

The line crested at Atigun Pass at 4,739 feet and had grades of as much as 55 degrees. It crosses 500 rivers and streams and three mountain ranges. [16] Where the line is buried, it is laid in an insulated, refrigerated ditch. Refrigeration plants must pump cold brine into the casings to keep the soil cooled. In some areas even the supports are cooled. Oil comes out of the ground at about 180 degrees F. and is transported at 120 degrees. Left at that temperature, the lines or supports would melt the permafrost causing the line to sink, possibly resulting in damage.

The first barrel of oil flowed through on June 20, 1977, and in 2006, the average flow was 759,000 barrels per day or 277 million barrels for the year. The linefill * is 9,059,057 barrels.

Mardi Gras Project

In 2000, BP began construction of a major deepwater system in the Gulf of Mexico. The system consists of five lines, each named after a Mardi Gras parade. The total mileage will be 490 with some lines as deep as 7,300 feet. When completed, the system will be able to

 move more than one million barrels of crude oil and 1.5 billion cubic feet of natural gas per day and will be the highest capacity deepwater system ever built. [17]

Some have defined the nation's pipeline system as a "sleeping transportation giant," and it has been said that no point in the continental U.S. is more than 200 miles from a pipeline. [18] This subterranean transportation system, the largest in the world, is recognized as the most economical and safest method of moving huge quantities of oil and gas from production points and refineries to users.

Questions for Understanding

1. Discuss the service characteristics of a pipeline versus other modes of transportation.

2. How does the cost structure of a pipeline differ from that of a motor carrier? Why?

3. Describe the various kinds of pipeline and their primary purposes.

---

* The total capacity of the pipeline from the beginning to the end.

4. Do you believe it would be possible to construct a transcontinental pipeline today? Why or why not?

5. What is the primary ownership structure of most pipelines?

Chapter 7: Domestic Water Carriers

> "He who does not know his way to the sea should take a river
> for his guide.
>
> - Blaise Pascal

The Early Years

There can be no disagreement that water transportation was the
first mode that facilitated commerce in the United States. Already
highly developed in many areas of the world, when the first settlers
arrived in the New World, they immediately began to apply those
familiar techniques to transportation in their new home. [1]

The first river boat can be traced back to 3500 BC when ships with
oars were used to transport goods along the rivers. [2] Indeed, had
it not been for water transportation, the New World would not have
been settled at all. But, although shipping routes between Europe
and the colonies were already established, the new internal systems
were hit and miss. It took three days to get from Philadelphia to
New York by the fastest land route then available; and in bad
weather, one could not get there at all. [3] With all the rivers,
streams, and natural harbors on the East Coast, it was only natural
that water transport would quickly become the first mode to be used
commercially.

The first recorded cargo shipment down the Mississippi River was a
load of 15,000 bear and deer hides in 1705; [4] but it was not until

1790 that flatboats and keelboats came into use on a regular basis. These boats were made of wood planks and were rowed or poled downstream. They sometimes were as long as 80 feet with a width of ten feet and could carry a large payload. When they arrived at their destination, they were sold for their wood content. [5] These boats obviously could not move back upstream with nothing but oars and poles to power them.

This basic system of river commerce was in use until 1900; but in the meantime, effort had been underway to try to utilize the newly invented steam engine in water commerce. In 1787, John Fitch made a successful run of a forty-five-foot steamboat on the Delaware River, [6] but it was Robert Fulton that made the steamboat a commercial success. In 1807, his steamboat, the *Clermont*, sailed from New York City to Albany in 32 hours, a distance of 150 miles. [7] By 1814, Fulton and his partners were offering regular service on the Mississippi between Natchez, Mississippi and New Orleans. [8]

During the next hundred years, river commerce was largely dependent on the steamboat. There were improvements along the way, such as moving the paddlewheel from the side to the rear of the boat and lashing barges to the side, but the diesel engine was not invented until 1892. And it was another 39 years until the first diesel-powered prototype for the modern towboat was built. [9]

The Equipment

Today, there are two basic kinds of equipment used in domestic water commerce – the towboat and the barge. A *towboat* is used primarily in river commerce. They have flat bottoms and a series of six rudders – two main and four flanking – that give them

Photography by Greg Thorpe
Courtesy: Ingram Barge Company

the maneuverability they need to push the large tows through relatively shallow water. They derive their name from the load they push, call the "tow." They have living quarters for their crews and are really quite comfortable.

116

The modern towboat varies in length from 40 to 200 feet and in width from 20 to over 50 feet, depending on where they are used. They range from 600 to over 10,000 horsepower and have the latest in navigation and communication tools.

They should not be confused with the tugboat that has a deeper hull and is used for moving large ships in and out of ports.

There are approximately 4,000 tow and tugboats in use in the country today.

Photography by Greg Thorpe
Courtesy: Ingram Barge Company

The *barges* which contain the cargo also have flat bottoms and typically are about 200 feet long and 35 feet wide. According to the American Waterways Operators, there are three basic types of barges used on the rivers. [10]

The *inland liquid cargo tank barge* is 297 feet long, with a one million gallon capacity, and is used for moving such commodities as petroleum, petroleum products, fertilizer, and chemicals.

An *open dry cargo barge* is 195 feet long, has a 1,530-ton capacity and carries coal, steel, ore, sand, gravel, and lumber.

117

The *covered dry cargo barge*, with a similar length and capacity, is used for grain, soybeans, coffee, salt, sugar, paper products, and packaged goods.

A fourth type, the *coastal ocean going tank barge*, is used in coastal service for petroleum and petroleum products. It is 550 feet long, has a 225,000-barrel capacity, and a deeper hull for maneuverability in ocean waters.

There are about 18,000 barges in use in the country today. While the average tow size is 15 barges, today's powerful towboats can push as many as 40. An uncovered barge costs about $500,000 and has an expected life of 25 to 30 years. [11]

The Inland Waterway System

The inland waterway system consists of five distinct subsystems; i.e., [12]

1. Great Lakes
2. Mississippi River
3. Coastal Rivers
4. Intracoastal Waterways
5. New York Barge Canal

The *Great Lakes System* consists of the great lakes – Superior, Michigan, Ontario, Huron, and Erie – plus the St. Lawrence Seaway.

The *Mississippi River System* consists of the Mississippi River and those rivers that feed into it, such as the Ohio, Illinois, Missouri and other smaller tributaries. This system is by far the most important.

118

The *Coastal Rivers* are other rivers in the country that flow into the oceans and gulf.

The *Intracoastal Waterway* runs from Massachusetts to the Mexican border along the coastline of the Atlantic Ocean and Gulf of Mexico.

The *New York Barge Canal* is a reconstruction and enhancement of the old Erie Canal.

Most of the country's navigable waterways are in the eastern United States. The total system includes about 25,000 miles of navigable bodies of water.

The river system, especially the Mississippi, is a constantly changing mosaic. With ebbs and flows, high water and low, the banks move, the channels shift, new islands are formed, and others disappear. In the words of Mark Twain, "The Mississippi River will always have its own way; no engineering skill can persuade it to do otherwise." As a result, maintenance and reconstruction are never-ending tasks.

The commercially important waterways (about 12,000 miles) are maintained by the U.S. Army Corps of Engineers. This work consists of almost constant dredging, channel maintenance, and lock and dam repair and upkeep. Most of these locks and dams are quite old and require almost continuous maintenance. For example, above St. Louis, on the Mississippi and

Photography by Greg Thorpe
Courtesy: Ingram Barge Company

Illinois Rivers alone, there are 37 locks and dams with an average age of 50 years.

In addition to their state of repair, they are inadequate for most of the tows on the river. The most frequently used 15-barge tow is about 1,200 feet long, and only three of the locks have 1,200-foot capacity. The remainder are only 600 feet long. [13] A 1,200-foot lock can accommodate one average length towboat and 17 barges while a 600-foot lock can accommodate only eight barges and a

119

towboat. In total, the waterway system has 191 active lock sites with 237 lock chambers. [14]

Photography by Greg Thorpe
Courtesy: Ingram Barge Company

The barge industry pays a 20-cent per gallon fuel tax into a trust fund which is obligated for 50 percent of the new construction and rehabilitation costs. The remaining 50 percent is supposed to come from the General Treasury, although individual project appropriations can vary. At the end of 2005, the Inland Waterways Trust Fund had a balance of $352.6 million. The 2008 budget for the USACE was $4.871 billion, with the bulk of that dedicated to construction, operations, and maintenance for the waterway system.

The Significance of the Industry

The significance of the industry can be measured, to a great extent, by its huge capacity and relatively low cost.

For example, one barge has a capacity of 1,500 tons; 62,500 bushels; or 453,500 gallons. A 15-barge tow can haul 22,500 tons; 767,500 bushels; or 6,804,000 gallons. Comparing these capacities to those of other forms of transport yields the following comparisons:

- One barge equals 15 jumbo rail hoppers or 58 trucks.
- One 15-barge tow equals 2 ¼ 100-car unit trains, or 870 trucks.

Photography by Greg Thorpe
Courtesy: Ingram Barge Company

Stated another way: [15]

- One 15-barge tow is ¼ mile in length.
- Two and a quarter unit trains are 2 ¾ miles.
- 870 trucks total 34 ½ miles (assuming 150 feet between rigs).

Generally speaking, the river charges are 63 percent lower than rail and 94 percent less than truck, second only to pipelines as the lowest cost mode of transport.

Water carriers are very fuel efficient. An average tow can carry one ton 514 miles on a gallon of fuel, compared with 202 miles by rail, and 59 by truck. [16]

Barges carry almost 30 percent of the coal moved in the country, enough to produce over 10 percent of the annual electricity usage. Over 60 percent of all grain exports ($8.5 billion) moves by barge to the ports. It has been estimated that the waterway system adds $5 billion annually to the nation's economy.

The following graph shows the predominant movements for 2006.

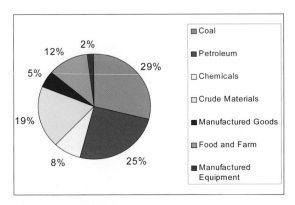

Source: USACE Waterborne Commerce Statistics Center

Figure 7-a. 2006 Inland Waterway Movement by Commodity

These movements consisted of

Commodity	Millions of Short Tons (2000 lbs.)
Coal	183.2
Petroleum	159.5
Crude Materials	120.4
Food and Farm	73.6
Chemicals	48.9
Manufactured Goods	30.9
Manufactured Equipment	9.5
Other	1.4
Total	627.4

According to the 2008 CSCMP State of Logistics Report, about $5 billion was spent on domestic water transportation in 2007.

Characteristics of the Industry

In addition to the large capacity and low cost of water transportation, there are several other advantages as well.

Water transportation is the safest mode of transportation. The industry works closely with the U.S. Coast Guard to prevent accidents and spills. Also, the newer barges all have double hulls which protect the cargo and the environment in case of collisions.

Compared with the congestion of the highways, airways, and (in some cases) railroads, the waterway system for the most part is underutilized.

There is little air and/or noise pollution associated with water traffic. Also, because of the confinement to often isolated waterways, there is no negative social impact. The rivers have always been there and will probably always be there.

There are disadvantages, as well, however. First of all, river transportation is slow. Other than pipelines, it probably is the slowest mode of transport, although with the increase in highway congestion and that of some railroads, that point might be debatable. For example, a trip from New Orleans to Cairo, Illinois takes eight days by water. Moving downstream is faster, of course, but the trip back still takes four days.

In some parts of the country, river traffic is seasonal. During the winter months some rivers and a portion of the Great Lakes are impassable. Rivers such as the Mississippi that do not freeze can nonetheless be impacted by droughts and floods. Droughts on the upper Mississippi, for example, have almost shut down commerce in that area for weeks at a time.

Finally, barge freight cannot be interchanged easily with other carriers. The barges must be loaded and/or unloaded to transfer freight to or from other modes.

Water carriers are subject to regulation by the Surface Transportation Board. This includes transportation on the inland waterways, between ports in the United States, and the U.S. and its territories. Since water carriers are exempt from economic regulation when hauling dry and liquid bulk commodities, however, the practical result is very little economic regulation in the industry.

Carriers can be private, contract, or common, just as in the motor carrier industry.

Cost Structure

The cost structure of the water carriers is very similar to that of motor carriers. The waterways are provided by nature and maintained by the government. Fixed costs consist primarily of lease costs and depreciation on the equipment, plus some other general expenses.

The major expenses (i.e., fuel, labor, and user charges) all vary with the amount of traffic. Operating costs for water carriers are approximately 15 percent fixed and 85 percent variable. [17]

Competition

The primary competition for water carrier for the movement of petroleum and petroleum products is the pipeline system and, to a lesser extent, rail and truck.

For the heavy, bulk products (i.e., coal, rock, etc.) rail carriers are the predominant competitor. The same is true for grain, soybeans, sugar, etc.

For the relatively small amount of package goods and manufactured equipment, the major competitors would be motor carriers.

Competition with the railroads has always been particularly emotional. Rail carriers, of course, maintain their own rights of way but must compete with motor carriers and water carriers that operate over natural or government-supplied and -maintained rights of way. On bulk commodities, there simply is no contest when comparing rail and water rates, and the rail carriers believe that the users of our rivers should contribute more to their maintenance and upkeep. This controversy revolves around the 50 percent of operating and maintenance expenses that come out of the U.S. Treasury General Fund. Advocates of this inequity position argue that barge operators should pay their "fair share," or the government should subsidize the addition of necessary new rail capacity.

Since the number of carriers operating between any two given points on the waterway system is relatively small, competition within the industry is minimal.

Questions for Understanding

1. Describe the various kinds of barges and their primary use.

2. What is the difference between a tugboat and a tow boat?

3. How are navigable waterways financed?

4. Discuss the capacity of a barge compared to that of a truck or rail car.

5. Compare the cost structure of a water carrier compared to that of a railroad.

6. What is the competitive disagreement between railroads and water carriers?

Chapter 8: *Specialized Carriers*

Things aren't always what they seem.

Historically, most shippers usually purchased transportation service directly from the carriers involved. Most transactions were single movements based on the specific agreement between the shipper and the carrier and the rates that were published. As the industry evolved, however, there were several entities that evolved with it and came to play an important role in transportation transactions.

Freight Brokers

A freight broker is a company or an individual that serves as a liaison between a company needing transportation services and the carriers that can provide that service. It does not function as a shipper or a carrier but as an agent that brings the buying and selling parties together. Brokers never take possession of the goods. To operate as a freight broker the individual or company must obtain a license from the Federal Motor Carrier Administration. They are expected to carry insurance and in some areas are required to maintain surety bonds, as well. [1]

While in recent years freight brokers have become more prominent, they are not a new entity by any means. They were recognized in the Motor Carrier Act of 1935 as parties who sell and arrange transportation but do not actually perform the transportation services. [2] As a profession, they have been around as long as the motor carrier industry itself.

 All too often, the term "freight broker" conjures up visions of Joe Bob parked in a booth at the Flying Z truck stop with his cell phone, a pad and pencil, and a generous portion of chicken fried steak. In a few cases, the image may not be too far from the truth. But for the most part, Joe Bob has gone the way of the dinosaur. Today, freight brokerage – the business of matching up shippers who have freight to be moved with carriers who can haul it – has grown into a sophisticated multimillion dollar profession. Brokers have been particularly successful during times of trucking capacity shortages.

Hit by soaring fuel and insurance costs in recent years, thousands of truckers have closed their doors. In ordinary times, that would simply mean more opportunity for the survivors, but truckers looking to expand quickly become discouraged by equipment prices. New engine emissions regulations pushed tractor prices up to record levels. Then there's the problem of finding more drivers. The new driver hours-of-service regulations only exacerbated an already existing driver shortage.

As the smaller, poorly managed fleets were squeezed out of the industry and the rest grappled with equipment and productivity constraints, shippers found themselves caught in a capacity crunch. Many of these shippers turned to brokers and their expansive networks.

Today brokers are larger and more customer-focused than ever before. For example, C. H. Robinson derives a significant amount of its gross profit from managing over-the-road freight even though it doesn't own a single truck.

In the early 2000's, several entrepreneurs launched Internet-based brokerage sites, but the idea never really caught on in a major way. Many logistics managers still prefer more direct, personal negotiations with carriers, particularly for their more service-sensitive customers.

That caution may be misplaced. As more asset-based industry veterans concentrate on brokerage, shippers can use their services with confidence that their shipments will be handled with the same dispatch and care they'd experience through direct dealings with the carriers. A number of responsible carriers have placed their reputation and credibility squarely on the line with their brokerage operations. One of those is Schneider National. Schneider's transportation management operation includes thousands of carrier partners that are qualified annually, and it has established an electronic marketplace to help carriers secure loads.

The one thing freight brokers can't do, of course, is create more trucks. But they can provide access to an expanded array of reliable hauling options. Shippers just have to follow one simple rule: Exercise the same care in selecting a freight broker that you would when buying any other logistics service.

Intermodal Marketing Companies

Somewhat similar to the freight broker is the intermodal marketing company or IMC. The IMC's facilitate intermodal transportation between shippers and rail carriers. They assume no legal liability but function as consolidators or facilitators.

Typically, an IMC will have a volume, "wholesale-priced" contract with various railroads. Because of the significant amount of tonnage they can offer to a rail carrier, the rates they are charted can be significantly lower than those the individual shippers can obtain for themselves. The IMC's will combine the tonnage of various shippers to offer the carrier a combined volume of business. Their profits are derived from the spread between the prices they charge the shippers and those which they pay to the rail carriers.

As intermodal traffic has increased, some IMC's have become quite large and branched into other businesses such as container ownership, brokerage, and drayage. One of the more successful

IMC's has been the Hub Group. Founded in 1971, for the year ending December 31, 2007, the company had revenues of $1.6 billion. A major portion of the revenues realized by an IMC is "pass though" or receipts that are in turn paid out to the carriers, and in the case of the Hub Group in 2007, this amounted to approximately $1.4 billion. The gross margin for the year was $232.2 million. [3]

The Hub Group has relationships with eight major railroads and several other service providers such as K-Line, Maersk Sea-Land, and Pacer International. Carriers in some cases have granted exclusive access to a certain number of containers for dedicated use on their railroads.

In addition, Hub Group functions as one of the larger truck brokerage firms in the country, negotiating rates, tracking shipments, and handling claims for its customers. [4]

One disadvantage in dealing with an IMC is in the area of liability. A shipper typically pays the IMC for the transportation service and it, in turn, reimburses the carrier. If, however, the IMC for any reason does not pay the carrier, the shipper is liable for the freight costs. In the unfortunate event that such a thing happens, a shipper could end up paying the same freight bill twice.

This is not a good reason to exclude IMC's from your transportation management process, however. It simply reinforces the importance of careful due diligence in selecting the provider, just as with any other carrier.

Drayage Companies

Another firm that has experienced rapid growth, along with that of intermodal service, is the drayage company. These companies are the "links" that complete the door-to-door chain of intermodal movement. These carriers, who own tractors, specialize in hauling containers from shippers and ports to the intermodal yards, or from the intermodal yards to the final destination. They haul either chassis they own or those provided by carriers or steamship lines.

Typically, they will operate within a relatively small metropolitan or regional area but, in some cases, may engage in longer hauls, as well. They provide a necessary and important function in intermodal movements.

Freight Forwarders

Freight forwarders can be defined as firms that consolidate the shipments of several shippers, often small- to medium-sized firms, into larger shipments for which they negotiate lower rates with the carriers. The process is very similar to that of an intermodal marketing company. One major distinction of freight forwarders, however, is that when the Interstate Commerce Commission was in existence, freight forwarders were considered to be common carriers and thus subject to regulation by the ICC. Although no longer subject to the same regulations, the freight forwarding industry tends to be a little more structured than brokerage firms, IMC's, and other similar entities. A freight forwarder, for example, must issue a bill of lading to the shipper.

Freight forwarders are generally divided into two basic categories – i.e., surface and air – although many firms function as both. Generally speaking, a surface forwarder utilizes the services of motor, rail, or domestic water carriers, while an air forwarder deals only with shipments by air. They can operate either domestically or internationally.

A surface forwarder will pick up shipments of a firm, consolidate them, provide for the transportation, and arrange for deconsolidation and delivery at the destination. They must issue a bill of lading and accept full responsibility for the shipment much as a motor carrier does. (See Figure 8-a.)

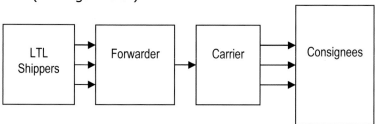

Figure 8-a. A Typical Freight Forwarder Movement

Air freight forwarders offer similar services, but utilize air rather than surface transportation. Because of the expense involved, typically air forwarders will be used by those firms shipping high value goods, having very time-sensitive delivery requirements, or both.

Due to the complexity of global shipments and regulations, international freight forwarders play a more important role than domestic forwarders for many firms. In addition to air forwarding services, an international forwarder will deal with ocean carriage, as well. These firms will be familiar with the import and export rules and regulations of the U.S. and foreign countries, methods of shipment, and the myriad of foreign trade documents.

Even before a sale is made, they can provide information on freight costs, port charges, insurance costs, consular fees, and documentation costs. After the transaction is complete, the forwarder can book the carrier space, complete the documentation, arrange for insurance and packing, advise on regulations, and provide customs clearance. With the growth in the global economy, they are playing a critical role in facilitating international movements.

Freight forwarders also have expanded beyond their basic business

model. UTi, for example, one of the leading forwarders, provides airfreight forwarding, ocean freight forwarding, customs brokerage, contract logistics, and other supply chain management services. By adding additional supply chain services to their basic competency, a freight forwarder can function as a single-source logistics service provider in some cases. This can be particularly important to those firms who lack global supply chain expertise or resources.

Shippers' Associations

Shippers' Associations are non-profit membership cooperatives that operate much as freight forwarders do. They combine the volume of their member companies, then negotiate with the carriers for lower rates than the shippers would be able to obtain individually.

A shippers' association is defined by the American Institute of Shippers Associations as a:

> "Non-profit membership cooperative which makes domestic or international arrangements for the movement of members' cargo. They are a means by which the small and medium sized shipper, and even the large shipper, can obtain economies of scale without the markups charged by other transportation intermediaries who perform consolidation services in order to obtain volume discounts." [5]

They are exempt from regulation, and there is no exposure to anti-trust laws.

The most important reason for joining a shippers' association is to reduce costs, while at the same time maintaining good service. This is particularly valuable to the smaller firm since, if left on its own, its smaller shipments would result in significantly higher costs and, in many cases, inferior service.

It is important to remember, however, that if a firm does not meet its volume commitments to the association, it may incur a penalty. Keep in mind also that if there are competitive firms in the same association, your tonnage may be helping your competitor.

Small Parcel and Express Carriers

As speed of delivery and reductions in inventory levels have become more important, the need for overnight or expedited service has become more prevalent. This is particularly important in the retail trade where consumers want their purchases in three days, two days, or even one day and are simply unwilling to wait longer. No longer are we satisfied to wait four to six weeks for delivery. We have become an instant gratification society.

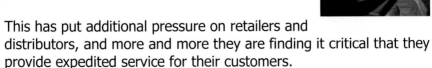

This has put additional pressure on retailers and distributors, and more and more they are finding it critical that they provide expedited service for their customers.

From an inventory perspective, firms have reduced stock levels to a point that if there is a production difficulty or other disruption in the normal process, expedited replenishment stocks can become necessary very quickly.

Two U.S.-based firms have emerged as the real giants in this industry; i.e., United Parcel Service and FedEx. Both have become true global providers and, in addition to their expedited services, have branched into other services, as well. Both, for example, have extensive less-than-truckload operations to complement their other businesses.

Photography by Clifford Lynch

FedEx

The founder of FedEx, Frederick W. Smith, has become almost a cult hero in the industry. In 1971, Fred Smith used a $4 million inheritance and over $90 million in other capital to acquire a Little Rock, Arkansas, used aircraft business. It was his intention to provide an overnight delivery service. [6]

In 1973, Federal Express, with 389 employees and 14 Dassault Falcon planes, began operations at the Memphis International Airport. By 2007, FedEx had revenues of $35.2 billion, 280,000 employees, and 672 aircraft. Its businesses include

- FedEx Express - express transportation
- FedEx Ground - small package delivery
- FedEx Freight - LTL
- FedEx Kinko's - document solutions and business services

For the year 2007, FedEx Express operations included the following:

Average Daily Volumes

U.S. overnight boxes	1,174,000
U.S. overnight envelopes	706,000
U.S. deferred delivery packages	898,000
U.S. freight pounds	9,569,000
International priority freight pounds	1,878,000
International airfreight pounds	1,831,000

FedEx Ground had an average daily package volume of 3,126,000. [7]

Memphis, Tennessee, functions as the major hub for FedEx Express, although other hubs in Anchorage, Alaska; Fort Worth, Texas; Indianapolis, Indiana; Newark, New Jersey; and Oakland, California are utilized as well. Packages are sent by air to these hubs where they are sorted and loaded for their final destinations. In order to accommodate pickup and delivery, FedEx operates an international network of pickup and delivery vehicles and facilities. According to the 2007 Annual Report, there were 45,000 vehicles, 1,401 stations, and over 50,000 drop-off locations.

Overnight delivery is available to most destinations in the United States and international deliveries to 220 countries can be accomplished within a few days.

United Parcel Service

Although best known for its brown trucks and domestic package delivery, UPS has become a worldwide provider of expedited services, as well. Founded in 1907, UPS has 428,000 employees, 3,000 operating facilities, 150,000 worldwide access points, 282 aircraft, and 94,500 package delivery vehicles. Revenues for 2006 were $47.5 billion. [8]

As in the case with FedEx, UPS has added additional businesses including a less-than-truckload carrier, freight forwarding, UPS stores, and UPS Supply Chain Solutions.

For the year 2006, UPS had the following statistics.

Average Daily Package Volume

Domestic Next Day Air	1,267,000
Domestic Deferred	993,000
Domestic Ground	11,537,000
International Domestic	1,108,000
International Export	689,000

The primary hub for UPS is at Louisville, Kentucky.

Both FedEx and UPS offer extremely good tracking systems and other technology, as well as a full line of freight forwarding and customs brokerage services for its expedited customers.

DHL

DHL, with 2007 revenues of $21.6 billion (US), is owned by the Deutsche Post and serves over 200 countries and territories. It is known primarily for its international capability, but has made a significant investment in marketing its services in the U.S. While it made some progress in the U.S. market, it is not considered to be a serious threat to either FedEx or UPS.

It does have the physical resources (400 aircraft, 450 hubs and terminals, and 170,000 employees) to be a factor in international shipping, but for whatever reason, it has not been able to capture the momentum of its competitors, at least in the U.S.

Courtesy: Memphis-Shelby County Airport Authority

In a 2008 move to attempt to do so, DHL completely shut down its air network in the U.S. and outsourced all air transportation to UPS. DHL also curtailed its ground structure in certain parts of the United States. This move was designed to generate a profit in the DHL U.S. Express business by 2012. [9]

Motor Carrier Expedited Service

There are also motor carriers who offer an expedited service, as well. For small domestic shipments, these can be a reliable, less expensive option.

These carriers usually have good shipment tracking capability and, in some cases, a guaranteed delivery schedule.

Household Goods Carriers

The movement of household goods is a specialized service that is handled by firms that are equipped to handle the unique requirements. Office movements fall into this same category. These firms can be national, local, franchised, or independent and operate quite differently than the traditional motor carrier.

The cost of a shipment is estimated by the carrier before the move is made, and the estimator, in turn, evaluates the services that may be required. Each item must be inspected prior to loading, and every scratch, scrape, or other damage must be noted and agreed to by the shipper. Once the shipment is loaded, it is weighed and sent to its destination. There it is unloaded, placed in the new location – apartment, house, or office – and inspected for damage.

Charges are based on the actual weight moved.

This specialized transportation can be very stressful for all. Moving itself is a stressful experience for most, and damage to personal items can be a very traumatic experience. In some cases, actual charges will be more than the estimated cost, creating even more stress and dissatisfaction.

Also, the combination of local, national, and franchise operators can be confusing, and it is sometimes difficult to determine who has the responsibility for adjustments.

A number of household goods carriers have discontinued their basic business and moved to the transportation of high value, electronic equipment. Using their fleets of cushion underframe equipment, as well as the blankets and braces used for household goods, many carriers have found the transportation of copy machines, computers, ATM's and other large electronic equipment to be much more rewarding – both financially and emotionally.

Owner-Operator

Finally, a discussion of specialized carriers would not be complete without a mention of owner-operators. These truck drivers usually

own their own tractors and, in some cases, their trailers. They hire out either to regular for-hire carriers or solicit their own loads, usually through brokers and other intermediaries. They are paid by the mile and pay their own expenses.

In the 1970's, this was a very popular occupation and conjured up visions of *Smokey and the Bandit* and CB radios. In recent years, however, the cost of the equipment, insurance and fuel costs, and hours-of-service regulations have made this occupation much less attractive. During the high fuel cost periods in the mid-2000's it became almost impossible for an owner-operator to earn enough to live decently. Even when they were able to do so, it required much more time and energy than some were willing and/or able to devote to the occupation.

While there no doubt will always be some owner-operators, it is unlikely that they will ever again be a major factor in the industry.

Questions for Understanding

1. Discuss the differences between a freight forwarder and a shippers' association.

2. Explain the function of a freight broker.

3. Does an intermodal marketing company add value to the transportation function?

4. Discuss the major issues facing household goods carriers.

5. Discuss the future of owner-operators.

Chapter 9: Transportation Pricing

"Who pays well is served well."
- The Mafia Manager

In previous chapters, the cost structures of the various modes of transport were discussed, and an understanding of these is important to the understanding of transportation pricing in general. It is also necessary to have some grasp of the underlying forces which drive the pricing of transportation services and markets in general.

Market Structures

Economic theory teaches us that there are four basic market structures:

- pure competition,
- monopoly,
- monopolistic competition, and
- oligopoly

The structures differ from each other in five ways: [1]

- number of sellers,
- number of buyers,
- whether seller or buyer influences prices,

- barriers to entry, and
- price elasticity of demand

The term *price elasticity of demand* describes the relationship between the changes in the demand for a product and the changes in price. It is developed from the following formula.

$$\text{price elasticity of demand} = \frac{\text{percentage change in quantity demanded}}{\text{percentage change in price}}$$

If the percentage change in the quantity demanded is greater than the percentage change in price, demand is elastic, or responsive to price changes. If the demand percentage is less than that of the percentage change in price, demand is inelastic, or not greatly influenced by price changes. [2]

Demand is considered to be perfectly elastic when a firm can sell all its output at one price, but nothing above that price. [3] This would be characteristic of pure competition where there are a large number of producers and buyers of the same product and no one firm is large enough to influence the market.

At the opposite end of the spectrum is a perfect monopoly. Here there is a single seller with many buyers of a necessary product or service in a market which is difficult for new sellers to enter. Demand is highly inelastic. An example of this type of structure might be a local utility from which households must buy electricity or natural gas or do without.

Monopolistic competition describes a market where there are many sellers offering slightly different products that can be substituted for each other. Sellers often will distinguish themselves on product or service characteristics. [4] Motor carriers, for example, operate in this type market. Price elasticity is fairly high.

An oligopoly has a relatively small number of sellers, but a large number of buyers. The products or services are somewhat similar, and often there is a price leader. If one seller drops its prices, others will follow suit in order to maintain market share. Barriers to entry will limit the number of suppliers, but when developing strategic plans, an oligopolistic firm must always plan for reactions by competitors to changes in its prices. In transportation, airlines and railroads operate within this environment.

Freight costs and fuel surcharges, like other costs such as production, marketing, etc., all are included in the price of a product; but whether continuing increases in freight costs will influence consumption depends on the elasticity of demand for the product, as well as the supply. [5] The less elastic the demand for a product is (i.e., the less its consumption is influenced by changes in price), the more likely it is that an increase in freight costs will raise the price of the product.

Figure 9-a [6] illustrates the impact of a price change on the consumption of a product which has a relatively inelastic demand, or a steep demand curve.

Since the demand is inelastic, the price change (P') results in only a slight curtailment of consumption.

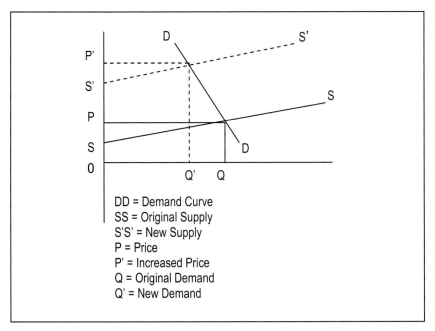

Figure 9-a. Inelastic Demand

If, however, the demand is elastic, the demand curve is less steep, and a price increase will have a more significant impact on consumption. See Figure 9-b. [7]

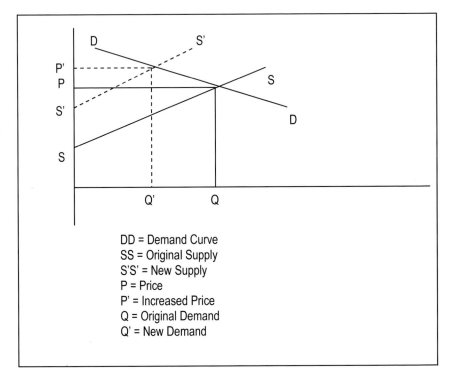

DD = Demand Curve
SS = Original Supply
S'S' = New Supply
P = Price
P' = Increased Price
Q = Original Demand
Q' = New Demand

Figure 9-b. Elastic Demand

In both examples it is assumed that supply curves will remain the same. It should be noted, however, that supplies can be elastic and inelastic, as well, and affected by changes in price. For a more detailed explanation, any good economics textbook will be helpful. Suffice it to say, for our purposes, freight costs have an impact on prices, the magnitude of which depends on elasticity of demand.

Other Costs

In addition to the fixed and variable cost components, other types of costs must be considered as well in order to develop a comprehensive pricing structure.

Common Costs are costs that cannot be traced to specific activities such as the cost of a rail line or terminal used for any number of services and products.

Direct Costs are those that can easily be allocated to a particular activity. The repair cost of a trailer or railcar, for example, can readily be assigned to the piece of equipment.

Indirect Costs, on the other hand, cannot be. The salary of the manager of the maintenance facility that repairs the trailer, for example, would be an indirect cost.

Sunk Costs are those that already have been incurred and will be uninfluenced by future activity.

Pricing

Cost of service pricing is used by carriers attempting to cover only the actual expense of providing the specific service. There is no contribution to overhead. Obviously, pricing everything in this manner would be unproductive over the long run, and at some point overhead and other costs such as those mentioned above must be covered, as well as some contribution made to profit.

Full cost pricing allows a carrier to cover all its variable costs plus a proportionate share of fixed costs. [8] This form of pricing allows the carrier to provide necessary maintenance and replace equipment when necessary. In the long term, only full cost pricing will allow a carrier to survive.

Value of service pricing is sometimes called whatever the traffic will bear. This form of pricing allows the carrier to maximize its revenue regardless of what its costs are. It will charge up to the price point that shippers will discontinue the use of the service.

These three methods represent the full spectrum of pricing. See Figure 9-c.

145

Maximum	Value of Service
Somewhere in Between	Fully Allocated
Minimum	Cost of Service

Figure 9-c. The Pricing Spectrum

Marginal cost pricing concentrates on contribution margin. In other words, as long as revenues are greater than variable costs, some contribution is being made to overhead and profits. An airline provides a good example of pricing of this type. Figure 9-d provides a hypothetical cost structure for Up, Up and Away Airlines.

Fixed Cost Per Flight	$10,000
Variable Cost Per Passenger	$300
Capacity	100
Passengers Booked	99

Figure 9-d. Up, Up and Away Airlines Cost Structure

In the above case, there is one ticket left to sell. If the marginal pricing method is used, the minimum charged for that ticket would be $300. Any revenue above that would contribute to the margin.

If, however, the airline wishes to recoup its full cost, the price of the ticket would be $300 plus the share of fixed costs ($10,000/100, or $100) for a total of $400. This would enable the airline to recover the total cost of $40,000 for the flight. While this would cover the total cost in this example, there is no profit. Also as a practical matter, one could argue that rather than let the plane take off with one empty seat, some revenue is better than none. This is the theory behind lower fares for Saturday night stayovers, for example.

In the final analysis, however, actual pricing will depend on competition and individual airline operating characteristics.

Breakeven Analysis

Breakeven analysis, while on the surface somewhat complicated, is actually a very simple concept. Breakeven is that point at which carrier operations operate at neither a profit nor a loss. [9] The formula for breakeven is

$$TR - VC - FC = 0$$

TR = units sold times unit price
VC = units sold times variable cost of each
FC = fixed costs

Figure 9-e provides the necessary data for a hypothetical XYZ Motor Freight.

Variable (per unit)	
Fuel	$10.00
Labor	7.00
Other	5.00
Total	22.00
Fixed (annual total)	
Salaries (management)	$150,000
Equipment Leases	100,000
Terminal Leases	50,000
Miscellaneous	30,000
Total	$330,000

Note: Example has been simplified for clarity.

Figure 9-e. Cost Structure XYZ Motor Freight

To understand the concept, a few simple exercises will be helpful.

(a) If XYZ Motor Freight charges $30 per unit, what is the breakeven number of units?

With "X" as the unknown number of units, the formula would be

147

$$TR - VC - FC = 0$$

$$30X - 22X - 330,000 = 0$$
$$8X - 330,000 = 0$$
$$8X = 330,000$$
$$X = 41,250 \text{ units}$$

In other words, to break even, XYZ Motor Freight would have to sell 41,250 units at $30 each.

(b) If XYZ Motor Freight believes it will only handle 27,000 units in 2008, what is the breakeven price per unit?

$$TR - VC - FC = 0$$

Where "SP" equals the unknown selling price:

$$27,000SP - 27,000 \times \$22 - \$330,000 = 0$$
$$27,000SP - \$594,000 - \$330,000 = 0$$
$$27,000SP = \$924,000$$
$$SP = \$34.22$$

The breakeven selling price will be $34.22.

(c) One could argue, however, XYZ Motor Freight is not in business to break even. Suppose it wants to make a profit of $90,000 this year. How many units does it have to handle, assuming a price of $30 per unit?

Again, with "X" as the unknown:

$$\$30X - 22X - \$330,000 = \$90,000$$
$$8X - \$330,000 = \$90,000$$
$$8X = \$420,000$$
$$X = 52,500$$

(d) Finally, revised plans indicate a softening in the business – possibly as low as 30,000 units. What does XYZ have to charge per unit to ensure the $90,000 profit?

$$30,000SP - 30,000 \times \$22 - \$330,000 = \$90,000$$
$$30,000SP - \$660,000 - \$330,000 = \$90,000$$
$$30,000SP = \$1,080,000$$
$$SP = \$36$$

When relying on breakeven analyses, it is important to remember that costs change frequently, and the analyses must be revised every time they do so. They can be extremely helpful, however, in setting transportation prices, particularly under fixed contracts.

Variables in Pricing

Bowersox and Closs have identified at least seven other variables that will influence pricing – volume, distance, liability, market factors, handling requirements, density, and stowability. [10]

Volume will, of course, affect economies of scale. Average costs will decline as volume increases, and these decreases should be reflected in the rates.

Distance is an important factor in that total costs will increase at a slower rate than the distance. This is demonstrated by the tapering rate principle illustrated in Figure 9-f.

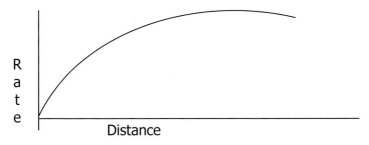

Figure 9-f. Tapering Rate Principle

Liability is a reflection of the products' susceptibility to loss and damage. More expensive and more fragile goods will command higher rates.

Market factors will affect rates, as well. The availability of equipment and competition have direct impacts on rate levels. The availability of backhauls, for example, also will influence a carrier's rates into a given market.

Handling requirements will impact costs and, therefore, prices. Special handling equipment, transloading, and other non-transportation handling will result in higher rates.

Density is the relationship between weight and cubic dimensions of the product. Assuming no violation of state weight restrictions, a truck can handle a bigger payload of canned goods than it can ready-to-eat cereals. The canned goods will weigh out before they cube out, and the cereals will do just the opposite. The rates per hundredweight on canned goods, therefore, will be lower than those on cereals.

Stowability is a similar concern. The best loads are tight and compact and yield little, if any, wasted space in the trailer or rail car.

Rate Systems

Rate making has changed dramatically since 1980. Prior to deregulation rate making was a complex, tedious, and often disputed process; and there was little room for creativity or innovation. Since that time, however, both carriers and shippers have been able to negotiate more competitive and reasonable arrangements. There are any number of pricing variations, the most important of which are discussed briefly.

Contracts

If the parties desire, prices can be contractual. Both rail and motor carriers can negotiate rate and service contracts with their shippers. These can be based on minimum volumes, provide for special delivery schedules or almost any consideration the parties agree to. These contracts do not have to be published in tariffs.

Mileage Rates

Most truckload shipments and many rail shipments move under mileage rates. Truckload carriers will publish rates per mile between points which they service without regard to the commodities hauled.

FAK (Freight All Kinds) Rates

These rates are not based on the commodity but on the value of the service. These rates are usually quoted in cents per hundredweight or total cost per truckload.

Multiple Car Rates

Published by rail carriers, these rates offer lower rates for multiple carloads than for single carloads. Grain shipments often are priced in this manner.

Trainload Rates

Rail carriers also publish rates for a trainload of a single commodity. Coal usually moves under such a pricing arrangement.

Spot Market Rates

These rates, often found on Internet sites or negotiated through brokers, match shippers and carriers for particular movements at a given point in time. Often lower rates may be obtained from a carrier trying to reposition equipment, for example.

Less-Than-Truckload (LTL) rates

LTL rates may be the most complex of the post-deregulation environment. These rates are based on the National Motor Freight Classification which provides a class rating for virtually every product that is shipped. The rates used to be based strictly on mileage, but today they can be negotiated.

This is usually done, however, through discounts from the classification rates. For example, a carrier may quote rates between any number of zip codes based on a discount from the class rates – for example, 60 percent of Class 70.

A more recent development has been the use of benchmark rate structures such as CzarLite, a product of SMC[3]. Many companies use this baseline as the scale against which to negotiate their LTL rates with individual carriers. This sophisticated model operates on a three and five digit zip code basis, and provides a more reliable and accurate tool for negotiating individual rates.

Collective Rate Making

One last vestige of regulation was finally eliminated on May 7, 2007, when the Surface Transportation Board finally snipped off one of the last remaining regulatory loose threads. In a ruling many shippers had awaited for over a quarter of a century, the board terminated its approval of the agreements among 11 motor carrier bureaus to collectively determine and set truck rates.

To understand the significance of the board's decision, a short review of the origins of motor carrier regulation in 1935 will be helpful. As discussed in Chapter 2, that year the Motor Carrier Act brought carriers under the purview of the Interstate Commerce Commission (ICC), which was given oversight over who could enter the trucking business, what routes they could serve, and what rates they could charge. The 1935 law, however, left the legal status of collective ratemaking unclear. After a number of investigations and lawsuits, Congress settled the matter by passing the Reed-Bulwinkle Act in 1948, which allowed motor carrier rate bureaus to set rates

collectively and granted them antitrust immunity for doing so.

And that's exactly what the carriers did for the next 30-plus years. Rates were set via a two-part procedure: First, the National Classification Committee established ratings for all products based on their transportation characteristics. Then, the bureaus established the rates. Those rates were what most shippers paid.

152

Then the deregulatory winds began to blow through the industry. With passage of the Motor Carrier Act of 1980, Congress for the most part deregulated the trucking business. It did not, however, lift all pricing restrictions. Nor did it rescind antitrust immunity for the collective ratemaking process. The practice was allowed to continue, although after 1980, many carriers chose not to participate.

In 1995, Congress passed the Interstate Commerce Commission Termination Act, which lifted the remaining restrictions on trucking rates with three exceptions: rates for household-goods moves, rates for certain joint motor-water movements, and rates set collectively by motor carrier bureaus. But in drafting the law, Congress also made provisions for the collective ratemaking issue to be revisited in the future. The law mandated a periodic review of existing motor carrier bureau agreements under a "public interest" standard – a task that would fall to the Surface Transportation Board. The May, 2007 decision was the result of the board's most recent review.

In that review, the STB concentrated on whether its continued approval of collective ratemaking agreements would be consistent with the public interest – specifically to fostering such national transportation policy goals as encouraging fair competition (with reasonable rates); allowing a variety of quality and price options to meet changing market demands and the diverse requirements of the shipping public; and maintaining a sound, safe, and competitive privately owned motor carrier system. After more than two years of deliberation, the STB concluded, among other things, that the current system put certain shippers at a disadvantage in bargaining and that collective rate increases had probably artificially inflated rates. From there, it wasn't much of a stretch to decide that the current arrangements fell short of meeting the national transportation policy's requirements.

This is significant in that twenty-seven years after deregulation, there finally was, and is, a truly competitive free motor carrier market.

FOB Terms

While technically not a part of transportation pricing, it is important

153

to understand the FOB terms used in conjunction with freight costs. The FOB (Free on Board) terms, or terms of sale, define when title passes to the buyer, who pays the freight charges, and which party is liable for loss and/or damage. [11]

There are six different terms of sale and freight payment options available to buyers and sellers of goods. [12] These are diagrammed below.

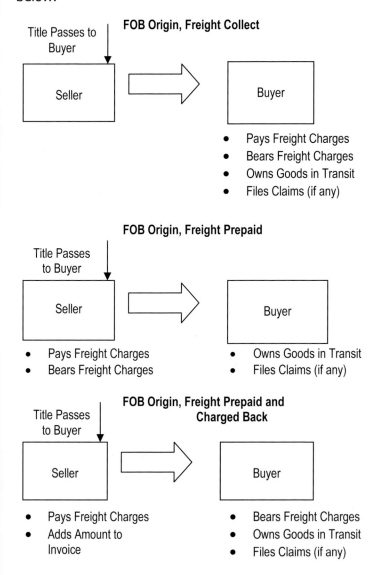

FOB Origin, Freight Collect

Title Passes to Buyer

Seller

Buyer

- Pays Freight Charges
- Bears Freight Charges
- Owns Goods in Transit
- Files Claims (if any)

FOB Origin, Freight Prepaid

Title Passes to Buyer

Seller

Buyer

- Pays Freight Charges
- Bears Freight Charges

- Owns Goods in Transit
- Files Claims (if any)

FOB Origin, Freight Prepaid and Charged Back

Title Passes to Buyer

Seller

Buyer

- Pays Freight Charges
- Adds Amount to Invoice

- Bears Freight Charges
- Owns Goods in Transit
- Files Claims (if any)

FOB Destination, Freight Collect

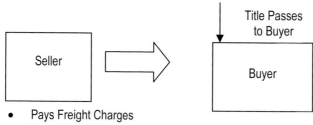

Title Passes
to Buyer

Seller

Buyer

- Owns Goods in Transit
- Files Claims (if any)

- Pays Freight Charges

FOB Destination, Freight Prepaid

Title Passes
to Buyer

Seller

Buyer

- Pays Freight Charges
- Bears Freight Charges
- Owns Goods in Transit
- Files Claims (if any)

FOB Destination, Freight Collect and Allowed

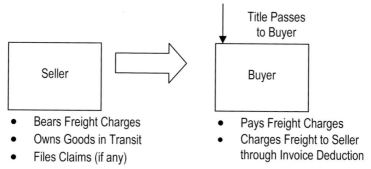

Title Passes
to Buyer

Seller

Buyer

- Bears Freight Charges
- Owns Goods in Transit
- Files Claims (if any)

- Pays Freight Charges
- Charges Freight to Seller through Invoice Deduction

As will be seen in Chapter 13, domestic FOB terms are not as complex as those for international shipments, but nevertheless are important to the understanding of transportation costing and pricing.

As discussed in Chapter 4, fuel surcharges have complicated the entire pricing structures and, to the extent possible, should not be treated as part of the basic transportation pricing structure.

Questions for Understanding

1. Discuss the differences between elastic and inelastic demand.

2. Discuss the ways in which market structures differ from each other.

3. Explain the breakeven analysis.

4. Discuss the differences between cost of service pricing and full cost pricing.

5. What are some of the variables in establishing freight rates?

6. Describe the difference between FOB Origin and FOB Destination.

Chapter 10: Transportation Management

Success is good management in action.
- William E. Holler

In the previous chapters we have described the various modes of transportation and the characteristics of each, pricing, and technology; but the major challenge will be in the management of the transportation function within the firm. As discussed in Chapter 1, transportation is a major expense for most companies, and its effective management will be critical to the success of the business enterprise.

Bloomberg, LeMay, and Hanna define transportation management as "the planning, implementation, and control of transportation services to achieve organizational goals and objectives." [1] Stated another way, it is the management of the time and place utility of your firm's products.

Planning

Planning should start with the definition of a transportation strategy that will be aligned with both the firm's overall goals as well as its supply chain strategy. The transportation manager must identify the objectives for the function and define those tactics that will be used to achieve them. These objectives will usually include those related to cost, service, and desired position in the marketplace.

Secondly, the manager must decide what type of organization will be necessary to efficiently manage the function. The size and complexity of the organization will depend on the size of the firm, but it will be necessary to provide for the management of such activities as:

- Strategy and planning
- Carrier selection
- Rate negotiations
- Service monitoring
- Technology
- Accounting
- Expediting and tracing
- Audit and payment
- Carrier management
- Documentation

Once the appropriate organization is in place, the manager will be in a position to concentrate on the more strategic issues.

Strategy

There will be four strategic decisions the transportation manager must make:

1. What modes will be used?
2. What carriers will be used within the selected modes?
3. Will transportation be outsourced, or will the firm provide its own resources; i.e., private fleet?
4. What type of technology will be used to manage the function and control costs?

Mode Selection

All modes of transportation offer unique advantages and disadvantages, but mode selection will be dictated primarily by the nature of the goods. For example, consumer goods will usually move by truck or small parcel carriers, sand and gravel will be moved by barge or rail, and crude oil will be transported by pipeline, rail, or truck. While there often will be more than one option, most

158

firms will settle on one or two primary modes. Some of the service components for each mode were discussed in Chapter 1.

Carrier Selection

Once the appropriate mode has been selected, the next important decision will be to decide which carrier(s) within that mode to utilize.

Price

Prior to deregulation in 1980, price was not a factor in the selection of a carrier. Since rates were regulated, with a few unique exceptions, all carriers charged the same rates for transporting the same products between the same two points over the same routes. Carrier selection decisions, for the most part, were based on factors other than price such as service and relationships. That is not the case today. All other things being equal, the shipper, more often than not, will select that carrier that can provide satisfactory service at the lowest price.

Contracts

The rates paid may take any number of different forms as described in Chapter 9; but for repetitive movements, it often will be desirable to enter into a contract with selected carriers. Each mode and each carrier will have unique contracts, but the one most traffic managers will encounter more often is the motor carrier contract.

While there is no one best form of document for this purpose, contract motor carrier agreements tend to be fairly straightforward. Often the selected carrier will be able to provide a contract form that requires little modification. In any case, while flexibility should be maintained, the agreement should be as brief as possible.

A contract may be entered into for either truckload or less-than-truckload services. These will be slightly different due to the differences in services required, but the general provisions will be very similar. Provisions of a representative truckload agreement will be discussed in the following paragraphs, and a sample contract is provided in Appendix 10-1. Please remember that the terms and conditions may not apply in all jurisdictions or to all situations.

Professional legal advice should be sought before any such document is executed.

Preamble

THIS CONTRACT is made and entered into this _____ day of _____, 20__, by and between _____, hereinafter referred to as Company and _____, hereinafter referred to as Carrier.

WHEREAS, Carrier is engaged in the business of transporting property for hire by motor vehicle, is duly authorized by the appropriate state and federal regulatory authorities to operate as a motor carrier transporting the property hereinafter described, within the territories hereinafter described, and desires to serve Company as a contract carrier by motor vehicle; and

WHEREAS, Company, having authority to choose the Carrier for transportation of freight to be tendered under this Agreement, desires to enter into an Agreement with Carrier providing for transportation of such quantities of Company's property as it, its suppliers and consignors may tender to Carrier for shipment, between designated origins and destinations;

NOW THEREFORE, in consideration of the mutual promises herein contained, the parties hereto agree as follows:

The Whereas Clause establishes that the carrier is ready, willing, and able to perform the services being contracted for and has the appropriate legal authority.

It is a good idea to incorporate a copy of the authority into the contract as an appendix, as well.

Scope of Agreement

Carrier shall transport between origins and destinations designated by Company, products named in Schedule A attached hereto, under such terms and conditions and at such rates and charges as set forth in Schedule B attached hereto, as the same may be supplemented or amended pursuant to Sections ___ and ___ hereof.

Shipments made under this Contract shall be subject to the rules and regulations attached as Schedule C. This Contract shall supersede any conflicting bill of lading or tariff provision. Amendments to rules must be made in the manner described in Sections ___ and ___ hereof to be effective as to transportation provided under this Contract.

This section identifies, through attached schedules, the origins, destinations, products, terms and conditions applicable to the contract.

Schedule A should designate all the products of the Company that will be covered by the contract.

Schedule B should outline all the terms and conditions of the transportation, including rates, accessorial charges, discounts, if any, and special waivers. (Examples shown in the appendix are just that, and should be modified according to individual situations.)

Schedule C will cover any unusual arrangements such as fuel surcharges.

Payment of Freight Charges

Payment of freight charges shall be the responsibility of the Company, consignee, or other party as set forth by the bill of lading. Payments shall be due within ____ days following receipt of invoice by Company. However, a late payment will not alter the application of discounts, rates and charges. Shipments must be invoiced as soon as practicable after delivery, but in no event more than ____ days thereafter; failure to bill charges to Company within the said ____ days shall waive forever any right of Carrier to bill to or collect from Company charges for any shipment not billed, regardless of any rule, regulation or understanding to the contrary.

Since the sunset of the Interstate Commerce Act, there are no regulatory requirements for the payment of freight charges, so the agreement for responsibility and timing must be included in the contract.

Minimum Volume Commitment

Company agrees to tender to Carrier and Carrier agrees to transport for Company a minimum of ___ shipments of Company's freight during the initial term of this Contract, and during each subsequent renewal hereof. Should this Contract be terminated at any time other than the conclusion of the initial term hereof or the end of any subsequent renewal period, the minimum quantity of freight provided in this section as applying to the final partial term hereof shall be reduced by the proportion the unexpired portion of the term bears to one year.

Should Shipper fail to tender or to have tendered to Carrier the minimum volume set forth in this Section, such failure shall not change in any respect the rates or charges due Carrier for shipments which Shipper did tender or have tendered for movement.

Contractual rates almost always are, or should be, lower than transactional rates, but require a minimum commitment by the shipper. The agreed-upon minimum number of shipments is incorporated into this section.

Rate and Rule Changes

Rates and charges in the Contract shall not be increased during the term of this Contract, and rules shall not be changed, except by mutual written agreement of Company and Carrier. Unless otherwise agreed in writing, no rate increase by Carrier shall take effect on less than ___ days' notice to Company.

Rate reductions (including cancellation of a proposed increase) may be made on ___ days' notice to Company.

These paragraphs outline the terms and conditions under which rates and charges may be increased or decreased. Rate increases usually require fifteen days' notice, but reductions only one. While this may seem somewhat biased in favor of the shipper, the shipper can adjust to a reduction much more readily than to an increase which may affect its own prices, relationships with customers, etc.

This section also should specify exactly how billing should be submitted and in what format. This will be particularly important if the shipper has a Transportation Management System or other automated process.

Loss and Damage

Carrier will be liable for loss or damage to the Goods only while in the care and control of the Carrier, and when it results from the negligence or intentional acts

of the Carrier, its employees, subcontractors, or agents. In no event will the Carrier be liable for concealed damage or where the loss or damage is caused by an act of God, the public enemy, and act of Company or its employees or agents, a public authority or the inherent nature of the Goods. Carrier's liability to Company for any loss or damage to the Goods shall not exceed the direct cost to the Company of the Goods involved, including transportation to the point of loss or damage, less its salvage value, if any.

A claim under this contract for loss, damage, injury or delay to a shipment shall be made in writing or electronically within ___ days after delivery or tender of delivery of the shipment, or, if it is not delivered or tendered for delivery, within ____ months after a reasonable time for delivery has elapsed. If shipment is made at a released value, it will be declared on the Bill of Lading.

Any action at law or suit in equity pertaining to a shipment transported by Carrier shall be commenced within ___ years from the date Company receives written notice from Carrier that Company's claim or any part thereof has been disallowed.

This section spells out liability and terms of settlement. Provision for released values, if any, should be included in this section. Also, if the company is successful in negotiating "offsets," the provisions will appear here; i.e.,

Company shall have the immediate right to offset freight or other charges owed to Carrier against claims for loss, damage or delay, or for overcharge and duplicate payment claims, unless Carrier disputes such claims.

Undercharges and Overcharges

Any action or proceeding by the Carrier to recover charges alleged to be due hereunder, and any action or proceeding by Company to recover overcharges alleged to be due hereunder, shall be commenced no more than ____ (___)

days after delivery or tender of delivery of the shipment with respect to which such charges or overcharges are claimed. To the extent permitted by applicable law, the expiration of the said ____-day period shall be a complete and absolute defense to any such action or proceeding, without regard to any mitigating or extenuating circumstance or excuse whatever. Undercharge claims may not be collected unless notice is received by company within ___ days of the original freight bill date.

The terms and conditions of collection of overcharges and/or undercharges by either party must be indicated.

For both loss and damage and undercharge and overcharge claims, the applicable law within the contractual jurisdiction should be reviewed before executing the Contract.

Distinct Needs of Shipper

A company may want to ensure that the carrier meets the continuing needs and requirements of the company. In the ever-changing environment of the twenty-first century this could be a very important provision. Examples of important considerations are shown in Schedule D of the contract in Appendix 10-1.

Carrier agrees that it will provide service to Company as a contract carrier by motor vehicle, which is and will be designed to meet the distinct needs of Company. Carrier shall tailor its service to meet those needs more particularly set forth in Schedule D attached hereto, as well as those indicated elsewhere in this Agreement.

There shall be a review on an ongoing basis on the requirement to alter or amend the service standards from those initially needed by Company, so as to make certain that the distinct needs of Company continue to be met. Carrier agrees to train its personnel who provide and will provide service to Company to ensure that Company receives that service which meets and will continue to meet Company's distinct needs.

Insurance

Carrier, at its own expense, agrees to carry and keep in force at all times public liability, property damage, cargo, and workmen's compensation insurance with such reliable insurance companies and in such amounts as Company may from time to time approve and such as will meet the requirements of federal and state regulatory bodies having jurisdiction of Carrier's operations under this Contract. Certificates of insurance showing Carrier's compliance with the provisions of this section shall be furnished to Company prior to any transportation under this Contract and whenever Carrier changes or renews its insurance coverage.

This paragraph covers the carrier's insurance obligations. The company should make sure that the carrier has the necessary insurance coverage in adequate amounts.

Independent Contractor

It is the specific intention of the parties that this Contract not be construed to make Carrier or any of its agents or employees in any sense a servant, employee, agent, partner or joint-venture participant of or with Company, and Carrier is not authorized or empowered by this Contract to obligate or bind Company in any manner whatsoever. Carrier shall conduct operations hereunder as an independent contractor, and as such shall have control over its employees and shall retain responsibility for complying with all federal, state and local laws pertaining in any way to this Contract. Said responsibilities include, but are not limited to, provision of safe equipment appropriate to haul Company's property tendered under this Contract, assumption of full responsibility for payment of all state and federal taxes for unemployment insurance, old age pensions, or any other social security law or laws as to all employees or agents of Carrier engaged in the performance of this Contract. Carrier shall not display Company's name on any motor vehicle equipment it provides under this Contract without specific authorization to do so from Company.

The Carrier must be identified as an independent contractor and in no manner affiliated with the Company.

Indemnification

Carrier agrees to indemnify and hold Company harmless from any and all claims for death or injury to persons, and loss or damage to property of any nature arising from Carrier's transportation of property for Company. Carrier further agrees to comply with all applicable federal and state statures, rules and regulations, including judicial interpretations thereof, and to also indemnify and hold Company harmless from any and all claims or fines arising from Carrier" transportation of property of Company in violation of any such statute, rule or regulation.

Force Majeure

Neither Company nor Carrier shall be liable for failure to perform caused by acts of God, public authority, revolutions or other disorders, wars, strikes, fires or floods.

Notices

All notices required or permitted to be given under this Contract shall be in writing and shall be deemed to have been sufficiently given when received if delivered in person, when deposited at the telegraph office if transmitted by telegraph, or when deposited in the mails of the United States Postal Service, certified, return receipt requested, postage and other charges prepaid, and addressed to the respective parties at the following addresses:

CARRIER:

_____

_____

_____

_____

COMPANY:

_____

_____

_____

_____

Confidentiality

Neither party shall disclose the terms of this Contract to any third party except: (1) to a parent, affiliate or subsidiary corporation; (2) as may be required by law; (3) to any attorney, auditor or consultant who has a need for the Contract in the performance of professional services for a party.

Term

This Contract shall remain in full force and effect for ___ (__) year(s) from the date hereof (herein referred to as the initial term of this Contract), (and from year-to-year thereafter,) subject to the right of termination by either party at any

166

time on _____ (__) days' notice to the other party sent by certified mail, return receipt requested.

The term may be any length desired but usually is one year. Regardless of the length, most contracts can be terminated by either party on thirty days' notice.

Amendment

This Contract shall not be amended or altered except in writing and signed by authorized representatives of both parties.

Assignment

Without the prior written approval of Company, Carrier shall not assign this Contract, and shall not assign any rights under this Contract to a third party. Any unapproved attempted assignment shall be null, void, and of no force or effect; should it be attempted, Carrier agrees to pay to Company any expenses including reasonable attorneys' fees that Company may incur in defending against any action or conduct related thereto. This Contract shall be binding upon each party's heirs, successors and assigns, if any, including any successor or assign by operation of law.

Execution

IN WITNESS WHEREOF, the parties have executed this Contract on the day and year first herein written.

> **_CARRIER:_**
> *By: _____*
> *Title: _____*
>
> **_COMPANY:_**
> *By: _____*
> *Title: _____*

With the revised hours-of-service rules, some firms have developed new systems and procedures that will help drivers get the most out of their time. These may be incorporated into the contract, and the traffic manager should try to obtain incentives for actions that will enhance carrier productivity.

Service

Service will be second only to price in considering which carriers to use; and in some cases when shipping time-sensitive or service-sensitive products, it will be more important. When selecting a carrier, it is critical to select one that will provide the necessary level of service; and the continued use of that carrier should be contingent upon the maintenance of such service.

Availability

Obviously, when the firm needs transportation, the service should be available to it. It is important to select carriers that will maintain such availability and have relationships that will facilitate this, particularly in times of tight capacity. As mentioned earlier, during the motor carrier capacity shortage of 2003 – 2004, those shippers who had maintained good relationships with their core carriers fared far better than those who had not.

Reliability

Reliability and consistency are important service components, as well. This is particularly true as we become more sensitive to inventory levels and utilize JIT, Efficient Consumer Response, and other time-focused inventory models. Referring again to our inventory example in Chapter 1, if a truck shipment from a manufacturing plant in Chicago to a distributor in Los Angeles consistently takes three days, the distributor will provide a three-day supply of stock to compensate for the transit time. If, however, 30 percent of the inbound shipments take four days, he must increase his inventory levels by one day even though he won't need it 70 percent of the time.

Several years ago, inventory managers did not really care (within certain limits, of course) how long transit times were as long as they were consistent. This is no longer the case. With current emphasis on speed and reliability, the preferred transit time will be both short *and* reliable.

Claims Record

It is not a perfect world; and from time to time, shipments will be damaged or lost. This can result in lost sales, lost profits, and unhappy customers. It is important to ensure that this does not happen often, and carriers' performances in this area should be examined carefully. It does no good to pay a low rate or achieve on-time delivery on a damaged product.

Industries Served

Some carriers specialize in certain industries such as grocery products, pharmaceuticals, cigarettes, chemicals, computers, and electronics. Others, while not advertised specialists, have come to be preferred by clients in particular industries.

The advantages to dealing with specialists are obvious. The knowledge and expertise they have in specific industries lend economies, efficiencies, and innovation to their operations.

There are, however, excellent generalists in the industry as well. Many of them have learned to operate with as much skill in a variety of industries as some of the specialists have in one.

Sources of Information

For the new traffic manager, just identifying qualified carriers can be a daunting task. There are several ways to approach this.

Word of Mouth

As with other business issues, the best sources of information will be from those who have had experience with the various carriers. Conversations with colleagues, customers, and competitors, as well as attendance at various seminars and conferences can yield invaluable, accurate knowledge of the industry and specific carriers.

169

Whatever the user industry might be, the chances are there is another firm that has had experience and is willing to offer advice and counsel and share thoughts. In the words of an old Chinese proverb, *A single conversation across the table with a wise man is worth a month's study of books.*

Trade Publications

In addition to carrier advertising, the leading trade journals all provide heavy coverage of industry developments. Numerous articles and accounts of user experiences can yield valuable information and contacts.

Some of the more popular trade and professional publications are listed in Appendix 10-2.

Some of these publications, such as *Inbound Logistics* and *Logistics Management*, publish annual listings of the top carriers and the services they offer.

Trade Associations

Trade Associations are another good source of information. Most of the major carriers will belong to one or more of these. Although membership does not necessarily guarantee excellence in performance, the association offices and directories are valuable resources.

The major groups are listed in Appendix 10-3.

Websites

Most carriers have informative websites which will outline the basic facts about the company, and the major ones also will provide case studies of solutions they have provided to clients with a particular need. These can be particularly helpful when seeking a carrier with a certain kind of experience.

Other types of information are available, as well. For example, the "Top 100 Motor Carriers" published annually by *Inbound Logistics* can be viewed at www.inboundlogistics.com.

Outsourced vs. Proprietary Transportation

Another strategic decision the traffic manager must make is whether to use for-hire transportation, a private fleet, or a combination of the two. As discussed in Chapter 4, there are several reasons a firm might want to utilize a private fleet. The most common of these is service.

Almost every company that operates its own fleet does so because it has unique service requirements that only a private fleet can reliably meet. For example, what common carrier do you call if, like Batesville Casket Co., you needed caskets delivered to some 16,000 funeral parlors twice daily? Where do you look if, like Walgreen's, you need a carrier that can make daily just-in-time deliveries to 4,800 stores around the country? The answer is "You don't." You do it yourself. For these companies and hundreds like them, there's no substitute for having their own drivers – drivers who understand their business, who know their customers, and who are available day or night.

Operating a fleet always looks more attractive when truck capacity is in short supply, but a word of caution is in order. Running your own fleet will not provide relief from rising truck rates. Private fleets face the same problems and cost pressures that common carriers struggle with. In fact, they're likely to find themselves at a disadvantage because they can't match the larger carriers' buying clout when they negotiate fuel prices or bid for new drivers. Before committing to a private fleet, it will be important to conduct a thorough financial analysis, comparing the cost of for-hire to proprietary transport.

Appendix 10-4 is a suggested form that can be used to manage transportation expenses or compare in-house and outside carrier costs.

Technology

In today's transportation management environment, it is almost impossible to effectively manage the function and control costs without good technology, preferably a state-of-the-art Transportation Management System. Transportation management information and systems are discussed at some length in Chapter 11.

Implementation

Once the transportation manager has made the four important strategic decisions, he or she will be faced with the tactical day-to-day operations referred to earlier.

 When asked to identify their major challenge in managing transportation, most managers say it is the identification, hiring, and keeping a quality workforce. It will be critical to hire and motivate dedicated, efficient employees to carry out the day-to-day activities. One of the most challenging aspects will be to keep employees motivated, sometimes during very hectic times or under stressful conditions.

There is no better way to do this than through recognition of their efforts. Too often, good performance is simply taken for granted, and many managers sometimes forget that approval and recognition are basic human needs. Ralph Waldo Emerson said, "The reward for a thing well done is to have done it;" but even if our employees take pride in their own performance, they take even more pride when it is acknowledged by others. Too often supply chain managers become so wrapped up in the operations and technology, they tend to forget their most important asset – their employees.

Everyone needs recognition for his accomplishments, but few people make the need known quite as clearly as the little boy who said to his father, "Let's play darts. I'll throw and you say, 'Wonderful.'"

(from *The Best of Bits and Pieces*)

Questions for Understanding

1. What is the major challenge in managing transportation?

2. Discuss the four strategic decisions a transportation manager must make.

3. What are the primary criteria for selecting a carrier?

4. Discuss the advantages and disadvantages of private carriage.

5. What will be the transportation manager's most important tool in today's environment?

Chapter 11: Transportation Management Information and Systems

A reliable transportation management system is no longer a "nice-to-have." It is critical to the management of the transportation function.

While information technology has been a fixture in the business community for a number of years, as the years pass, new innovations appear, and technological advances are made, it becomes even more critical. In some respects, it is a self-fulfilling prophecy in that the more information we have, the more there is to manage, and the more we need technology and systems. In no industry is this more relevant than in transportation.

As indicated in an earlier chapter, transportation costs in the U.S. totaled about $848 billion in 2007. These costs as a percentage of a manufacturing or distributing company's revenue can be anywhere from 10 to 40 percent depending on the value of the product and the modes of transport utilized. In *any* company, it is a significant expense and one which must be managed carefully.

Capacity constraints, rising oil prices, and increasing rates have become major concerns for most firms, and there is a tremendous amount of ongoing pressure on logistics and supply chain managers to monitor and manage expenses as closely as possible. They are finding that they are expected to do more with less while, at the same time, maintain excellent levels of customer service.

In order to protect their firms' costs, service, and positions in the marketplace, increasingly today's managers are relying on technology as a necessary measurement and management tool.

In order to understand how technology can be used in the management of the transportation function, however, it is important to be aware of the basic types of information and documents that must be dealt with

Sources of Information

As we learned earlier, the demand of transportation is a derived demand. If there is no demand for products to move from one point to another, there is no demand for transportation. Thus the demand for the transportation service is "derived" from, or a result of, the demand for the goods that will need to be transported.

While the principle is the same for supplies, raw materials, ingredients, and other inbound commodities; for the sake of this discussion, we will begin with the need or desire for a finished product.

Purchase Order

The purchase order will be the initial request for product to be shipped. It will almost always originate with the buyer but may be routed through a sales representative. Whatever the routing process, the order will identify the specific items desired and the amount of each. The order usually will state when the product is needed (or should be shipped), the mode, and sometimes the specific carrier. Price may be indicated, as well.

176

Pick Ticket

Once a purchase order is received at the seller's shipping location, the warehouse management system will convert this purchase order to a pick list or loading sheet. If there is no warehouse management system, this will be done manually, but in either case, the end product will be a document for the order picker which will contain the SKU number, item description, amount to be picked, location in the warehouse, and disposition of the product (i.e., door number, order number, etc.). In many instances, the warehouse will be equipped with scanning equipment, bar codes, RFID, etc., and the process will be more automated.

Once the order is picked and ready for shipment, a bill of lading must be issued.

Bill of Lading

After the carrier is contacted, a bill of lading for the shipment will be prepared.

A bill of lading is a contract between the shipper and the carrier for the movement of the product, and it serves as

1. a receipt for the goods,
2. a description of the shipment,
3. an operating document describing special handling or other unique requirements, and
4. the contract between the shipper and the carrier outlining all terms and conditions of the carriage.

While it is the responsibility of the carrier to issue a bill of lading, most are customized and generated by the shipper. The signing of the bill of lading by a carrier constitutes issuance.

A bill of lading may be a *straight* bill of lading or an *order* bill of lading. A *straight* bill is the type most commonly used and is non-negotiable. The terms of sale between the shipper and receiver are the binding conditions of title passage.

However, an *order* bill of lading is negotiable, and title to the goods described in the bill of lading will be transferred only when the endorsed bill of lading is surrendered to the carrier. Order bills of lading are usually handled by banks and given to the buyer upon

receipt of payment for the goods. The bill of lading is then surrendered to the carrier in exchange for the shipment.

Both types of bill are subject to predetermined terms and conditions.

First of all, the carrier liability is clearly spelled out. The carrier is liable for all loss, damage, or delay to the shipment except for:

1. Act of God – an unavoidable catastrophe.
2. Act of Public Enemy – terrorists or aggressors against the country.
3. Act of Shipper – poor packaging, false declaration of contents.
4. Inherent Nature of the Goods – normal loss or shrinkage.
5. Act of Public Authority – seizures by governmental agencies.

Also, the carrier is bound to deliver the goods only with "reasonable dispatch," not on a fixed schedule.

Pages 179 and 180 show a Uniform Straight Bill of Lading and its terms and conditions.

VICS Bill of Lading

The Voluntary Interindustry Commerce Solutions Association (VICS) was founded in 1986 to improve the efficiency and effectiveness of the supply chain. Its members believe that cross-industry standards can facilitate better customer service, lower costs, and improvements in competitive positioning. Their efforts have been quite effective, and among other initiatives, they have adopted a standard bill of lading to afford better electronic interchange of the information. Terms and conditions are standard. Only the format was changed for consistency. For example, the bill of lading shown on pages 181 and 182 is made available by FedEx Freight for the customers that desire to use it. [1]

Waybill

A waybill is the term used for the shipment of a rail car. It is similar in form and content to a motor carrier bill of lading, although it does contain more specific information about train assignments, routes, junctions, and switching points. [2]

NATIONAL MOTOR FREIGHT CLASSIFICATION 100-Z

RULES

(To be printed on white paper)

UNIFORM STRAIGHT BILL OF LADING

ORIGINAL—NOT NEGOTIABLE

Carrier's Pro No. _____
Shipper's Bill of Lading No. _____
Consignee's Reference/P.O. No. _____
Carrier's Code (SCAC)_____

Name of Carrier _____

RECEIVED, subject to individually determined rates or contracts that have been agreed upon in writing between the carrier and shipper, if applicable, otherwise to the rates, classifications and rules that have been established by the carrier and are available to the shipper, on request:

From _____ Date _____
Street _____ City _____ County _____ State _____ Zip _____

the property described below, in apparent good order, except as noted (contents and condition of contents of packages unknown) marked, consigned, and destined as shown below, which said carrier agrees to carry to destination, if on its route, or otherwise to deliver to another carrier on the route to destination. Every service to be performed hereunder shall be subject to all the conditions not prohibited by law, whether printed or written, herein contained, including the conditions on the back hereof, which are hereby agreed to by the shipper and accepted for himself and his assigns.

Consigned to _____
On Collect on Delivery Shipments, the letters "COD" must appear before consignee's name.

Destination Street _____
City _____ County _____ State _____ Zip _____
Delivering Carrier _____ Trailer No. _____
Additional Shipment Information _____

Collect on Delivery $ _____ and remit to: _____ | C.O.D. charge | Shipper ☐
Street _____ City _____ State _____ | to be paid by | Consignee ☐

Handling Units No. Type	Packages No. Type	⊙ HM	Kind of Package, Description of Articles, Special Marks and Exceptions (Subject to correction)	Weight (Subject to Correction)	Class or Rate Ref. (For Info. Only)	Cube (Op-tional)

⊙ Mark "X" to designate Hazardous Materials as defined in DOT Regulations.

NOTE (1) Where the rate is dependent on value, shippers are required to state specifically in writing the agreed or declared value of the property as follows:

"The agreed or declared value of the property is specifically stated by the shipper to be not exceeding _____ per _____."

NOTE (2) Liability Limitation for loss or damage on this shipment may be applicable. See 49 U.S.C. § 14706(c)(1)(A) and (B).

NOTE (3) Commodities requiring special or additional care or attention in handling or stowing must be so marked and packaged as to ensure safe transportation with ordinary care. See Sec. 2(e) of NMFC Item 360.

Freight charges are PREPAID unless marked collect.
CHECK BOX IF COLLECT ☐

FOR FREIGHT COLLECT SHIPMENTS:
If this shipment is to be delivered to the consignee, without recourse on the consignor, the consignor shall sign the following statement:
The carrier may decline to make delivery of this shipment without payment of freight and all other lawful charges.

(Signature of Consignor)

Notify if problem en route or at delivery _____ (for informational purposes only)
Name   Fax No.   Tel. No.

Send freight bill to: _____
Company Name   City   Street   State   Zip
Shipper _____ Carrier _____
Per _____ Per _____ Date _____

Shipper Certification	Carrier Certification
This is to certify that the above-named materials are properly classified, described, packaged, marked and labeled, and are in proper condition for transportation according to the applicable regulations of the DOT. Per _____ Date _____	Carrier acknowledges receipt of packages and required placards. Carrier certifies emergency response information was made available and/or carrier has the DOT emergency response guidebook or equivalent document in the vehicle. Per _____ Date _____ Package Nos. _____

UNIFORM STRAIGHT BILL OF LADING
Terms & Conditions

Sec. 1. (a) The carrier or the party in possession of any of the property described in this bill of lading shall be liable as at common law for any loss thereof or damage thereto, except as hereinafter provided.

(b) No carrier shall be liable for any loss or damage to a shipment or for any delay caused by an Act of God, the public enemy, the authority of law, or the act or default of shipper. Except in the case of negligence of the carrier or party in possession, the carrier or party in possession shall not be liable for loss, damage or delay which results: when the property is stopped and held in transit upon request of the shipper, owner or party entitled to make such requests; or from faulty or impassible highway, or lack of capacity of a highway bridge or ferry; or from a defect or vice in the property; or from riots or strikes. The burden to prove freedom from negligence is on the carrier or the party in possession.

Sec. 2. Unless arranged or agreed upon, in writing, prior to shipment, carrier is not bound to transport a shipment by a particular schedule or in time for a particular market, but is responsible to transport with reasonable dispatch. In case of physical necessity, carrier may forward a shipment via another carrier.

Sec. 3. (a) As a condition precedent to recovery, claims must be files in writing with: any participating carrier having sufficient information to indentify the shipment.

(b) Claims for loss or damage must be filed within nine months after the delivery of the property (or, in case of export traffic, within none months after delivery at the port of export), except that claims for failure to make delivery must be filed within nine months after a reasonable time for delivery has elapsed.

(c) Suites for loss, damage, injury or delay shall be instituted against any carrier no later than two years and one day from the day when written notice is given by the carrier to the claimant that the carrier has disallowed the claim or any part of parts of the claim specified in the notice. Where claims are not filed or suits are not instituted thereon in accordance with the foregoing provisions, no carrier shall be liable, and such claims will not be paid.

(d) Any carrier or party liable for loss of or damage to any of said property shall have the full benefit of any insurance that may have been effected, upon or on account of said property, so far as this shall not avoid the policies or contracts of insurance, PROVIDED, that the carrier receiving the benefit of such insurance will reimburse the claimant for the premium paid on the insurance policy or contract.

Sec. 4. (a) If the consignee refuses the shipment tendered for delivery by carrier or if carrier is unable to deliver the shipment, because of fault or mistake of the consignor or consignee, the carrier's liability shall then become that of a warehouseman. Carrier shall promptly attempt to provide notice, by telephonic or electronic communication as provided on the face of the bill of lading, if so indicated, to the shipper or the party, if any, designated to receive notice on this bill of lading. Storage charges, based on carrier's tariff, shall start no sooner than the next business day following the attempted notification. Storage may be, at the carrier's option, in any location that provides reasonable protection against loss or damage. The carrier may place the shipment in public storage at the owner's expense and without liability to the carrier.

(b) If carrier does not receive disposition instructions within 48 hours of the time of carrier's attempted first notification, carrier will attempt to issue a second and final confirmed notification. Such notice shall advise that if carrier does not receive disposition instructions within 10 days of that notification, carrier may offer the shipment for sale at

(c) Where carrier has attempted to follow the procedure set forth in subsections 4(a) and (b) above and the procedure provided in this section is not possible, nothing in this section shall be construed to abridge the right of the carrier at its option to sell the property under such circumstances and in such manner as may be authorized by law. When perishable goods cannot be delivered and disposition is not given within a reasonable time, the carrier may dispose of property to the best advantage.

(d) Where a carrier is directed by consignee or consignor to unload or deliver property at a particular location where consignor, consignee, or the agent of either, is not regularly located, the risk after unloading or delivery shall not be that of the carrier.

Sec. 5. (a) In all cases not prohibited by law, where a lower value than the actual value of said property has been stated in writing by the shipper or has been agreed upon in writing as the released value of the property as determined by the classifications or tariffs upon which the rate is based, such lower value plus freight charges if paid shall be the maximum recoverable amount for loss or damage, whether or not such loss or damage occurs from negligence.

(b) No carrier hereunder will carry or be liable in any way for any documents, coin money, or for any articles of extraordinary value not specifically rated in the published classification or tariffs unless a special agreement to do so and a stipulated value of the articles are endorsed on this bill of lading.

Sec. 6. Every party, whether principal or agent, who ships explosives or dangerous goods, without previous full written disclosure to the carrier of their nature, shall be liable for and indemnify the carrier against all loss or damage caused by such goods. Such goods may be warehoused at owner's risk and expense or destroyed without compensation.

Sec. 7. (a) The consignor or consignee shall be liable for the freight and other lawful charges accruing on the shipment, as billed or corrected, except that collect shipments may move without recourse to the consignor when the consignor so stipulates by signature or endorsement in the space provided on the face of the bill of lading. Nevertheless, the consignor shall remain liable for transportation charges where there has been an erroneous determination of the freight charges assessed, based upon incomplete or incorrect information provided by the consignor.

(b) Notwithstanding the provisions of subsection (a) above, the consignee's liability for payment of additional charges that may be found to be due after delivery shall be as specified by 49 U.S.C. §13706, except that the consignee need not provide the specified written notice to the delivering carrier if the consignee is for-hire carrier.

(c) Nothing in this bill of lading shall limit the right of the carrier to require the prepayment or guarantee of the charges at the time of shipment or prior to delivery. If the description of articles or other information on this bill of lading is found to be incorrect or incomplete, the freight charges must be paid upon the articles actually shipped.

Sec. 8. If this bill of lading is issued on the order of the shipper, or his agent, in exchange or in substitution for another bill of lading, the shipper's signature on the prior bill of lading or in connection with the prior bill of lading as to the statement of value or otherwise, or as to the election of common law or bill of lading liability shall be considered as part of this bill of lading as fully as if the same were written on or made in connection with this bill of lading.

Sec. 9. If all or any part of said property is carried by water over any part of said route, such water carriage shall be performed subject to the terms and provisions and limitations of liability specified by the "Carriage of Goods by Sea Act" and any other pertinent laws applicable to water carriers.

FedEx Freight

VICS Bill of Lading

SHIP FROM	
Name:	Bill of Lading Number: _____
Address:	CARRIER: _____ TRAILER: _____
Address:	
City/State/Zip:	SCAC: _____ Pro Number: _____
SID#: _____ SID#: _____	

SHIP TO	
Name: [ ]	
Address:	PLACE PRO LABEL HERE
Address:	
City/State/Zip:	
CID#:	

THIRD PARTY FREIGHT CHARGES BILL TO	
Name:	**Freight Charge Terms:**
Address:	Prepaid _____ Collect _____ 3rd Party _____
City/State/Zip:	Freight charges are to be prepaid unless marked collect.

SPECIAL INSTRUCTIONS:

☐ Master Bill of Lading: with attached underlying Bills of Lading

CUSTOMER ORDER INFORMATION

CUSTOMER ORDER NUMBER	# PKGS	WEIGHT	CIRCLE ONE PALLET/SLIP		ADDITIONAL SHIPPER INFO
			Y	N	
			Y	N	
			Y	N	
			Y	N	
			Y	N	
GRAND TOTAL					

CARRIER INFORMATION

HANDLING UNIT		PACKAGE			(✔)	COMMODITY DESCRIPTION	NMFC #	CLASS
QTY	TYPE	QTY	TYPE	WEIGHT	H.M.	Commodities requiring special or additional care or attention in handling or stowing must be so marked and packaged as to ensure safe transportation with ordinary care. (See NMFC, Sec. 3c, item 360)		
				GRAND TOTAL				

NOTE: (1) Where the rate is dependent on value, shippers are required to state specifically in writing the agreed or declared value of the property as follows:
"The agreed or declared value of the property is specifically stated by the shipper to be not exceeding _____ per _____."

NOTE: (2) Limitation for loss or damage on this shipment may be applicable. See 49 U.S.C. § 14706(c)(1)(A) and (B). NOTE: (3) Commodities requiring special or additional care or attention in handling or stowing must be so marked and packaged as to ensure safe transportation with ordinary care. See Sec. 2(e) of NMFC item 360.

RECEIVED, subject to individually determined rates or contracts that have been agreed upon in writing between the carrier and shipper, if applicable, otherwise to the rates, classifications and rules that have been established by the carrier and are available to the shipper, on request, and to all applicable state and federal regulations.

COD Amount: $ _____ Collect:☐ Prepaid:☐
Customer check O.K.:☐ Cashier's check only:☐
"COD" must appear with consignee's name above.

The carrier shall not make delivery of this shipment without payment of freight and all other lawful charges (Section 7).

_____ Shipper Signature

SHIPPER SIGNATURE / DATE
This is to certify that the above named materials are properly classified, described, packaged, marked and labeled, and are in proper condition for transportation according to the applicable regulations of the Department of Transportation.

Trailer Loaded:
☐ By Shipper
☐ By Driver
☐ By OSL

Freight Counted:
☐ By Shipper
☐ By Driver/pallets said to contain
☐ By Driver/Pieces

CARRIER SIGNATURE / PICKUP DATE
Carrier acknowledges receipt of packages and required placards. Carrier certifies emergency response information was made available and/or carrier has the D.O.T. emergency response guidebook or equivalent documentation in the vehicle.

SS

Original not negotiable. See last page for further terms and conditions.

VICS COMPATIBLE BILL OF LADING
Terms & Conditions

Sec. 1. (a) The carrier or the party in possession of any of the property described in this bill of lading shall be liable as at common law for any loss thereof or damage thereto, except as hereinafter provided.

(b) No carrier shall be liable for any loss or damage to a shipment or for any delay caused by an Act of God, the public enemy, the authority of law, or the act or default of shipper. Except in the case of negligence of the carrier or party in possession, the carrier or party in possession shall not be liable for loss, damage or delay which results: when the property is stopped and held in transit upon request of the shipper, owner or party entitled to make such requests; or from faulty or impassible highway, or by lack of capacity of a highway bridge or ferry; or from a defect or vice in the property; or from riots or strikes. The burden to prove freedom from negligence is on the carrier or the party in possession.

Sec. 2. Unless arranged or agreed upon, in writing, prior to shipment, carrier is not bound to transport a shipment by a particular schedule or in time for a particular market, but is responsible to transport with reasonable dispatch. In case of physical necessity, carrier may forward a shipment via another carrier.

Sec. 3. (a) As a condition precedent to recovery, claims must be filed in writing with: any participating carrier having sufficient information to identify the shipment.

(b) Claims for loss or damage must be filed within nine months after the delivery of the property (or, in the case of export traffic, within nine months after delivery at the port of export), except that claims for failure to make delivery must be filed within nine months after a reasonable time for delivery has elapsed.

(c) Suits for loss, damage, injury or delay shall be instituted against any carrier no later than two years and one day from the day when written notice is given by the carrier to the claimant that the carrier has disallowed the claim or any part or parts of the claim specified in the notice. Where claims are not filed or suits are not instituted thereon in accordance with the foregoing provisions, no carrier shall be liable, and such claims will not be paid.

(d) Any carrier or party liable for loss of or damage to any of said property shall have the full benefit of any insurance that may have been effected, upon or on account of said property, so far as this shall not avoid the policies or contracts of insurance, PROVIDED, that the carrier receiving the benefit of such insurance will reimburse the claimant for the premium paid on the insurance policy or contract.

Sec. 4. (a) If the consignee refuses the shipment tendered for delivery by carrier or if carrier is unable to deliver the shipment, because of fault or mistake of the consignor or consignee, the carrier's liability shall then become that of a warehouseman. Carrier shall promptly attempt to provide notice, by telephonic or electronic communication as provided on the face of the bill of lading, if so indicated, to the shipper or the party, if any, designated to receive notice on this bill of lading. Storage charges, based on carrier's tariff, shall start no sooner than the next business day following the attempted notification. Storage may be, at the carrier's option, in any location that provides reasonable protection against loss or damage. The carrier may place the shipment in public storage at the owner's expense and without liability to the carrier.

(b) If the carrier does not receive disposition instructions within 48 hours of the time of carrier's attempted first notification, carrier will attempt to issue a second and final confirmed notification. Such notice shall advise that if carrier does not receive disposition instructions within 10 days of that notification, carrier may offer the shipment for sale at a public auction and the carrier has the right to offer the shipment for sale. The amount of sale will be applied to the carrier's invoice for transportation, storage and other lawful charges. The owner will be responsible for the balance of charges not covered by the sale of the goods. If there is a balance remaining after all charges and expenses are paid, such balance will be paid to the owner of the property sold hereunder, upon claim and proof of ownership.

(c) Where carrier has attempted to follow the procedure set forth in subsections 4(a) and (b) above and the procedure provided in this section is not possible, nothing in this section shall be construed to abridge the right of the carrier at its option to sell the property under such circumstances and in such manner as may be authorized by law. When perishable goods cannot be delivered and disposition is not given within a reasonable time, the carrier may dispose of property to the best advantage.

(d) Where a carrier is directed by consignee or consignor to unload or deliver property at a particular location where consignor, consignee, or the agent of either, is not regularly located, the risk after unloading or delivery shall not be that of the carrier.

Sec. 5. (a) In all cases not prohibited by law, where a lower value than the actual value of said property has been stated in writing by the shipper or has been agreed upon in writing as the released value of the property as determined by the classification or tariffs upon which the rate is based, such lower value plus freight charges if paid shall be the maximum recoverable amount for loss or damage, whether or not such loss or damage occurs from negligence.

(b) No carrier hereunder will carry or be liable in any way for any documents, coin money, or for any articles of extraordinary value not specifically rated in the published classification or tariffs unless a special agreement to do so and a stipulated value of the articles are endorsed on this bill of lading.

Sec. 6. Every party, whether principal or agent, who ships explosives or dangerous goods, without previous full written disclosure to the carrier of their nature, shall be liable for and indemnify the carrier against all loss or damage caused by such goods. Such goods may be warehoused at owner's risk and expense or destroyed without compensation.

Sec. 7. (a) The consignor or consignee shall be liable for the freight and other lawful charges accruing on the shipment, as billed or corrected, except that collect shipments may move without recourse to the consignor when the consignor so stipulates by signature or endorsement in the space provided on the face of the bill of lading. Nevertheless, the consignor shall remain liable for transportation charges where there has been an erroneous determination of the freight charges assessed, based upon incomplete or incorrect information provided by the consignor.

(b) Notwithstanding the provisions of subsection (a) above, the consignee's liability for payment of additional charges that may be found to be due after delivery shall be as specified by 49 U.S.C. §13706, except that the consignee need not provide the specified written notice to the delivering carrier if the consignee is a for-hire carrier.

(c) Nothing in this bill of lading shall limit the right of the carrier to require the prepayment or guarantee of the charges at the time of shipment or prior to delivery. If the description of articles or other information on this bill of lading is found to be incorrect or incomplete, the freight charges must be paid based upon the articles actually shipped.

Sec. 8. If this bill of lading is issued on the order of the shipper, or his agent, in exchange or in substitution for another bill of lading, the shipper's signature on the prior bill of lading or in connection with the prior bill of lading as to the statement of value or otherwise, or as to the election of common law or bill of lading liability shall be considered a part of this bill of lading as fully as if the same were written on or made in connection with this bill of lading.

Sec. 9. If all or any part of said property is carried by water over any part of said route, such water carriage shall be performed subject to the terms and provisions and limitations of liability specified by the "Carriage of Goods By Sea Act" and any other pertinent laws applicable to water carriers.

Freight Bill

Finally, the freight bill is the invoice for the carrier's transportation and other charges. It contains much of the same information shown on the bill of lading in addition to the actual rates and charges. Freight bills can be submitted manually or via EDI.

Once the freight bill is received by the shipper or the freight bill audit and payment company described in Chapter 12, it is matched with the bill of lading and paid, either electronically or by check. Freight bills may be rendered through EDI, mail, or via the Internet.

Technology

When one considers the mass of paper represented in the manual handling of the documents described above, it is no wonder that transportation users and providers have been so quick to embrace technology.

ISBN 0-918894-28-X

EDI – Electronic Data Interchange

Electronic data interchange has been used in the transportation industry since the early 1970's. *Supply Chain Terminology* by Philip Obal defines it as

> "Computer-to-computer communication between two or more companies that such companies can use to generate bills of lading, purchasing orders, and invoices. It also enables firms to access the information systems of suppliers, customers, and carriers, and to determine the up-to-the-minute status of inventory, orders, and shipments."

Using standardized transaction sets, promulgated by the American National Standards Institute, the administrative aspects and documents of the transportation management process can be transferred electronically, along with other important pieces of  information such as order status, delivery, and payment. EDI transmissions can be handled directly or through a VAN (Value Added Network).

There are hundreds of terms or transaction sets utilized in the transportation industry. Some of the most commonly used sets are shown in Figure 11-a.

The most frequently used in the motor carrier industry will be [4]

- 204- Motor Carrier Load Tender
- 990- Response to the Load Tender
- 211- Bill of Lading
- 212- Delivery Trailer Manifest
- 214- Shipment Status Message
- 210- Freight Details and Invoice
- 820- Payment Order/Remittance Advice

Transaction Sets	Definition
104	Air Shipment Information
160	Transportation Automatic Equipment Identification
180	Return Merchandise Authorization and Notification
204	Motor Carrier Shipment Information
210	Motor Carrier Freight Details and Invoice
211	Bill of Lading
212	Delivery Trailer Manifest
213	Motor Carrier Shipment Status Inquiry
214	Transportation Carrier Shipment Status Message
217	Motor Carrier Loading and Route Guide
218	Motor Carrier Tariff Information
300	Reservation (Booking Request) (Ocean)
301	Confirmation (Ocean)
303	Booking Cancellation (Ocean)
309	U.S. Customs Manifest
310	Freight Receipt and Invoice (Ocean)
313	Shipment Status Inquiry (Ocean)
317	Delivery/Pickup Order
350	U.S. Customs Release Information
358	U.S. Customs Consist Information
361	Carrier Interchange Agreement (Ocean)
404	Rail Carrier Shipment Information
425	Rail Waybill Request
426	Rail Revenue Waybill
466	Rate Request
820	Payment Order/Remittance Advice
858	Shipment Information
940	Warehouse Shipping Order
990	Response to a Load Tender

Source: Philip Obal, *Supply Chain Terminology*, 2005

Figure 11-a. Commonly Used EDI Transaction Sets

The typical flow would be as follows:

204   The tender of a load to a carrier.

990   The carrier's response to the load tender; i.e., accept or reject.

211   This transaction set will provide a bill of lading for the shipment.

212   Allows carriers to provide consignees with contents of load.

214   Provides shipment status.

210   This is the freight bill or invoice for the shipment.

820   This set is used to make a payment or send a remittance advice.

EDI has been an invaluable tool for the transportation industry. It provides *speed* of transmission as opposed to mail and telephone calls, and data is available immediately.

Accuracy is enhanced since there is no manual handling and re-handling of hundreds of documents.

In summary it allows all parties to the transportation process to function more efficiently and at a lower cost.

Internet

It is difficult to imagine where we would be without the Internet, and indeed some of us will not ever remember the time when it did not exist. (One of the leading transportation textbooks of 1980 contained no reference to it whatsoever.)

Just as the Internet has enhanced our personal lives and activities, it has also greatly improved our ability to function and communicate within the transportation community. The uses for the Internet can be divided into three basic categories: [5]

- Information Resources
- Communications

186

- Transactions

Virtually all carriers, and shippers for that matter, now have Internet sites from which company, product, and other information can be determined. Many carriers provide information on individual shipments which can be accessed by the parties to the contract. Delivery receipts can be provided as well.

For those companies that prefer to do so, EDI transmissions also can be handled on the Internet. Any number of other communications can be transmitted as well. Almost any piece of information the parties wish to share can be made available over the Internet. Some shippers and carriers will conduct transactions on the Internet. Load matching and brokerage sites, for example, enable a shipper and/or a carrier to complete a transaction electronically.

More and more carriers are making it possible for shippers to consummate transactions on their websites. The carriers provide forms, EDI transaction sets, and other important and necessary information at one location.

Future Internet enhancements no doubt will make it even more valuable to its users, and there is every reason to believe that, for the foreseeable future, it will be an important transportation management tool.

Transportation Management Systems

Transportation management systems (TMS) have been used by shippers since the 1980's, but the technology of today has made much more sophisticated and effective systems available. Broadly defined, a TMS is part of a

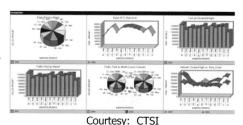

Courtesy: CTSI

group of systems commonly referred to as supply chain execution systems that are used to manage a firm's transportation function. It usually refers to a form of online or software system.

Some firms have developed their own TMS, but many systems are provided by software vendors and freight bill audit and payment firms. They have become a critical requirement for the successful management of a transportation function. According to Adrian Gonzalez, Director of ARC's Logistics Executive Council, the TMS market surpassed $1 billion in 2006, "reflecting the growing desire of companies to gain better visibility and control of their transportation processes and spend." [6]

There are any number of advantages to utilizing a transportation management system, and many of these will vary by individual firm. High Jump Software, a leading TMS vendor, identified five basic advantages, however, that they believe can save a firm up to 30 percent of its freight spend. [7]

1. *Contract Management* (10%)
   A single repository for all contracts will prevent errors in carrier selection and freight payment.

2. *Optimal Load and Route* (5 – 17%)
   Optimizing the carrier base and transportation plan.

3. *Least-Cost Mode/Carrier Selection* (2 – 7%)
   Selection of least-cost transportation without compromising customer service.

4. *Shipment Execution* (1 – 5%)
   Automation will breed accuracy.

5. *Performance Improvements* (1 – 3%)
   The ability to accurately measure performance will foster improvements.

Most firms will realize some variation of these advantages through the use of a TMS.

The selection of the system itself can be a daunting task. A TMS can be complex and expensive, and there are hundreds of vendors to choose from. The systems can be purchased outright, they can be hosted by the vendor, and in some cases can be on-demand. With the latter, one accesses the system only when necessary and "pays as he goes." Most users will agree, however, that a good system will have two main components – transportation planning and transportation execution. Most users also would agree that the data capture is the major challenge to implementing a useful system. One of the advantages of using a TMS from a freight bill audit and payment company is that it has already captured its clients' data and, therefore, is in an excellent position to provide an effective system. And these are not rudimentary systems. They are web-based applications for organizations seeking an enterprise-wide solution, managed through centralized administrative tools. (See Chapter 12.)

In some cases, a firm will not require an extensive and expensive TMS. If not, one of the "cafeteria plans" may be more applicable. Under this type arrangement, some vendors offer their TMS in modules. A company can simply purchase what they need and add on as they need to.

Available modules provide systems for such functions as

- *Carrier Selection:* Solutions for selecting least-cost carriers, routing guides and maps, vendor management, and compliance reporting.

- *Information Management modules:* Provide tools for mapping, graphing, trend reporting, carrier report cards, and dashboards.

- *Load Planning/Optimization Modules:* Aid in load consolidation, route optimization, mode selection and bill of lading preparation.

- *Modeling/Benchmarking:* Enables freight audit and payment, 3PL, warehouse

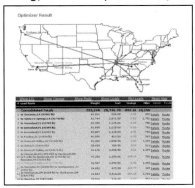

Courtesy: CTSI

189

relocation, and network design scenarios, as well as batch rating.

- *Order Management/Bill of Lading:* Provides a variety of options such as claim filing, order view, printing of packing lists and bills of lading.

- *Posting/Tendering modules*: Enable least-cost carrier tendering, spot quotes, expedited shipments and centralized dispatching.

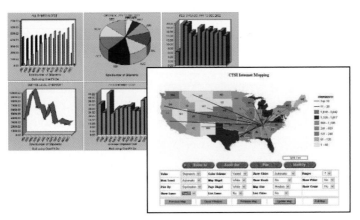

Courtesy: CTSI

- *Rate Management:* In the current transportation environment, this module is a must. It provides valuable assistance for centralized maintenance, transit time calculations, fuel surcharge and accessorial charge pricing, carrier rate files, major mileage programs, and capabilities for rating all modes of transportation.

Other firms have found the On-Demand TMS to be more effective for their transportation management process. These network-based systems often can provide unique opportunities for benchmarking and the identification of best practices. [8]

Whatever TMS is selected, the primary objectives should be to increase visibility, improve service levels, and reduce transportation expenditures.

Questions for Understanding

1. Discuss the functions of a bill of lading.

2. What is the difference between a straight bill of lading and an order bill of lading?

3. Under what circumstances is a carrier not liable for loss, damage, or delay to a shipment?

4. Discuss the advantages of EDI.

5. Discuss the value of the Internet in transportation management.

6. What are the basic advantages to utilizing a Transportation Management System?

Chapter 12: Freight Bill Payment Services [*]

The value of the service is not in the payment, but in the capture of the data.

At some point, the traffic manager must decide how to capture the information he or she needs to manage the function. As discussed in Chapter 11, one effective way of doing so is through the use of a freight bill audit and payment provider.

Any firm that ships anything at all is familiar with freight bills and the process for paying them; but less understood is the fact that there is a substantial industry built around the outsourcing of these payment activities.

Simply stated, a freight bill payment company receives its clients' freight bills directly from the carriers. When the bills are received, either electronically (Electronic Data Interchange) or manually, they are entered into the provider's system. This gives immediate visibility to the bills themselves.

Once the bills are entered into the system, they are audited, or checked for accuracy. Experienced auditors will verify, either manually or electronically depending on the circumstances, such things as

---

[*] This chapter is adapted from *The Role of Freight Bill Payment in the Supply Chain Industry* by J. Kenneth Hazen and Clifford F. Lynch.

- Validity of the bill (Did it go to the right party?)
- Weight
- Accessorial charges
- Use of correct tariff, classification, discount, etc.
- Extensions
- Mileage, origin, and destination accuracy
- Proper application of tariff rules
- Duplicate payments

When the bills have been checked for validity and accuracy, the charges are coded according to client specifications, then reconciled with the original data input.

From there, the bills are organized for payment, funding requirements are identified and communicated; and when funds are received, checks are written and mailed, or wire transfers initiated.

This is only part of the process, however. The freight bill payment firms have become much more progressive and sophisticated and offer an impressive array of services such as internal account coding, benchmarking, customized reporting, and transportation management systems. These will be discussed later in more detail. Suffice it to say, however, because the freight bill payment companies serve a number of clients, they have achieved a critical mass that enables them to keep abreast of the latest information technology; and often they are able to provide more information in a better format than the client firms themselves.

The Industry

While there has been significant consolidation in the freight bill payment industry, the best estimate is that there still are several hundred U.S. firms providing these services. Most of these operators are small, many are unsophisticated; and it is not surprising that a handful of larger, robust firms pay most of the bills.

It is estimated that freight bill payment firms pay 20 to 25 percent of the intercity freight in the United States. Since intercity freight totals hundreds of billions of dollars annually, this suggests a large market. [1] This, then, is an important industry that can serve any type of firm using any mode of transportation. According to ongoing studies, freight bill auditing and payment is outsourced frequently. [2] But, even though 50 percent of U.S. firms outsource this activity, there still is room to grow. While competition among the leading freight bill payment companies is brisk, the major competition continues to be the internal accounting function of the prospective clients.

History of the Freight Bill Payment Industry

The origins of the freight bill payment industry are somewhat unclear, but it is safe to assume that there has been some sort of freight bill payment outsourcing almost as long as there have been freight bills. The industry as we know it, however, generally is considered to have originated about 1956. This is the year CTSI was formed and also the year that Cass Bank began offering the service. Cass had been in business since 1906, but in 1956 formed a "clearing house" whereby both the shippers and the carriers were required to maintain accounts at the bank.

At the time, the Interstate Commerce Commission had very stringent credit regulations, requiring payment of freight bills within seven days of the postmark of the invoice. By clearing the funds within the same bank, customers were better able to keep current on their payments.

Originally, CTSI was a post-audit firm, but later developed a joint program with the Union Planters Bank in Memphis, Tennessee to provide services similar to Cass. There was one major difference, however. For some clients, CTSI actually audited freight bills before they were paid – a service most programs did not offer at the time.

Shortly thereafter, the Bank of Boston initiated freight bill clearance services; and by 1958, a total of thirty-four banks in the U.S. offered similar programs.

By then the structure of the plans had changed, as well. The banks no longer required carriers to keep an account at the bank, but would issue checks to non-depositors.

The industry continued to grow although many banks discontinued the offering, and services and reporting became more sophisticated. In the 1970's, a significant number of non-bank firms began to enter the market. Not only did these new firms pay bills, but invoices were pre-audited for accuracy and duplication; and reporting was even more developed than it had been before.

By the late 1990's, the progressive providers had developed Internet tools and provided their clients with full visibility to their bills and other reports.

Growth continued through the 1990's, and by 2000, 59 percent of U.S. firms were outsourcing at least some freight bill payment. In 2001, however, the industry hit a "bump in the road."

Basically, according to the late Bob Delaney of Cass Information Systems, there were two reasons why inferior freight bill payment companies were inferior. They did not provide good service, and they did not know how to manage money. This was confirmed in 2001 when interest rates dropped significantly. Unable to generate cash flow from a diminished float (funds advanced to the provider for later payment to carriers), a number of companies floundered. Many of them found themselves with minimal float income and non-compensatory transaction fees. Several bankruptcies occurred; and it was determined that, in more than one firm, the owners of the businesses had lived lavishly off the float.

The negative results were criminal charges, irate carriers, and clients that had advanced funds for bills that had not been paid, only to find themselves still liable for the charges. In early 2002, for example, one leading company was granted Chapter 7 bankruptcy relief. The company confirmed that it owed $25 million in unpaid bills to shipper clients, but had only $5 million in assets. [3]

These misdeeds were confined to a limited number of firms, however, and the remaining firms are stronger because of them.

The positive result of this was that there now is an industry that is wiser, more responsible, and prices services according to the cost of providing them. Client interest has increased, and there is every reason to believe that the market for freight bill payment and related services will continue to be strong.

Since most corporate long-range goals include a strategy for paperless transactions, the more innovative companies have realized that, to survive, they must become true information companies, rather than freight bill

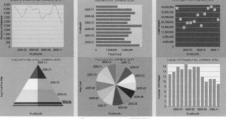

Courtesy: CTSI

processors. Services such as imaging, report writing, Internet access to bill status, etc. that were "value-added" a few years ago now are simply the "price of admission." The successful FBP firm will be the one that has global capability and capitalizes on its vast information resources and returns information to their clients in meaningful ways, such as transportation management systems, benchmarking, and carrier compliance reports.

Why Outsource Freight Bill Payment Services?

There are several good reasons to outsource freight bill payment to a qualified provider, but the one that will have the most appeal is the strong possibility of reduced costs. It can cost a large company from $10.00 to $50.00 [4] in fully allocated costs to pay a freight bill. If a freight bill payment company pays these same bills, the cost to the client will be approximately 5 to 10 percent of the internal expenses. Add to this another 2 to 5 percent

197

saved through the reduction in incorrect and/or duplicate freight bills, and savings to the client can be significant. [5]

While the cost reduction can be significant in and of itself, the real value is added through the business intelligence generated by the provider. Before the bill is paid, the FBP firm auditors' experience, combined with the latest technology, will ensure that clients pay the correct rate, including accessorial and surcharges.

Post-payment activity can include almost any type reporting the client wishes, including such things as routing compliance, expense by mode or carrier, or even product.

The technology of most freight bill payment companies is superior to that of many of its clients, thus enabling them to manage costs more effectively. Internet tools include report writing, visibility to freight bills, and improved data integrity.

Because of a provider's broad client base, a firm's freight expenses can be benchmarked against those of firms shipping comparable products.

Finally, the availability of comprehensive rate information for each client enables the provider to offer a broad range of consulting services without expensive data collection.

Thousands of firms around the world have found the outsourcing of the FBP function to be one of their more successful and beneficial partnerships.

Selecting the Right Freight Bill Payment Company

Although the outsourcing of any logistics function should be accompanied by a thorough due diligence, due to the financial sensitivity, extra effort should go into the selection of a freight bill payment provider.

While freight bill payment providers are listed in directories and trade journals and on the Internet, as with other business issues, the best sources of information will be those who have had experience with

198

the various providers. Conversations with colleagues, customers, and competitors, as well as attendance at various seminars and conferences can yield invaluable, accurate knowledge of the industry and specific providers. This will be particularly true in the more complex area of information technology.

Whatever the user industry might be, chances are good that there is another firm that has had FBP outsourcing experience and is willing to offer advice and counsel and share thoughts

Pay attention to their experiences – both good and bad.

On the other hand, the various publications and associations will provide the hard information such as website, addresses, telephone numbers and, in some cases, basic facts about the providers.

The identification of providers is the point in the process where due diligence starts to become critical. Before a contact can be made or a Request for Proposal or Request for Information issued, it is absolutely vital to have a clear understanding of the available providers, their reputations, and their suitability for client needs.

Once potential providers have been identified, it is time to begin a careful evaluation and selection process. Each client firm's needs will be unique, but there are certain basic criteria against which potential freight bill companies should be measured.

Financial Stability – The most important criterion will be financial stability. This has become very important, particularly for companies paying billions of dollars in freight bills. The potential client should know how long the provider has been in business, and whether they have the resources to survive economic downturns. Do they pay carriers promptly? What are their investment policies? What type of fiduciary responsibility and protection are provided?

Business Experience – The client firm should research the provider carefully to determine its experience in the industry and with its other clients. How many bills do they pay annually and for whom?

Commitment to Technology – The provider should have the technology to take advantage of its own critical mass and provide the output the client desires. More importantly, there must be a visible commitment to providing the most current technology for its own operations, and to maintaining systems that can be integrated with those of the clients. Finally, there must be an ongoing ability to provide for each client's unique needs as they change.

Management Depth and Strength – When outsourcing, it is important to remember that one of the products being purchased is expertise in providing the required service. The provider must have a strong, skilled organization, as well as adequate, qualified management.

"Bench strength" is a problem for some providers in any industry, and it is critical that the client have a clear understanding of the management and labor force that will be devoted to its relationship.

Reputation With Other Clients–The best substitute for personal experience is that of other customers and clients. The provider should be asked to provide a client list with contacts and telephone numbers.

When talking with other clients, it is important to determine if the provider simply does well what they are told or if they are proactive and have a commitment to continuous improvement in performance and customer satisfaction.

Carrier relationships are second only to client relationships for the successful freight bill payment company. At least three carrier references should be explored. These should be carriers that have had at least one year's experience with the FBP firm.

Continuous Improvement Programs – The progressive freight bill payment provider usually will have a formal quality or continuous improvement program. Some may be ISO certified, while others may have lesser, but meaningful programs in place.

It is absolutely critical that the provider selected must be one who is committed to ongoing performance enhancement, and has an

200

identified procedure for accomplishing this. The RFI should require a detailed description of the programs in place.

Growth Potential – Most firms project ongoing growth through volume increases, new products, or new markets; and it is important for the payment company to be in a position to support that growth.

While there probably will not be excess capacity immediately available, the selected provider should be in a position to provide that capacity or new services over a short or long term, depending on client requirements.

Security – While security is not a new issue in outsourcing, in the past it has not always received the attention it should have. Before September 11, 2001, and subsequent events, the prospects of terrorist attacks and workplace violence seemed so remote that very little thought was given to them. The same was true for natural disasters until the 2005 devastation of the U.S. gulf coast. Now in addition to the risk of theft and pilferage, we have a much greater need to secure our supply chain, its products, and its information.

Most client firms have adopted more stringent security standards; and when considering a freight bill payment provider, it is imperative that it be in a position to secure facilities, equipment and information as well as or better than the client.

Information systems must be fully protected from outsiders, and information technology personnel should ensure that all necessary log-ins, passwords, and firewalls are in place. There should be off-site, back-up storage of all data.

If your company is publicly traded, you will be bound by the Sarbanes-Oxley Act. While technically, the providers are not bound by the act (unless they are publicly traded), you still will want to make sure that they are SOX-compliant. Specifically, the provider should be asked to provide a Statement of Auditing Standards (SAS 70, Type II). This certifies that the provider has adequate financial controls in place, and that they are effective.

Cost – While it should not necessarily be last in importance, neither should cost be the first and foremost consideration. While it must be considered in the selection process, it should be a factor only in deciding among firms that meet all the other criteria.

The manager who selects a provider solely on the basis of cost has committed to an outsourcing strategy that will have little chance of success.

Ethics – It is an unfortunate sign of the times that we must check the moral fiber of the people and firms with which we deal. But when one looks at the actions of Enron, World-Com, and other former pillars of American business, it is clear that firms must be extremely careful about the providers they deal with.

Some of the large providers will have formal ethics policies. Other smaller providers may not have such formal written policies, but they should at least have some code of ethics for their employees. This does not necessarily have to be a written policy as much as a state of mind. In the words of Mason Cooley, "Reading about ethics is about as likely to improve one's behavior as reading about sports is to make one into an athlete." [6]

Once the criteria for selection have been agreed upon, they should be used by the outsourcing team in the preparation of the Request for Proposal and in the evaluation of the various responses. To facilitate this evaluation and conduct it in a more scientific and quantifiable way, the various factors should be weighted according to their importance. It is also important that the providers understand the criteria against which they are being measured.

By giving a numerical value to each, and rating them accordingly, a mathematical result can be determined for each provider being considered. Figure 12-a illustrates a form that may be used for such an evaluation.

202

LOGISTICS SERVICE PROVIDER
EVALUATION SUMMARY

5 = Highest
1 = Lowest

Criteria	Weight	Provider Scores		
		A	B	C
Financial Stability				
Business Experience				
Management Depth and Strength				
Reputation with Other Clients				
Strategic Direction				
Physical Facilities and Equipment				
Operations				
Information Technology				
Quality Initiatives				
Growth Potential				
Security				
Chemistry and Compatibility				
Cost				
Total	**100.0%**			

Figure 12-a. Evaluation of Potential Freight Bill Payment Companies

It is important that the Request for Proposal be as complete as possible. The provider can respond only to what the potential client firm provides; and if the information is incorrect and/or incomplete, the proposal will no doubt be so, as well.

While each outsourcing firm will have unique requirements, there are certain informational needs that will apply to almost every potential relationship.

The RFP should be clear and concise and provide for responses in a pre-determined format. The format should be designed in a manner that facilitates the evaluation of the criteria already identified.

At a minimum, it should contain the following.

Background Information About Outsourcing Company – This section should describe the outsourcing firm and its basic businesses. It should include a general description of products manufactured or distributed, annual revenues, methods of distribution, and other helpful information, such as mission statements, numbers of facilities, and numbers of employees.

If publicly held, one effective method of providing such information is through the inclusion of the firm's most recent annual report with appropriate information highlighted.

Purpose of the Request For Proposal – This is simply the reason for the request. The objectives of the process should be described. This section should explain in detail what the outsourcing firm hopes to accomplish.

Scope of Work – For the freight bill payment company to submit an informed pricing proposal, it will be necessary for the potential client to provide a considerable amount of information about its payment activity. While it may be tempting to guess at the information – remember – that the more accurate the input, the more accurate the pricing.

Obviously, each payment provider will have its own informational needs and hopefully a template for addressing them, but Appendix 12-1 is an example of a checklist that will be helpful in preparing the RFP.

As the number of firms operating within a global economy continue to increase, it is becoming necessary for freight bill payment companies to have the experience and resources necessary to handle international invoices, as well.

If your firm falls into this category, there are some additional questions you should be prepared to answer. These are shown in Appendix 12-2.

Project Schedule – The firm should set forth the timetable of the project, including due dates, as well as the schedules for notification and further decisions, including estimated start-up dates.

Evaluation Criteria – As mentioned earlier, evaluation criteria should be listed and explained clearly so the provider will know by what benchmarks it will be evaluated.

Response Guidelines – This section should describe the format for responses. Hard copies or electronic formats, or both may be requested.

Rules for making oral presentations, if required, should be presented here.

Respondent Qualifications – Keeping in mind the evaluation criteria, this next section should request specific information about the provider. It is difficult to outline a precise list of the questions that should be asked; but the RFP should at least contain the following inquiries.

- What is your basic business?
- What services do you provide?
- When was the company founded?
- Is the company public or private? If public, please provide copy of latest annual report.
- If there is a parent organization, describe the relationship of businesses and strategies.

- Please provide the most recent three years' statements of profit and loss and cash flow, as well as balance sheets.
- Describe projected annual growth for the next three years. What will be the source?
- Describe strategies to be pursued in achieving this growth.
- Discuss your long- and short-term business visions.
- Provide resumés of key managers and charts for the remainder of the organization.
- Describe staffing policies for new account start-ups.
- What is your overall approach to the management of ongoing relationships?
- What is your annual employee turnover?
- Describe your information technology platform, hardware, software, and operating systems. Recount your experience with ERP systems and clients utilizing SAP, etc.
- Describe your IT staff including development, integration, operation and support personnel.
- How would you organize your systems and staff to meet our needs?
- How many transactions do you process annually, EDI and manual?
- What percentage of your total revenue is accounted for by your largest client?
- Please provide names, contacts and telephone numbers for five largest clients.
- How do you measure performance of your operations and report it to clients?
- How do you handle client communications? How often?
- Have you had a contract terminated in the last three years? If so, why? May we contact the client for more detail?
- Describe in detail your approach to ethics, security, risk management and disaster recovery.
- What are your processes and requirements for freight bill payment, including such things as short pays, accuracy, duplicates, coding accessorial charges, accruals, funding, reporting, etc.?
- Describe a typical implementation for your services. What is the procedure? What is the usual timeline?

Financial Stability
- Is an audited financial statement available?
- What is the net worth (financial strength) of the firm?
- What types of external (independent) audits are performed on the outsourcing firm? What type of risk coverage is provided?
- Is the company public or private?
- Is it part of a financial institution?
- What type of fiduciary responsibility and protection are provided?

Customer Support
- Are individual account representatives assigned to your company?
- Is a formal inquiry response system used to insure follow-up to all calls?
- Are all inquiries documented?
- Is there a dedicated EDI implementation group?
- Are there Internet and automated telephone inquiry capabilities available?
- Do you offer Internet services/tools specifically targeted to the needs of your clients?
- Describe your knowledge of the carrier industry.
- Describe your familiarity with logistics industry "best practices."
- How can you help our company identify logistics opportunities available to us based on the data you capture from our invoices?
- Can you offer benchmarking of a company's current transportation contracts and pricing with industry averages?

Technology
- Is the firm using the latest hardware and software technology?
- What are the future plans for handling data processing requirements?
- Can the firm handle all forms of electronic commerce?
- Describe in detail your EDI capabilities.
- Does the firm handle all EDI standards as well as proprietary EDI formats?

- Does the firm have a separate EDI implementation staff?
- Can information be accessed via the Internet?
- Are Internet database applications available?
- What is the size of the information technology support staff?
- Is there a formal disaster recovery plan in place?
- What operating systems are compatible with your software?
- Do you offer a transportation management system/solution software package?
- What length of time is historical data kept within the system?

Evaluation – Once the responses have been received, they should be evaluated according to the established criteria. Using the rating sheets, the top three should be identified, notified and scheduled for oral presentation, as well as personal visits by the selection team.

Oral presentations often will reveal weaknesses, strengths, and provide other impressions not readily identifiable in the written responses.

Site Visits – Finally, there is no substitute for an in-depth inspection of the physical facilities and operations of the finalist providers. These should be conducted by qualified members of the selection team or other internal or external experts brought in for the purpose.

With ready access to computer software and sophisticated graphics, almost anyone can generate an attractive, convincing document; but

 a thorough site examination by knowledgeable personnel will quickly reveal whether the physical facts support the salesmanship.

During these inspections facilities, operations, management, information technology and other aspects of the business can be examined closely; and the written responses can be compared to the visual conclusions.

208

How Are Freight Bill Payment Services Priced?

As mentioned earlier, since 2002 virtually all freight bill payment companies have priced their services based on the cost of providing them. Beware of providers that are only interested in being the "low bidder." A well-managed FBP firm will submit a bid based on their own costs, not on those of a competitor. Here again, each provider will have its own formula, but generally speaking a client can expect some variation of the following:

Implementation Fee – This will be an important part of the payment start-up. This fee covers the cost of FBP personnel going to the client's site to gather specifications, loading rates into the provider system, customized programming, loading reference files, edits and safeguards, and a myriad of other client-specific start-up activities. This fee is not intended to be a profit center, but simply to cover the cost of the activity.

There will be an individual charge that covers pre-audit, processing, and payment of each individual bill. Pricing will be higher for manual bills than for EDI invoices, and for both there will be an additional charge per bill for line item activity such as account allocation, accessorial data, etc.

A certain number of reports will be provided at no charge, but customized reports or services usually will be available for a small fee.

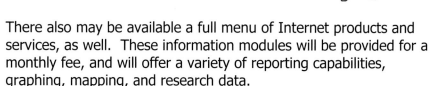

There also may be available a full menu of Internet products and services, as well. These information modules will be provided for a monthly fee, and will offer a variety of reporting capabilities, graphing, mapping, and research data.

The latter services will no doubt be the most valuable to the client. The modern freight bill payment provider is most importantly a supply chain information company. With its wealth of accumulated data on its clients' shipping practices and pricing, it is an invaluable and irreplaceable source of information, both current and historical.

The Freight Bill Payment Contract

As with any other outsourcing relationship, there should be a contract between the provider and the client.

The service agreements usually are brief compared to those for other outsourced logistics activities, but will vary in length and content, depending on the provider and the requirements. While the agreement need not be lengthy, it must be very clear on the services to be performed and the compensation therefore. At a minimum it should include the following:

Preliminary statements define the parties and their intentions and provide for the engagement of the provider by the client to perform certain services.

Services should be clearly defined and will include such responsibilities as pre-audit, payment of bills, data capture, and reports. The provider should confirm in this section that it has EDI capability.

This section also should describe any Internet services that will be provided and should clearly define the confidentiality requirements for the software and materials.

The *term* of the contract, along with any termination privileges should be included.

The *fee schedule* should be clearly outlined and based on a profile that has been provided by the client. The profile should be incorporated into the contract in order for all parties to understand the assumptions on which the pricing was based.

Finally, the agreement should contain *a confidentiality clause*, as well as provisions for *severability, governing law, insolvency, force majeure*, and the *relationship of parties*.

210

There will be variations of these provisions since individual clients may have unique requirements. Whatever agreements are executed, the terms should be clear, flexible, and mutually satisfactory. Both parties must remember that while they are working toward common goals, these goals may change, or each party's interests may differ from time to time. The contract must allow for these dynamics through reasonable non-adversarial language.

A sample contract is shown in Appendix 12-3.

Questions for Understanding

1. Why would a firm want to use a freight bill audit and payment (FAP) company?

2. Discuss the criteria for selecting a FAP firm. What are the most important?

3. How are FAP services priced?

4. What are some of the key questions a potential client should ask a FAP firm?

Chapter 13: International Transportation

*Globalization has been the creator of much of the
world's increased prosperity over the past decades.*
                                           - Alan Greenspan (2007)

Foreign Commerce

No supply chain development in recent years has impacted the
transportation function as much as the increase in foreign goods
entering the United States. Estimates of the amount of goods some
retailers bring in from abroad range from 50 to 85 percent of the
products in their stores. [1]

Foreign commerce has
always been important
to the U.S. but never as
much so as during the
past 20 years. In 1988,
U.S. exports of goods
totaled $320.2 million,
and imports amounted
to $545.7 million. In
2007, exports totaled
$1.2 billion and imports were $2.0 billion. This was an increase in
exports of 359 percent and 360 percent in imports. (See
Figure 13-a.)

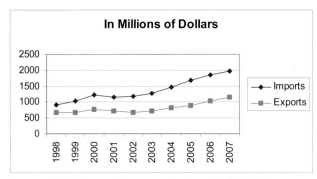

Source: U.S. Census Bureau – Foreign Trade Division

Figure 13-a. Foreign Trade 1998 - 2007

While the top six U.S. trading partners have remained constant over time, their rank within the group has changed rather dramatically. Figure 13-b shows the top six and their total trade (exports and imports) with the U.S. during the year 2007.

Country	Total in Billions of U.S. $
Canada	561.55
China	386.75
Mexico	347.34
Japan	208.13
Federal Republic of Germany	144.02
United Kingdom	107.19

Source: U.S. Census Bureau

Figure 13-b. Top Six U.S. Trading Partners – 2007

Comparing the 2007 rank to that of 1985, however, shows a very different picture, particularly in the case of China which rose from number six to number two. (See Figure 13-c.)

As can be seen from Figure 13-c, the most significant shift has been in trade with China, and most of this has been a result of imports. Since 2003, the value of Chinese imports has increased by 210 percent.

214

Country	1985 Rank	2007 Rank
Canada	1	1
Japan	2	4
Germany	3	5
Mexico	4	3
UK	5	6
China	6	2

Source: U.S. Census Bureau

Figure 13-c. Top Six U.S. Trading Partners

As most know, this country has been the source of the majority of the retail goods mentioned earlier, but it also is a major source for electrical machinery and equipment. In 2006, China's major exports by volume fell into these two categories. [2]

While this growth may slow with the economy, there is every indication that the trend will continue. A survey by the Foundation for the Malcolm Baldrige Quality Award revealed that 95 percent of CEO respondents identified "more globalization" as their top challenge over the next three to five years. Eighty percent identified improving their global supply chains as their top challenge. Needless to say, CEOs' objectives quickly become the objectives of everyone in their organizations, logistics and supply chain managers included.

As business has spun out of its purely domestic orbit, transportation managers have been caught up in the tumult. Their jobs have changed; they need new tools, new services and new skills. But most importantly, they are encountering new challenges in managing the business's most basic functions. Managing a domestic transportation network can be challenging enough. Combine these issues with customs, foreign cultures, currency, language, packaging, labeling, erratic transit times, and port congestion; and the task becomes formidable indeed.

Global or international transportation can be defined as importing and/or exporting goods and/or services beyond the boundaries of a country. [3] Within North America products may move by rail, motor carrier, air, or water; but outside the continental boundaries, there are only two options – ocean or air.

International Air Freight

In terms of weight, air freight accounts for less than one percent of the international volume; although if measured by value, the percentage would be much higher. [4] Air freight is handled by various cargo airlines, as well as FedEx, UPS, and DHL; and most major U.S. airports handle a significant amount of air cargo. Figure 13-d show the top ten U.S. airports ranked by international tonnage received during 2007.

Rank	Airport	Pounds
1	Anchorage	9,639,573,667
2	Miami	3,649,191,653
3	New York Kennedy	2,955,131,058
4	Los Angeles	2,458,646,909
5	Chicago O'Hare	2,420,131,519
6	Atlanta	1,009,942,899
7	San Francisco	1,003,175,114
8	Dallas-Ft. Worth	813,857,899
9	Memphis	760,656,095
10	Newark	570,743,518

Source: Traffic World, May 5, 2008

Figure 13-d. Top 10 U.S. Airports for International Freight - 2007

Worldwide, considering both international and domestic tonnage, the top ten airports in 2007 were

Rank	Airport	Millions of Metric Tons
1	Memphis	3.8
2	Hong Kong	3.8
3	Anchorage	2.8
4	Seoul	2.6
5	Shanghai	2.5
6	Paris	2.3
7	Tokyo	2.3
8	Frankfort	2.2
9	Louisville	2.1
10	Miami	1.9

Source: www.aci.aero/cda/aci/6/26/08

Figure 13-e. Top 10 Cargo Airports - 2007

Air cargo may move in space ranging from the belly of a passenger jet to a fully loaded 747 cargo plane. Boeing has even modified a 747 cargo jet called the Dreamlifter that is large enough to haul large sections of its new 787 passenger jet currently under development.

The Dreamlifter has capacity enough to transport fuselages from Italy, rudders from China, and wings from Japan. [5] All three of the large package carriers – FedEx, UPS, and DHL – operate high capacity cargo jets, as well.

Even so, the major concern for most traffic managers will be the supervision of the movement of goods by ocean carrier.

International Ocean Freight

The lower-valued, high-density products usually move by ocean carrier. These would include such commodities as iron ore, bauxite, coal, etc. For example, most of the bauxite used in the United States comes from Australia. [6] Higher-valued consumer goods, on the other hand, also move via ocean carrier on specially designed container ships.

Ships

Ocean going vessels must be registered but not necessarily in the country in which their owner firm is domiciled. They may register in countries such as Liberia or Panama, for example, or any country where regulations may be more relaxed. These countries are referred to as *flags of convenience*. It is not unusual, therefore, to see a U.S.-owned ship on a regular route between Shanghai and Long Beach flying a Liberian flag.

Bulk Vessels

The bulk ships tend to be very large and can be either a conventional bulk vessel or a tanker. They may operate either on a schedule or as a "tramp." (A tramp ship operates on no fixed schedule and sails when it is full to wherever its cargo is destined.) The largest bulk carrier ship in the world is the MS *Berge Stahl*, registered in Stavanger, Norway. It has a capacity of 364,767 metric tons and is so large it can tie up at only two ports in the world when it is fully loaded – Terminal Maritomo de Ponta da Madeira in Brazil and the Europort near Rotterdam. [7]

Container Ships

The movement of goods in containers has brought an entirely new dimension to ocean transportation. Containers are moved on specially designed ships that are quite different from the traditional ocean going vessel.

Container shipping was pioneered by Malcolm McLean some fifty years ago. On April 27, 1956, the *Ideal X*, a 524-foot long, ocean-going tanker with a metal platform fastened over the pumps and pipes on its deck, sailed from Newark to Houston with 58 fully-loaded truck trailers. [8] Visionary though he was, McLean probably had no idea what he had started on that April day in 1956. Today, over 70 percent of general ocean cargo is shipped in containers, and 15 million containers enter the U.S. every year.

The newer ships are designed so that no space is wasted. The larger ships carry no cranes or other loading or unloading gear, and they are loaded and unloaded by port equipment. Containers are lashed onto the deck and stacked six or seven containers high. Propelled by diesel engines, they have crews of between 20 and 40 seamen and can carry up to 1,500 TEU's (about 750 40-foot containers). * This is roughly equivalent to 35 100-car, double stacked intermodal trains.

Today, larger and larger ships are being built, and as a result most of the new ships will not fit through the Panama Canal. As of May 2008, the largest containership in service was the *Emma Maersk*. The ship is 1,304 feet long and has a beam of 184 feet. It can carry about 11,000 containers. By way of comparison, the largest ship that will fit through the Panama Canal can be no more than 951 feet long and 106 feet wide. A ship that can traverse the canal is called a Panamax ship, while the larger vessels are termed post-Panamax.

The major difficulty with modern containerships is that the ships are surpassing their ability to be handled efficiently.

---

* Container statistics and ship capacities are measured in TEU's. TEU stands for Twenty Foot Equivalent Unit and represents one container, 20 feet in length, 8 feet in width, and 8.5 feet in height. One forty-foot container is equal to two TEU's, as is one forty-five-foot container.

Containers

Containerization was no doubt one of the most important logistics innovations of the twentieth century. The savings in labor and freight costs are almost incalculable; and there is little doubt that they have contributed immeasurably to world trade flows. They have revolutionized international shipping.

The containers themselves come in three lengths – 20, 40, and 53 feet – with the 40-foot container being the most commonly used. Each will hold a significant amount of product, with inside dimensions of a 40-foot container being 39 feet 4 inches long, 7 feet 6 inches high, and 7 feet 8 inches wide. Cubic capacity is about 2,261 feet.

All containers are equipped with the necessary locks and latches to hold them in place on the ships and rail flatcars and to lock together when they are stacked. They are easily handled by modern cranes at port and rail intermodal facilities.

Double-stack Container Train

They may be owned by steamship lines, rail carriers, intermediaries, or shippers, themselves, and the widespread use of ISO standard containers has made them easily interchangeable. [*]

---

[*] ISO containers are built to standard specifications established by the International Organization for Standardization. This group sets worldwide standards for industrial and commercial activity.

Ports

Without ports, global ocean transportation would be cumbersome indeed; and with the explosion in global shipping as well as the construction of larger ships, it would be hard to find a port that is not undergoing some type of renovation, whether it is increasing the depth of the channels and harbors, adding state-of-the-art handling equipment,  or both. In 2008, twelve U.S. ports had some form of capital improvement underway.

The top 20 U.S. ports ranked by 2007 tonnage in TEU's is shown in Figure 13-e.

The Port of Long Beach is the fifteenth busiest in the world; and if the ports of Long Beach and Los Angeles were combined, together they would constitute the fifth busiest port complex.

In 2007, the Port of Long Beach handled

- 5,300 vessels
- 7.3 million TEU's
- 87 metric tons of cargo
- 13 percent of all cargo moving through U.S. ports [9]

In many cases, ports in the rest of the world "outclass" those in the United States, however. Singapore, for example, is the world's busiest port and plans another $2 billion expansion project scheduled for completion in 2013. The port of Singapore has a main channel depth of 52 feet and in 2007 handled [10]

- 140,000 vessels
- 27 million TEU's
- total cargo of 533,090 tons
- bulk cargo of 185,956 tons
- containerized cargo of 318,672 tons

Rank	Port	TEU's
1	Los Angeles	5,740,261
2	Long Beach	4,994,949
3	New York	3,935,262
4	Savannah	2,041,521
5	Norfolk	1,573,273
6	Oakland	1,451,326
7	Houston	1,415,657
8	Charleston, SC	1,408,434
9	Seattle	1,289,364
10	Tacoma	1,150,590
11	Port Everglades	691,645
12	Miami	684,793
13	Baltimore	427,902
14	New Orleans	254,782
15	San Juan	208,265
16	Portland, OR	206,900
17	Philadelphia	196,827
18	Wilmington, DE	185,231
19	Gulfport	171,835
20	West Palm Beach	168,014

Source: www.intermodal.org/statistics_files/stats4.shtml

Figure 13-e. Top 20 U.S. Ports – 2007

Port Jebal Ali, Dubai is the world's largest manmade harbor and the largest port between Rotterdam and Singapore. By 2030, it is expected to have a capacity of 80 million TEU's. In 2007, it handled [11]

- 128,568 vessels
- 10.7 million TEU's

The *world's* top container ports in 2007 were

222

Port	Millions of TEU's
Singapore	27.9
Shanghai	26.1
Hong Kong	26.0
Shenzhen	21.1
Pusan	13.3
Rotterdam	10.8
Dubai	10.7
Kaohsiung	10.3

The Asia Pacific influence is quite evident in this display.

As larger ships are built and global trade increases, port congestion will continue to loom on the horizon, and enhancements will no doubt be ongoing.

The Panama Canal

Second in importance to ocean commerce only to ports is the Panama Canal. Work began on the Panama Canal in 1882 by a Frenchman, Ferdinand de Lesseps, who had been active in the development of the Suez Canal. At the time, Panama was a republic of Columbia. From the beginning, the project was plagued with yellow fever, malaria, and financial difficulties. The volcanic ground was too much for the steam shovels and dredges; and finally, Lesseps gave up his idea of a sea level canal. [12]

In 1885 the plan was changed to a lock canal, but in 1889, Lesseps' company was forced into liquidation. In 1894 a new company was formed in France to complete the canal, but it too gave up five years later and began to search for a buyer. (Its lease on the land was not up until 1903.)

In 1889 the United States had begun construction of a canal in Nicaragua, but in 1893 a stock panic halted the construction. At that point many wanted to continue the Panama Canal instead, and after a long series of arguments, negotiations, and personal fortunes lost, in 1902 the Senate and House surprisingly voted to build in Panama instead. The Spooner Act gave President Theodore Roosevelt $40 million for the canal and the authority to negotiate with Columbia. The latter became impossible, and Panama planned a revolution which was quietly supported by the U.S. Navy. After that, the rest was easy.

Construction was not easy, however, and disease was a major problem. (Between 10,000 and 20,000 had died between 1882 and 1888.) U.S. doctors, however, were able to conquer the mosquitoes which carried yellow fever and malaria with insecticides and screened tents, and after nine years of seemingly insurmountable construction obstacles, in 1914 the canal was completed. Today it remains a marvel of engineering and construction expertise.

As indicated earlier, however, it is too small for the new ships, and often vessels that do pass through it must wait for days to traverse the canal. The post-Panamax ships must unload at west coast ports or move through the Suez Canal to ports on the East Coast of the United States.

The Americans ran the Panama Canal until 1999 when, by advance agreement, it was turned over to Panama. In 2006 Panama voters agreed to expand the canal, and at a cost of $5.25 billion, a third "lane" will be added. One set of locks will be constructed at the Atlantic end and one at the Pacific end. Each set of locks will have three chambers, each of which will be 1,400 by 180 feet and 60 feet deep. They will accommodate ships of up to 1,200 feet long and 160 feet wide with a draft of up to 50 feet.

The new locks are expected to be operational by 2015, and it is believed that the expansion will result in increased volumes at gulf and east coast ports thereby relieving congestion on the West Coast.

Global Intermediaries

Intermediaries play a much more crucial role in international transportation than they do in the domestic management of the function. With their unique expertise it is almost impossible for a firm to ship internationally without utilizing the services of one or more intermediaries. The most common types of these are international freight forwarders, customs brokers, non-vessel-operating common carriers, ship agents, and ship brokers.

International Freight Forwarders

International freight forwarders operate much like the domestic freight forwarders discussed in Chapter 8. They can be ocean or air and consolidate small shipments into larger ones, arranging for transportation on behalf of their clients. In addition, however, international freight forwarders provide a number of other services, as well. [13] They

- Negotiate rate quotations with international carriers.

225

- Charter vessels and book space.
- Pay the freight charges on behalf of the shipper.
- Provide tracing and expediting services.
- Purchase marine insurance when necessary.
- Complete the necessary documentation required at port of debarkation and embarkation.
- Contract for inland transportation.
- Obtain packaging cost quotations.
- Provide advice on shipping, packing, and documentation.
- Assist in language translation when needed.

Customs Brokers

Customs brokers perform a number of services, the most important of which is ensuring that documentation is accurate so that products can move through customs smoothly. Export and import documentation is a complex task for the inexperienced, and customs brokers have a good base of knowledge concerning the rules and regulations of the various countries.

Non-Vessel-Operating Common Carriers (NVOCC)

NVOCC's function much like a freight forwarder in that they consolidate less-than-container shipments into full container loads. They also have a good knowledge of export and import requirements. A NVOCC sometimes will deconsolidate container loads at destination inland cities, as well.

Ship Agent

These agents act on behalf of the carrier and are particularly helpful in ports where the shipping company has no facilities. They manage the loading, unloading, clearance, etc. that the carrier would provide for itself in larger ports.

Ship Broker

A ship broker operates in much the same way as a domestic truck broker, arranging for tramp service for shippers. Their activities are very similar to the arrangements and relationships between a domestic broker and an owner-operator trucker.

In addition to the above intermediaries it sometimes will be necessary or helpful to utilize *trading companies* (marketers who take title to the goods and minimize the shipper's financial risk), *export management firms* that do not take title but market a firm's products in other countries, or *packers* who have the necessary expertise required to safely package and label an export shipment.

Managing the Process

As indicated earlier, managing the international transportation can be a daunting task and careful attention to documentation, rules, and regulations are critical.

Terms of Sale

To many, the relationship between the buyers and sellers will be the most difficult to understand. In an effort to simplify this process and clearly describe the duties of each party, the International Chamber of Commerce has standardized International Commercial Terms referred to as INCOTERMS. These thirteen terms, first used in 1936, were designed as a terminology bridge between various countries and languages. They define the agreements for the purchase and shipment of goods internationally.

INCOTERMS sometimes are divided into four groups to facilitate the applicability of each.

- An E term is a term indicating origin.

- F terms are those applicable when the international transportation is not paid by the seller.

- C terms cover arrangements in which the seller does pay the freight.

- D terms are the arrival or destination terms.

E Terms

Ex-Works gives the buyer total responsibility for the shipment. Delivery is accomplished when the product is given to the buyer's representative at the shipper's plant or distribution center. The buyer is responsible for freight costs, insurance, export and import clearance, and all customs charges.

F Terms

FOB (Free on Board) means that the seller is responsible for getting the goods to a port. (Example, FOB Singapore) The buyer bears cost and responsibility from that point on.

FCA (Free Carrier) provides that the seller fulfills his responsibility when he delivers the product to a carrier. (Example, FCA Matson Dock, Singapore)

FAS (Free Alongside Ship) requires the seller to deliver the product alongside a given vessel at a port. (Example, FAS, *USS Bobby Matson*, Pier 3, Singapore)

C Terms

Here the seller pays the freight, and there are four terms that describe the relationships and responsibilities.

CFR (Cost and Freight) deals with the cost of the merchandise as well as the freight costs. The seller pays for the products and the transportation costs to the destination port, and the buyer is responsible for the product as soon as it is loaded on the ship. (Example, CFR Long Beach)

CIF (Cost, Insurance, and Freight) again provides that the seller pays for the transportation, but also the insurance. (Example, CIF Long Beach)

CPT (Carriage Paid To) is similar, but in addition the seller must purchase cargo insurance naming the buyer as the insured. He must also provide export clearance. (Example, CPT Long Beach)

228

CIP (Carriage and Insurance Paid To). This term is used primarily for multi-modal transportation and is the same as CPT except that the seller must purchase cargo insurance in the name of the buyer. (Example, CIP Long Beach)

D Terms

Finally, the D terms cover the delivery or destination arrangements. There are five of these.

DAF (Delivered at Frontier). Here delivery is accomplished when products are cleared for export at a named frontier or border point. The buyer takes delivery here and is responsible for clearing customs into the destination country. (Example, DAF Juarez, Mexico)

DES (Delivered Ex Ship) The seller's duties are discharged when the ship arrives at the destination. The buyer assumes responsibility for unloading and import clearance. (Example, DES *USS Bobby Matson*, Long Beach)

DEQ (Delivered Ex Quay). This is similar except the seller assumes responsibility for getting the goods off the ship. (Example, DEQ Dock, Long Beach)

DDU (Delivered Duty Unpaid). The seller provides transportation and risk assumption to the destination except the buyer must pay customs duties and taxes. (Example, DDU Los Angeles)

DDP (Delivered Duty Paid). This is the maximum obligation that can be assumed by a seller. The seller is responsible for all risk and charges up to the consignor's door. (Example, DDP Los Angeles)

Since INCOTERMS are standard, they can be found on a number of carrier or other websites. One exceptionally good chart of INCOTERMS can be found at www.ups.com.

Documentation

The amount of documentation required for international trade and transportation almost boggles the mind. Requirements will vary by country and product, but the most commonly used documents will be[*]

- *Shipper's Export Declaration.* The SED is the most common of all export documents and must be completed for all shipments over $2,500 in value and all shipments to certain countries.

- *Commercial Invoice.* A bill for the goods from the seller to the buyer. These invoices are often used by governments to determine the true value of goods when assessing customs duties. Governments that use the commercial invoice to control imports will often specify its form, content, number of copies, language to be used, and other characteristics.

- *Certificate of Origin.* The Certificate of Origin is only required by some countries, and in many cases, a statement of origin printed on company letterhead will suffice. Special certificates are needed for countries with which the United States has special trade agreements, such as Mexico, Canada and Israel.

- *Bill of Lading.* A contract between the owner of the goods and the carrier (as with domestic shipments). For vessels, there are two types: a straight bill of lading which is non-negotiable and a negotiable or shipper's order bill of lading. The latter can be bought, sold, or traded while the goods are in transit. The customer usually needs an original as proof of ownership to take possession of the goods.

- *Temporary Import Certificate/ATA CARNET.* An ATA Carnet (a.k.a. "Merchandise Passport") is a document that facilitates the temporary importation of products into foreign countries by eliminating tariffs and value-added taxes (VAT) or the

---

[*] This list was compiled from www.export.gov/logistics where sample forms and explanations are available. For FedEx shipments an excellent resource is the *International Shipping Reference Guide* found at www.fedex.com. Similar information may also be found at www.ups.com.

posting of a security deposit normally required at the time of importation.

- *Insurance Certificate.* Used to assure the consignee that insurance will cover the loss of or damage to the cargo during transit. These can be obtained from your freight forwarder.

- *Export Packing List.* Considerably more detailed and informative than a standard domestic packing list, it itemizes the material in each individual package and indicates the type of package, such as a box, crate, drum, or carton. Both commercial stationers and freight forwarders carry packing list forms.

- *Import License.* Import licenses are the responsibility of the importer. Including a copy with the rest of your documentation, however, can sometimes help avoid problems with customs in the destination country.

- *Consular Invoice.* Required in some countries, it describes the shipment of goods and shows information such as the consignor, consignee, and value of the shipment. If required, copies are available from the destination country's Embassy or Consulate in the U.S.

- *Air Waybills.* Air freight shipments are handled by air waybills, which can never be made in negotiable form.

- *Inspection Certification.* Required by some purchasers and countries in order to attest to the specifications of the goods shipped. This is usually performed by a third party and often obtained from independent testing organizations.

- *Dock Receipt and Warehouse Receipt.* Used to transfer accountability when the export item is moved by the domestic carrier to the port of embarkation and left with the ship line for export.

- *Destination Control Statement.* Appears on the commercial invoice and ocean or air waybill of lading to notify the carrier and all foreign parties that the item can be exported only to certain destinations.

One other form that should be mentioned is the *North American Free Trade Agreement (NAFTA) Certificate of Origin.* It is required for shipments between the U.S., Canada, and Mexico and is required to ensure that these shipments enjoy the reduced or eliminated duty provided for.

Pricing

International rates are established by individual carriers or steamship conferences. The latter operate much like the domestic rate bureaus and publish rates on behalf of those carriers who are members. The tramp ships usually will charter either for one trip or for some period of time. A "barefoot charter" occurs when the vessel is chartered, but the chartering firm provides the crew and operates the ship.

In many cases it will be necessary to classify products much like the methods used in classifying domestic products. For international trade the classifications are contained in the *Harmonized Tariff Schedule of the United States.* This schedule is based on the international *Harmonized Commodity Coding and Classification System* (*Harmonized System*) established by the World Customs Organization. [14]

The publication is updated periodically by the U.S. International Trade Commission and is available in electronic format.*

Foreign Trade Zones

One of the obvious results of expanding international trade has been the rise in the number of Foreign Trade Zones (FTZ) in the United States. In 1970 there were only eight in the country, and by 2008

---

* Harmonized classification numbers, for example, are necessary to complete the NAFTA Certificate of Origin.

there were 263. Utilized properly, depending on the nature of a firm's business, the transportation manager can use an FTZ to both financial and operational advantage.

By definition, a Foreign Trade Zone is a government-sanctioned site where foreign and domestic materials remain in a kind of international commerce limbo. While they remain in the zone, the materials may be stored, manipulated, mixed with domestic and/or foreign materials, used in assembly or manufacturing processes, or exhibited for sale without triggering the payment of U.S. Customs duties and excise taxes. Though the FTZ may technically lie within the United States' boundaries, the goods residing there are essentially considered to be goods without a country – and so, remain outside U.S. Customs' clutches.

FTZ's were created in 1934 to "expedite and encourage foreign commerce." From a customs perspective, goods in a North Mississippi foreign trade zone are treated the same way as those located in, say, China. Imports may flow directly into the zone and be held there indefinitely duty free. Duty is assessed only when those goods are shipped out of the zone to destinations in the United States.

FTZ's can offer a number of benefits, including:

- *Eliminating delays in customs clearance.* This is particularly important in this time of unprecedented port congestion.

- *Eliminating duty drawback.* Goods that are imported and stored in an FTZ may be re-exported without ever incurring duties. This eliminates the need to file for duty drawback refunds, a lengthy procedure that ties up funds.

- *Avoiding duty on waste or scrap.* If for some reason goods in the zone must be destroyed or returned, no duties will be charged.

- *Providing relief from inverted tariffs.* There are instances where companies are actually penalized for manufacturing at home. When the duty on raw materials is higher than that on the finished product, an importer of finished goods has an advantage over the U.S. producer. If the manufacturing takes place in an FTZ, however, the owner pays duty on his end products as they are shipped, thus leveling the playing field. For example, an FTZ-located company can import parts and components and ship assembled motorcycle and jet ski engines at a duty rate of 0 to 4 percent, depending on type. If, however, the same company operated outside the FTZ, the import duty on the parts and components would range from 0.2 to 11 percent.

- *Major savings in processing fees.* The 2000 Trade and Development Act contained a provision that provided for "weekly entry" procedures in all FTZ's. This may not seem like a big deal, but companies located outside the zones pay a 0.21 percent (value of merchandise) fee for every shipment processed by U.S. Customs. The minimum fee is $25, and maximum (which applies to any shipment valued at $230,952 or above) is $485, regardless of the amount of duty paid.

  Example: Suppose a company located in an FTZ received ten shipments, each with a value of $250,000, every week. At $485 each, the processing fees outside the zone would be $4,850 weekly or $252,200 annually. Within the zone, however, these same ten receipts would be processed as a single shipment of $2,500,000 for a total fee of $485 per week.

The advantages to be gained from doing business in a foreign trade zone vary by industry and company, but transportation managers of U.S. companies involved in importing would do well to examine this option carefully. For more information on Foreign Trade Zones, visit the National Association of Foreign Trade Zones' website at www.naftz.org.

Land Bridges

Land bridge is a term that is commonly used in international transportation; and there are three types of bridges that the transportation manager will encounter from time to time.

A *land bridge* refers to a movement from Asia to Europe, for example, that moves across the Pacific Ocean to a U.S. west coast port, then by rail to an east coast port where it is transferred to a ship for passage along the Atlantic. This is in lieu of an ocean movement through the Panama Canal.

A *mini-bridge* refers to a movement from Asia to the West Coast, for example, then by rail across the U.S. to another port such as Charleston, Savannah, etc. This replaces an all-water route to one of these ports.

A *micro-bridge* substitutes a U.S. interior city for the destination port city. For example, a shipment from Shanghai via water to Long Beach, then rail to Memphis would be a micro-bridge movement.

North American Free Trade Agreement

The North American Free Trade Agreement (NAFTA) was signed by the U.S., Canada, and Mexico in 1993 and ratified by Congress in 1994. The objectives of the treaty were based on three principles: [15]

- the unimpeded flow of goods
- most favored nation status
- a commitment to enhance the movement of goods and services across the borders.

Under the original schedule, NAFTA would have opened U.S. roadways to both Canadian and Mexican truckers on Jan. 1, 2000. In 1995, however, the Clinton administration put the trucking provisions of NAFTA on hold – but only for Mexican truckers – citing concerns about the trucks' ability to meet U.S. safety standards.

In 2001, Congress enacted legislation requiring U.S. government agencies to meet 22 safety requirements before Mexican truckers would be allowed to travel beyond the commercial zones. The following year, Transportation Secretary Norman Mineta confirmed that those requirements had been met. Legal challenges, however, kept the initiative tied up in court until 2004, when the U.S. Supreme

Court resolved the matter, ruling that Mexican truckers should be allowed into the United States.

Finally, in February 2007, the Department of Transportation (DOT) announced a one-year pilot program that would allow selected Mexican carriers to make deliveries beyond the U.S. commercial zones. To participate, truckers must pass a safety audit by U.S. inspectors, including a complete review of driver records, insurance policies, drug and alcohol testing programs, and vehicle inspection records.

This test has come under fire and vehemently protested by some legislators, the Owner-Operator Independent Drivers Association, and the Teamsters Union. The controversy no doubt will continue for some time to come.

Canadian truckers, on the other hand, have met no such resistance and have operated without controversy into and out of the U.S.

The benefits from NAFTA have been clear. In 2008 imports and exports between the United States and Canada totaled $562 billion, and U.S.-Mexico trade totaled $347 billion. Well over $2 billion in trade moves among the three countries every day. [16]

One interesting development since the passage of NAFTA has been the growth in the *maquiladora* operations. Located along the U.S.-Mexico border, the maquiladoras provide manufacturing or assembly for partially finished products. One good example involved a firm in El Paso that manufactured cloth dolls. The dolls were assembled in El Paso, then shipped across the border to Juarez where the facial features were sewn on by Mexican seamstresses. The dolls were then returned to El Paso for final inspection, packaging, and shipping.

Inland Ports

Recent years have seen the genesis of another new term in logistics – the *inland port.*

As import traffic has continued to increase, resulting in serious congestion at the traditional west coast ports, carriers and shippers have searched for ways of bypassing some of the significant delays at the ports of entry.

While the enhancements to the Panama Canal will increase the potential of gulf and east coast ports, the project will not be completed until 2014. In the meantime, with the continuing construction of newer post-Panamax ships, these vessels, by necessity, will continue to clog west coast ports.

One answer has been the growth of the inland port concept. According to the Center for Transportation Research at the University of Texas, an inland port is *a site located away from traditional land, air, and coastal borders. It facilitates and processes international trade through strategic investments in multimodal transportation assets and by promoting value-added services as goods move through the supply chain.* Several cities lay claim to the title; i.e., Dallas, Chicago, Kansas City, Atlanta, and Memphis; and at least three of these have the necessary infrastructure with a minimum of congestion. Over time, others may as well.

Dallas/Fort Worth is served by three major railroads, and largely through the efforts of the BNSF and more recently the Union Pacific, it has become a well-positioned inland port. Containers are loaded directly from ships to rail cars where they are transported to DFW, a more efficient and less congested transfer point. Facilities are excellent, and there are any number of motor carriers and logistics service providers serving the area. Foreign Trade Zones are also present for those who need or want them.

Kansas City also is a large rail center and among its other attributes is advertising its position on the KCS Railroad as an added and unique advantage. The KCS in conjunction with its Mexican subsidiary can move containers from the uncongested west coast port of Lazaro Cardenas directly to Kansas City. Kansas City has good highway transportation availability and over 10,000 acres of FTZ space.

Memphis is fast becoming one of the preferred inland ports. With FTZ space, excellent highway transportation resources, and a number of outstanding LSP's, Memphis is a leading distribution center. It also has a significant rail infrastructure, one of only three U.S. cities served by five Class I railroads.

With the opening of the new Canadian port at Prince Rupert, BC, the Canadian National will be able to bring containers from this less congested port (two days closer to Shanghai) directly to Memphis, giving the area still another option.

Inland Ports...

Prince Rupert
Edmonton
Vancouver
Winnipeg
Memphis, TN
Montreal
Chicago
Memphis
Jackson

Shanghai to Memphis – 18 Days
Via Prince Rupert

Security

Since September 11, 2001, one of the major concerns regarding international transportation has been security. Because of the overwhelming volume of containers and other tonnage moving into U.S. ports, it is almost impossible to be

100 percent secure, but there are certain steps that have been taken to protect the ships, cargo, personnel, facilities, and citizens.

The *Twenty-Four Hour Advance Cargo Manifest Declaration Rule* was published in the U.S. Customs Regulations in 2002 and is applicable to all cargo destined for the U.S.

The rule requires all ocean carriers or NVOCC's to submit a complete cargo manifest to U.S. Customs at least 24 hours prior to cargo loading. Failure to comply with this rule can result in cargo being held at origin port, significant penalties against the carrier and the removal of container for inspection by U.S. Customs and/or the denial of permission to unload vessel cargo and the possibility of returning the cargo to the origin port.

More information can be found at http://www.customs.gov/xp/cgov/import/carriers/24hour_rule/.

C-TPAT (Customs-Trade Partnership Against Terrorism) is a partnership between U.S. Customs and Border Protection (CBP) and the shipping community designed to facilitate legitimate cargo and conveyances while securing the global supply chain. According to the 2004 CBP Strategic Plan, [17]

> "In joining C-TPAT, companies sign an agreement to work with CBP to protect the supply chain, identify security gaps and implement specific security measures and best practices. Additionally, C-TPAT partners provide CBP with a security profile outlining the specific security measures the company has in place. C-TPAT applicants must address a broad range of security topics including personnel security; physical security; procedural security; access controls; education, training and awareness; manifest procedures; conveyance security; threat awareness; document processing; business partners and relationships; vendors; and suppliers. Security profiles also list action plans that companies implement to align security throughout their supply chain."

Benefits of participating in the C-TPAT program include [18]

- A reduced number of inspections and reduced border wait times.
- A C-TPAT supply chain specialist to serve as the CBP liaison for validations, security issues, procedural updates, communication and training.
- Access to the C-TPAT members through the Status Verification Interface.

- Self-policing and self-monitoring of security activities.
- In the Automated Commercial System (ACS), C-TPAT certified importers receive reduced selection rate for Compliance Measurement Examinations and exclusion from certain trade-related local and national criteria.
- Certified C-TPAT importers are eligible for access to the FAST lanes on the Canadian and Mexican borders.
- Certified C-TPAT importers are eligible for the Office of Strategic Trade's (OST) Importer Self-Assessment Program (ISA) and have been given priority access to participate in the Automated Commercial Environment (ACE).
- C-TPAT certified highway carriers, on the Canadian and Mexican borders, benefit from their access to the expedited cargo processing at designated FAST lanes. These carriers are eligible to receive more favorable mitigation relief from monetary penalties.
- C-TPAT certified Mexican manufacturers benefit from their access to the expedited cargo processing at the designated FAST lanes.
- All certified C-TPAT companies are eligible to attend CBP-sponsored C-TPAT supply chain security training seminars.

TWIC is a common identification credential which will be issued to any individual who will have "unescorted access to secure areas of facilities and vessels and all mariners holding Coast Guard-issued credentials or qualification documents." [19] Workers will be issued a tamper-resistant "Smart Card" with a fingerprint template.

TWIC is considered to be a critical component of the Department of Homeland Security's efforts to protect U.S. ports.

Cargo Scanning, sometimes referred to as non-intrusive inspection (NII) refers to non-destructive methods of identifying the contents of containers. Congress has mandated that 100 percent of all containers entering the U.S. will be scanned. As of 2007, only 5 percent of these containers were being scanned. [20] To achieve 100 percent compliance is an ambitious goal and will be accomplished only through significant investment in advanced technology.

Port Security is, of course, handled by individual ports, and most have made a concerted effort to enhance and maintain security at and around their facilities. They rely on very sophisticated techniques in some cases (such as the underwater surveillance submersibles at Long Beach), dive teams, and careful employee and visitor screening, as well as such agencies as harbor patrols, local law enforcement agencies, the U.S. Coast Guard, Department of Homeland Security, and Customs and Border Protection. Even so, constant attention is required to ensure the safety of cargo and personnel.

The Future

There seems to be little doubt that the supply chains of many firms will continue to expand globally. Global end-to-end solutions will become increasingly valuable, and those logistics practitioners who are able to operate in this environment should be quite successful.

The chances of moving away from offshore-produced products are very slight.

Nick LaHowchic, former President of Limited Logistics Services, put it this way.

"Our retail supply chain which already sources or sells our [Limited] products in over 50 countries will only further expand globally to successfully compete in the 21st century. Our core competency has to remain, relying on what we think our customers want, in what categories, what channels, what market segments and geography and how we make it in the best factory and country alternatives supported by the fastest and most reliable supply chain network. Retailers that stay ahead of competition share this interdependence of their business challenge with experts in the 3PL field along with physical and cultural capabilities to get the best return of time, money and talent. Only together, can retails and 3PLs make the best consumer-driven business decision using and sharing the most we all can about the status of plans and products across the globe."

This will be a challenge for the manager. There will be several considerations not often encountered in domestic operations; i.e. [21]

- Understanding of cultural differences around the world.
- Understanding of various political environments.
- Documentation requirements.
- Ability to develop economic rationalization for international operations.

Additionally, such functions as inventory management will be more complex. Longer, more erratic transit times will require more inventory or necessitate new management techniques. Unfortunately, the Chinese have more port loading resources than the United Sates has unloading facilities; and for the time being, port congestion and delays at home will be the norm. Those delays, combined with inland transportation capacity problems, ensure that lead times will be long and delivery dates erratic.

There will be a continuing push for more and better technology. The complexity of global logistics will raise the bar where technology is concerned. Shippers charged with overseeing duty management, compliance screening, landed cost calculations, customs clearance and document filing will require systems far more sophisticated than the warehouse and transportation management systems they currently use for domestic activities. These will have to be enhanced, if not replaced.

There will be an increasing demand for education. It has been estimated that less than half of the logistics executives in the country currently have global responsibilities. And it's hard to imagine that anyone out there could be fully conversant with all of the complexities of managing all aspects of global trade. Education will be a necessity. Given that the Customs regulations for import shipments alone run well over 500 pages, it's clear the training process won't be quick or easy. But it will be necessary. It will be the price of living – and thriving – in a global market.

Questions for Understanding

1. Discuss the significance of Asia Pacific product origins to U.S. transportation.

2. Discuss the services provided by an international freight forwarder.

3. What is the significance of INCOTERMS? How are they used?

4. Discuss the most important documents utilized in international trade.

5. What are the benefits derived from utilizing a Foreign Trade Zone?

6. What were the objectives of NAFTA?

7. What are the major benefits derived from participation in the C-TPAT Program?

8. Discuss the significance of the Panama Canal to U.S. global trade.

Chapter 14: Shipper/Carrier Relationships

> *It is a socialist idea that making profits is a vice. I consider the*
> *real vice is making losses.*
>
> > - Winston Churchill

Managing a transportation relationship is not an easy assignment. Even if carriers, contracts, procedures, and personnel are all in place, from time to time carrier and shipper priorities and goals will differ. Inevitably, conflicts will arise, and must be dealt with. Even when differences are minimal, managing the relationship will be a full time job.

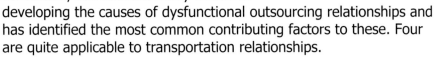

Everest Group, Inc., an outsourcing consultant, has assisted many clients in developing the causes of dysfunctional outsourcing relationships and has identified the most common contributing factors to these. Four are quite applicable to transportation relationships.

- Pricing and service levels are established at the start of the contract and usually contain no meaningful mechanism for continuous improvement.

- Differences in buyer and supplier cultures often cause misunderstanding and distrust. Even if the cultures are compatible, the two parties still have fundamentally different goals and objectives that are frequently difficult to harmonize.

- All outsourcing contracts are based on key assumptions regarding technologies, business conditions, personnel, and other relevant issues. As soon as the contract is signed, these assumptions begin to change. However detailed the contract or favorable the terms, most contracts cannot anticipate the changes in an evolving environment. This phenomenon tends to ensure that one, if not both of the parties will become disenchanted with the relationship. Longer-term contracts that lack flexibility tend to increase the likelihood of dissatisfaction.

- Once the contract is in force, there is a great temptation for both parties to sub-optimize the relationship and attempt to better their lot at the expense of the other. The inflexible nature of the contract usually favors the supplier. [1]

In discussing outsourcing relationships, Peter Bendor–Samuel, Editor of the *Outsourcing Journal*, has made an interesting distinction between partnerships and alliances. In suggesting that most contemporary outsourcing arrangements are alliances rather than partnerships, he said,

"A partnership is an association with another entity in a joint endeavor, where both parties have joint interests, joint risks and rewards. In a partnership, the interests are undivided. In an alliance, there is a pact or agreement between the parties to cooperate for a specific purpose and to merge their separate interests and efforts for that common purpose. The two work together for each other's good. Their pact (or the contract) establishing their alliance and agreement to perform a specified function together provides for flexibility. It also recognizes that their interests will differ at times." [2]

Such an arrangement by its very nature will produce cultural differences, and this is particularly true in transportation.

Both carriers and shippers alike have individual goals and objectives, and often the goals are conflicting. For example, a carrier strives for

(and is entitled to) a reasonable profit on the services it provides; and at the same time, shippers are attempting to pay the lowest rates consistent with the required service. Inevitably, conflicts will arise; and in recent years, these have been exacerbated by capacity shortages, a booming then declining economy, increased imports, and skyrocketing fuel costs.

For example, in June 2004, the president of the Truckload Carriers Association described conditions in the trucking industry as a "perfect storm" – four major forces (fuel, insurance, labor, equipment shortages) had all come to bear at once. Carriers quickly raised rates; and as a result, many turned in record profits in 2004.

And their management could hardly contain their glee: A 2004 article in *Traffic World* quoted several senior trucking executives who sounded like kids on Christmas morning. "It's a great time to be in trucking," said one. Another said, "I'm smiling again. Trucking is fun." A director of business development reported, "We are getting rate increases. We are culling accounts." This did not exactly endear them to the shipping public.

Industry consolidation in the "storm's" aftermath altered the market dynamics. After years of what could best be described as a buyer's market where trucks were in plentiful supply, the tables turned. Demand for trucks far outstripped supply, which meant truckers had the upper hand. They could afford to be selective about whose freight they would handle and what they would charge. Shippers had to adjust to a very different reality.

Fast forward to 2007 when the economy took a downturn, and suddenly there was more supply than demand for transportation service. Some shippers, recalling truckers' attitudes of a few years prior reacted with predictable tough negotiations.

This was complicated even further by soaring fuel costs. In 2008, with diesel fuel approaching $5.00 per gallon, carriers were declaring bankruptcy or parking tractors they could not afford to operate. Some shippers have simply refused to pay higher fuel surcharges because they believed they were being overcharged or simply could not afford to pay more.

The end result was that shippers and carriers simply weren't treating each other well, and relationships deteriorated in some cases to an all-time low.

As a transportation manager for a shipper or a carrier executive, it is important to try to find some common ground. The transportation relationship should not be one of "getting even," but one of mutual respect and integrity. We must be honest and forthright and foster collaboration and integration among the transportation partners. Success will come only after we truly understand that the transportation business is more about relationships than it is operations.

Questions for Understanding

1. Discuss the differences between a partnership and an alliance.

2. What are the major contributing factors to a deterioration in carrier/shipper relationships?

Endnotes

Endnotes

Introduction

(1) www.inventors.about.com/library/inventors
(2) CSCMP, *19th Annual State of Logistics Report*, June 2008.

Chapter 1

(1) http://inventors.about.com
(2) www.endoftheoregontrail.org
(3) Handfield, Robert B.; Nichols, Jr., E. L., *Introduction to Supply Chain Management*, Prentice Hall, 1999, p. 2.
(4) Coyle, John J.; Bardi, Edward J.; Novak, Robert A., *Transportation*, Thomson, 2006, p. 15.
(5) This table was based on the work of Bowersox, Closs, and Cooper in *Supply Chain Logistics Management*, McGraw-Hill, 2002.

Chapter 2

(1) Roy J. Sampson, Martin T. Farris, *Domestic Transportation*, Houghton Mifflin Company, Boston, 1979, p. 314.
(2) Ibid, p. 315.
(3) Ibid, p. 315.
(4) www.britannica.com/eb/article-9054289/Munn.v.Illinois
(5) Gibbons v. Ogden re-stated that Article 1, Section 8, Clause 3 of the Constitution empowers Congress "to regulate Commerce with foreign nations, and among the several States, and with the Indian Tribes."
(6) 57th Congress, Sess. 2, ch. 708, 32 Stat. 847.
(7) 61st Congress, ch. 309, 36 Stat. 539.
(8) Sampson, Farris, *Domestic Transportation*, p. 353.
(9) www.wikipedia.org/wiki/United_States_Railroad_Administration
(10) Sampson, Farris, *Domestic Transportation*, p. 330, 331.
(11) Locklin, Philip D., *Economics of Transportation*, Richard D. Irwin, Inc., Chicago 1949, p. 668.
(12) Sampson, Farris, *Domestic Transportation*, p. 350.
(13) 24 Stat. 379 (49 U.S.C.A. § 1 et seq.)
(14) Kennedy, John F., "Special Message to Congress on Transportation," April 5, 1962.
(15) Moore, Thomas Gale, "Trucking Deregulation," www.econlib.org
(16) John J. Coyle, Edward J. Bardi, Joseph L. Cavinato, *Transportation* 2nd ed., West Publishing Company: St. Paul 1986, p. 320.
(17) www.wikipedia.org/wiki/Railroad_Revitalization_and_Regulatory_Reform_Act
(18) Coyle, Bardi, Novack, *Transportation* , 5th ed., South-Western, Mason, Ohio, p. 59.

Chapter 3

(1) Johnny Mercer, Harry Warren, "On the Atchison, Topeka, and Santa Fe," 1945.
(2) Charlton Ozburn, "Railroad: The Great American Adventure," National Geographic Society, 1977.
(3) "Railroad History," www.sdrm.org/history/timeline
(4) http://inventors.about.com/library/inventors/brailroad
(5) www.historycentral.com/railroad/TThumb
(6) Ibid.
(7) D. Philip Locklin, *Economics of Transportation*," Richard D. Irwin, Inc., Chicago, 1949, pp. 90 – 91.
(8) Ibid., pp. 90 – 91.
(9) Ibid., p. 89.
(10) www.rakan.com/american_wealth/railroad_barons/railroad_tycoons2.asap
(11) Ibid.
(12) http://en.wikipedia.org/wiki/Robber_baron_(industrialist)
(13) Bear Stearns, "Railroad Industry," May, 2007, p. 58.
(14) Ibid. p. 56.
(15) *Railroad Facts – 2006 Edition*, (Association of American Railroads), p. 47.
(16) *BNSF Annual Report – 2003.*
(17) *Norfolk Southern Annual Report – 2006.*
(18) *Railroad Facts*, p. 44.
(19) Ibid., p. 18.
(20) Coyle, Bardi, Novak, *Transportation*, Thomson, Mason, Ohio, 2006, p. 144.
(21) *Railroad Facts*, pp. 3, 56.
(22) Ibid., p. 61.
(23) Bear Stearns, "Railroad Industry," p. 1.
(24) *Increased Railway Rates, Fares & Charges, 1942*, 255 I.C.C. 357, 386 (1943).
(25) http://en.wikipedia.org/wiki/Amtrak.
(26) CSCMP, *State of Logistics Report*
(27) www.amtrak.com
(28) www.railfaneurope.net/tgv/acela

Chapter 4

(1) CSCMP, *State of Logistics Report.*
(2) Ibid., p. 21
(3) www.student-brittanica.com, "Trucks and Trucking"
(4) www.wikipedia.org/wiki/Truck
(5) CSCMP, *State of Logistics.*
(6) Ibid. p. 31
(7) www.fhwa.dot.gov/infrastructure/hwyhisto4.cfm
(8) American Trucking Association, *American Trucking Trends 2005 – 2006*
(9) Eno Transportation Foundation, *Transportation in America*, 20th Edition
(10) Coyle, Bardi, Novak, *Transportation*, p. 105
(11) American Trucking Associations, *American Trucking Trends 2005 - 2006*
(12) www.teamster.org

(13)   *Global Insight*, "The U.S. Truck Driver Shortage: Analysis and Forecasts," May, 2005
(14)   www.cargobusinessnews.com, May 27, 2008.
(15)   Bear Stearns & Company, "Inside Freight," November 13, 2007
(16)   Ibid.
(17)   www.artba.org

Chapter 5

(1)   www.wikipedia.org/wiki/Aviation_history
(2)   Ibid.
(3)   Sampson, Farris, *Domestic Transportation*, p. 756.
(4)   www.wikipedia.org/wiki/Aviaation_history
(5)   Air Transport Association, 2007 Economic Report.
(6)   www.airlines.org/products/AirlineHandbookCh3
(7)   www.wikipedia.org/wiki/Low_cost_carrier
(8)   Air Transport Association, 2007 Economic Report.
(9)   Ibid.
(10)   Coyle, Narki, etc., *Transportation*, p. 166.
(11)   www.airlines.org/products/AirlineHandbookCh.8
(12)   Ibid.
(13)   Coyle, Nardi, etc., *Transportation*, p. 169.
(14)   Air Transport Association, 2007 Economic Report.
(15)   www.iata.org/whatwedo/economics/fuel
(16)   Air Transport Association, 2007 Economic Report.
(17)   Ibid.
(18)   Kelly Yamanouchi, "Airlines Look for a Bit of Stability," *Memphis Commercial Appeal*, June 29, 2008, p. C2.

Chapter 6

(1)   Philip D. Locklin, *Economics of Transportation*, Richard D. Irwin, Chicago: 1949,
       p. 650.
(2)   Ibid., p. 656.
(3)   www.phmsa.dot.gov/portal/site/PHMSA
(4)   www.aopl.org
(5)   www.pipeline101.com
(6)   Coyle, Bardi, Novack, *Transportation*, p. 198.
(7)   Ibid., p. 203.
(8)   www.wikipedia.org/wiki/Pipeline_inspection_gauge
(9)   Ibid.
(10)   Coyle, Bardi, Novack, *Transportation*, p. 203 – 204.
(11)   www.aopl.org
(12)   Ibid.
(13)   John Birger, "What Pipeline Problem," *Fortune*, September 4, 2006, pp. 23 – 24.
(14)   Ibid.

(15)   www.wikipedia.org/wiki/Trans_Alaska_Pipeline_System
(16)   www.alyeska-pipe.com
(17)   www.bp.com
(18)   Roy J. Sampson and Martin T. Farris, *Domestic Transportation*, Houghton Mifflin Company, Boston: 1979, p. 38.

Chapter 7

(1)   Ibid., p. 18.
(2)   www.inventors.about.com/library/inventors
(3)   Sampson and Farris, Transportation, p. 19.
(4)   www.caria.org/iwns
(5)   www.mainland.cctt.org
(6)   www.inventors.about.com/library/inventors
(7)   Ibid.
(8)   www.caria.org/iwns
(9)   Ibid.
(10)   www.americanwaterways.com
(11)   Jane Roberts, "Barge Bonanza," *Memphis Commercial Appeal*, April 10, 2008.
(12)   Philip D. Locklin, *Economics of Transportation*, Fifth Edition, Richard D. Irwin, Chicago: 1949, pp. 709 – 710.
(13)   Paul Bertek, *Cost Recovery on the Inland Waterway System*, July, 1998.
(14)   www.en.wikipedia.org/wiki/inland_waterways_of_the_United_States
(15)   www.ingrambarge.com
(16)   Ibid.
(17)   Coyle, Bardi, Novak, *Transportation*, p. 192.

Chapter 8

(1)   www.wisegeek.com
(2)   Sampson/Farris, p. 342.
(3)   Hub Group 10-K, February 22, 2008.
(4)   Ibid.
(5)   www.shippers.org
(6)   Richard Thompson, "FedEx Home Delivery Has County Covered," *Memphis Commercial Appeal*, September 18, 2002, p. C2.
(7)   FedEx 2007 Annual Report.
(8)   UPS 2006 Annual Report.
(9)   Stifel Nicolaus, "DHL Restructures U.S. Operations; UPS Wins Air Business," May 29, 2008.

Chapter 9

(1)   Bloomberg, LeMay and Hannon, *Logistics*, Prentice Hall, 2002, Upper Saddle River, New Jersey, p. 109.
(2)   www.CliffsNotes.com. *Elasticity*. April 3, 2008.
(3)   Coyle, Bardi, et.al., p. 263.

(4)   Ibid.
(5)   Locklin, Philip D., *Economics of Transportation*, Richard D. Irwin, Inc., Chicago 1949.
(6)   Ibid., p. 27.
(7)   Ibid., p. 27.
(8)   Bloomberg, LeMay and Hannon, *Logistics*, p. 122.
(9)   Bloomberg, LeMay and Hannon, *Logistics*, p. 251.
(10)   Donald J. Bowersox and David J. Closs, *Logistical Management: The Integrated Supply Chain* (New York: McGraw-Hill, 1996), pp. 365 – 67.
(11)   Bloomberg, LeMay and Hannon, *Logistics*, p. 124.
(12)   Ray Bohman, "Know the Terms of Sale, *Logistics Management*, October 1, 2006.

Chapter 10

(1)   David J. Bloomberg, Stephen LeMay, Joe B. Hanna, *Logistics*, Prentice Hall, New York, NY 2002, p. 118.
(2)   Marc Liebman, "Outsourcing Relationships: Why Are They Difficult to Manage?," Everest Group, Inc., 1999.
(3)   Peter Bendor-Samuel, "A Pact for Difference," *Outsourcing Journal*, November, 1999, p. 1.
(4)   "Truckers in the Driver's Seat," *DC Velocity*, June 2004.

Chapter 11

(1)   www.abf.com
(2)   Coyle, Bardi, Novak, *Transportation*, p. 357.
(3)   www.dcs-is-edi.com/Trucking
(4)   Coyle, Bardi, Novak, Transportation, p. 376.
(5)   Adrian Gonzalez, *On Demand TMS: An Ideal Platform for Enabling Continuous Improvement.*
(6)   High Jump Software, *The Five Key Ways Transportation Management Systems Can Rapidly Reduce Costs By Up to 30 Percent*, 2005.
(7)   Gonzalez, *On Demand TMS.*

Chapter 12

(1)   CSCMP *State of Logistics Report*, 2006.
(2)   Langley, van Dort, Topp, Dengel, and Sykes, *2006 Third-Party Logistics – Results and Findings of the 11th Annual Study*, 2006.
(3)   Clayton Boyce, "Computrex, Inc. Bankrupt," *Traffic World*, January 7, 2002, p. 9.
(4)   Aberdeen Group, "Achieving Closed-Loop Transportation Spend Management," January, 2008.
(5)   Lisa Harrington, "Getting Finance in Ship Shape," *Inbound Logistics*, September 2005, p. 97.
(6)   Mason Cooley, *City Aphorisms, Fifth Selection*, New York, 1988.

Chapter 13

(1)   Ted C. Fishman, "How China Will Change Your Business," *Inc. Magazine*, March 2005, p. 70.

(2)   Alexandra Harney, *The China Price*, New York, 2008, p. 5.

(3)   Bloomberg, LeMay and Hannon, *Logistics*, p. 109.

(4)   Ibid., p. 291.

(5)   www.npr.org/templates/story

(6)   www.wikipedia.org

(7)   Bloomberg, LeMay and Hannon, *Logistics*, p. 291.

(8)   Arthur Donovan and Joseph Bonner, *The Box That Changed the World*, East Windsor, NJ, 2006, p. 51.

(9)   www.polb.com

(10)   "Wide World of Ports," *Inbound Logistics*, March 2008, p. 38.

(11)   www.pancanal.com/eng/history

(12)   Ibid., p. 40.

(13)   Adapted from Bloomberg, LeMay and Hannon, *Logistics*, p. 295.

(14)   www.wikipedia.org/wiki/Harmonize-Tariff_Schedule_for_the_United_States

(14)   Coyle, Bardi, Novak, *Transportation*, Thomson, Mason, Ohio, 2006, p. 234.

(16)   www.census.gov

(17)   U.S. Customs and Border Protection, *Securing the Global Supply Chain*, 2004.

(18)   Ibid.

(19)   www.tsa.org

(20)   United States House of Representatives, *Waste, Abuse, and Mismanagement in Department of Homeland Security Contracts*, July 2006, pp. 12 – 13.

(21)   David Closs, "The Global Experience of the Supply Chain Management Professional," *Logistics Quarterly*, October 2006, p. 34.

Chapter 14

(1)   Marc Liebman, "Outsourcing Relationships: Why Are They Difficult to Manage?," Everest Group, Inc., 1999.

(2)   Peter Bendor-Samuel, "A Pact for Differences," *Outsourcing Journal*, November 1999, p. 1.

Glossary

(1)   Adapted from   Kate Vitasek, Supply Chain Visions, "Glossary of Supply Chain Terms,"

                                    and

Coyle, Bardi, & Novak, *Transportation*, 5th ed., South-Western College Publishing, 2000.

Appendices

Appendix 10-1

SAMPLE
CONTRACT FOR MOTOR CARRIAGE

Contract Number _____ (Provided by carrier)

THIS CONTRACT is made and entered into this _____ day of
_____, 20___, by and between _____, hereinafter
referred to as Company and _____, hereinafter referred
to as Carrier.

WHEREAS, Carrier is engaged in the business of transporting
property for hire by motor vehicle, is duly authorized by the
appropriate state and federal regulatory authorities to operate as a
motor carrier transporting the property hereinafter described, within
the territories hereinafter described, and desires to serve Company
as a contract carrier by motor vehicle; and

WHEREAS, Company, having authority to choose the Carrier for
transportation of freight to be tendered under this Agreement,
desires to enter into an Agreement with Carrier providing for
transportation of such quantities of Company's property as it, its
suppliers and consignors may tender to Carrier for shipment,
between designated origins and destinations;

NOW THEREFORE, in consideration of the mutual promises herein
contained, the parties hereto agree as follows:

1. SCOPE OF AGREEMENT - Carrier shall transport between origins
and destinations designated by Company, products named in
Schedule A attached hereto, under such terms and conditions and at
such rates and charges as set forth in Schedule B attached hereto,
as the same may be supplemented or amended pursuant to
Sections ____ and ____ hereof.

Shipments made under this Contract shall be subject to the rules
and regulations attached as Schedule C. This Contract shall
supersede any conflicting bill of lading or tariff provision.
Amendments to rules must

255

be made in the manner described in Sections ____ and ____ hereof to be effective as to transportation provided under this Contract.

2. PAYMENT OF FREIGHT CHARGES - Payment of freight charges shall be the responsibility of the Company, consignee, or other party as set forth by the bill of lading. Payments shall be due within ____ days following receipt of invoice by Company. However, a late payment will not alter the application of discounts, rates and charges. Shipments must be invoiced as soon as practicable after delivery, but in no event more than ____ days thereafter; failure to bill charges to Company within the said ____ days shall waive forever any right of Carrier to bill to or collect from Company charges for any shipment not billed, regardless of any rule, regulation or understanding to the contrary.

3. MINIMUM VOLUME COMMITMENT - Company agrees to tender to Carrier and Carrier agrees to transport for Company a minimum of ____ shipments of Company's freight during the initial term of this Contract, and during each subsequent renewal hereof. Should this Contract be terminated at any time other than the conclusion of the initial term hereof or the end of any subsequent renewal period, the minimum quantity of freight provided in this section as applying to the final partial term hereof shall be reduced by the proportion the unexpired portion of the term bears to one year.

Should Shipper fail to tender or to have tendered to Carrier the minimum volume set forth in this Section, such failure shall not change in any respect the rates or charges due Carrier for shipments which Shipper did tender or have tendered for movement.

4. RATE AND RULE CHANGES - Rates and charges in the Contract shall not be increased during the term of this Contract, and rules shall not be changed, except by mutual written agreement of Company and Carrier. Unless otherwise agreed in writing, no rate increase by Carrier shall take effect on less than ____ days' notice to Company.

Rate reductions (including cancellation of a proposed increase) may be made on ____ days' notice to Company.

5. LOSS AND DAMAGE - Carrier will be liable for loss or damage to the Goods only while in the care and control of the Carrier, and when it results from the negligence or intentional acts of the Carrier, its employees, subcontractors, or agents. In no event will the Carrier be liable for concealed damage or where the loss or damage is caused by an act of God, the public enemy, and act of Company or its employees or agents, a public authority or the inherent nature of the Goods. Carrier's liability to Company for any loss or damage to the Goods shall not exceed the direct cost to the Company of the Goods involved, including transportation to the point of loss or damage, less its salvage value, if any.

A claim under this contract for loss, damage, injury or delay to a shipment shall be made in writing or electronically within ____ days after delivery or tender of delivery of the shipment, or, if it is not delivered or tendered for delivery, within _____ months after a reasonable time for delivery has elapsed. If shipment is made at a released value, it will be declared on the Bill of Lading.

Any action at law or suit in equity pertaining to a shipment transported by Carrier shall be commenced within ____ years from the date Company receives written notice from Carrier that Company's claim or any part thereof has been disallowed.

Company shall have the immediate right to offset freight or other charges owed to Carrier against claims for loss, damage or delay, or for overcharge and duplicate payment claims, unless Carrier disputes such claims.

6. UNDERCHARGES AND OVERCHARGES - Any action or proceeding by the Carrier to recover charges alleged to be due hereunder, and any action or proceeding by Company to recover overcharges alleged to be due hereunder, shall be commenced no more than _____ (___) days after delivery or tender of delivery of the shipment with respect to which such charges or overcharges are claimed. To the extent permitted by applicable law, the expiration of the said ____-day period shall be a complete and absolute defense to any such action or proceeding, without regard to any mitigating or extenuating circumstance or excuse

whatever. Undercharge claims may not be collected unless notice is received by company within ___ days of the original freight bill date.

7. DISTINCT NEEDS OF THE SHIPPER - A company may want to ensure that the carrier meets the continuing needs and requirements of the company. In the ever-changing environment of the twenty-first century this could be a very important provision. Examples of important considerations are shown in Schedule D of the contract in Appendix 9-4.

Carrier agrees that it will provide service to Company as a contract carrier by motor vehicle, which is and will be designed to meet the distinct needs of Company. Carrier shall tailor its service to meet those needs more particularly set forth in Schedule D attached hereto, as well as those indicated elsewhere in this Agreement. There shall be a review on an ongoing basis on the requirement to alter or amend the service standards from those initially needed by Company, so as to make certain that the distinct needs of Company continue to be met. Carrier agrees to train its personnel who provide and will provide service to Company to ensure that Company receives that service which meets and will continue to meet Company's distinct needs.

8. INSURANCE - Carrier, at its own expense, agrees to carry and keep in force at all times public liability, property damage, cargo, and workmen's compensation insurance with such reliable insurance companies and in such amounts as Company may from time to time approve and such as will meet the requirements of federal and state regulatory bodies having jurisdiction of Carrier's operations under this Contract. Certificates of insurance showing Carrier's compliance with the provisions of this section shall be furnished to Company prior to any transportation under this Contract and whenever Carrier changes or renews its insurance coverage.

9. INDEPENDENT CONTRACTOR - It is the specific intention of the parties that this Contract not be construed to make Carrier or any of its agents or employees in any sense a servant, employee, agent, partner or joint-venture participant of or with Company, and Carrier is not authorized or empowered by this Contract to obligate or bind Company in any manner whatsoever. Carrier shall conduct operations hereunder as an independent contractor, and as such shall have control over its

employees and shall retain responsibility for complying with all federal, state and local laws pertaining in any way to this Contract. Said responsibilities include, but are not limited to, provision of safe equipment appropriate to haul Company's property tendered under this Contract, assumption of full responsibility for payment of all state and federal taxes for unemployment insurance, old age pensions, or any other social security law or laws as to all employees or agents of Carrier engaged in the performance of this Contract. Carrier shall not display Company's name on any motor vehicle equipment it provides under this Contract without specific authorization to do so from Company.

10. INDEMNIFICATION - Carrier agrees to indemnify and hold Company harmless from any and all claims for death or injury to persons, and loss or damage to property of any nature arising from Carrier's transportation of property for Company. Carrier further agrees to comply with all applicable federal and state statures, rules and regulations, including judicial interpretations thereof, and to also indemnify and hold Company harmless from any and all claims or fines arising from Carrier" transportation of property of Company in violation of any such statute, rule or regulation.

11. FORCE MAJEURE - Neither Company nor Carrier shall be liable for failure to perform caused by acts of God, public authority, revolutions or other disorders, wars, strikes, fires or floods.

12. NOTICES - All notices required or permitted to be given under this Contract shall be in writing and shall be deemed to have been sufficiently given when received if delivered in person, when deposited at the telegraph office if transmitted by telegraph, or when deposited in the mails of the United States Postal Service, certified, return receipt requested, postage and other charges prepaid, and addressed to the respective parties at the following addresses:

CARRIER: COMPANY:

_____   _____

_____   _____

_____   _____

_____   _____

13. CONFIDENTIALITY - Neither party shall disclose the terms of this Contract to any third party except: (1) to a parent, affiliate or subsidiary corporation; (2) as may be required by law; (3) to any attorney, auditor or consultant who has a need for the Contract in the performance of professional services for a party.

14. TERM - This Contract shall remain in full force and effect for ___ (__) year(s) from the date hereof (herein referred to as the initial term of this Contract), (and from year-to-year thereafter,) subject to the right of termination by either party at any time on _____ (__) days' notice to the other party sent by certified mail, return receipt requested.

15. AMENDMENT - This Contract shall not be amended or altered except in writing and signed by authorized representatives of both parties.

16. ASSIGNMENT - Without the prior written approval of Company, Carrier shall not assign this Contract, and shall not assign any rights under this Contract to a third party. Any unapproved attempted assignment shall be null, void, and of no force or effect; should it be attempted, Carrier agrees to pay to Company any expenses including reasonable attorneys' fees that Company may incur in defending against any action or conduct related thereto. This Contract shall be binding upon each party's heirs, successors and assigns, if any, including any successor or assign by operation of law.

IN WITNESS WHEREOF, the parties have executed this Contract on the day and year first herein written.

CARRIER:

By: _____

Title: _____

COMPANY:

By: _____

Title: _____

SCHEDULE A
TRANSPORTATION CONTRACT

PRODUCTS COVERED BY CONTRACT

**SCHEDULE B
TRANSPORTATION CONTRACT**

REPRESENTATIVE TERMS, CONDITIONS, RATES, CHARGES ETC.

1. The provisions of this schedule apply on interstate and intrastate LTL shipments handled direct and joint line between points in the USA served by the Carrier, and to any additional direct or joint line points added during the period of this Contract.

2. Classification: Shipments must be on the bill of lading and shipping orders by commodity in accordance with the National Motor Classification. However, all outbound and inbound shipments will be subject to FAK class ____ for all class 50 through ____, FAK ____ for all commodities carrying class rating in excess of ____ and commodities less than class ____ will be rated at actual class rates less the discounts shown herein. These classes will likewise apply to all inbound collect shipments and third-party billing.

3. Rates: Except as otherwise specifically provided herein, all shipments will be subject to the provisions of the National Motor Freight Classification, ICC NMF 100 Series, and class rates and/or minimum charges as determined from Czar-Lite base January 1, 1996 rates.

4. Discount: Except as otherwise specifically provided herein, minimum charges and charges resulting from the application of class rates subject to weight groups of less than 20,000 pounds as provided in paragraph 3 above will be reduced (discounted) by:

    A. Discount ____% on outbound direct shipments and ____% on joint line shipments.
    B. Discount ____% on inbound direct shipments and ____% on joint line shipments.

In no case will the freight charges applicable to any shipment be reduced or discounted below $_____.

5. Shipments tendered to Carrier hereunder may, at Carrier's discretion, be randomly selected for verification of weight and inspection as to the commodity description and its being in compliance with the National Motor Classification descriptions.

6. Waiver of Increase: Rates will be frozen for one year of signed agreement by both parties to this Contract. In the event of circumstances arising affecting the cost of transportation, the terms of this Contract will be renegotiated.

7. Third-party billing provisions will apply on any bill paid by Company.

8. Carrier agrees to waive single shipment charges.

9. Carrier agrees to waive linear foot rule.

10. Carrier agrees to waive any charges for bill of lading or delivery receipts copies.

11. Carrier agrees to waive any applicable cubic minimum charges.

12. Carrier agrees to waive notification charges.

13. Carrier agrees to waive sorting and segregating charges.

14. Carrier agrees to waive inside delivery charges.

SCHEDULE C
TRANSPORTATION CONTRACT

FUEL ADJUSTMENT SCHEDULE (EXAMPLE)

The base fuel price shall be $_____ per gallon based on the national average published on Monday of each week in *Transport Topics*.

The surcharges based on deviations from this price will be as follows:

This surcharge will appear on the freight bill as a separate line item, and is not subject to discount.

The surcharge will be adjusted each Monday, depending on the published cost of fuel.

SCHEDULE D
TRANSPORTATION CONTRACT

DISTINCT NEEDS OF SHIPPER (EXAMPLE)

- Appointment time provisions

- Schedules

- Type of equipment

- Unique delivery requirements

Appendix 10-2

Trade Publications

Air Cargo World
1270 National Press Building
Washington, DC 20045
(202) 661-3387, Fax (202) 783-2550
www.aircargoworld.com

American Shipper
300 West Adams Street, Suite #600
P.O. Box 4728
Jacksonville, FL 32201
(800) 874-6422
www.americanshipper.com

CSCMP Supply Chain Quarterly
Tower Square, Number 4
500 East Washington Street
North Attleboro, MA 02760
(800) 554-7470
www.supplychainquarterly.com

DC Velocity
Tower Square, Number 4
500 East Washington Street
North Attleboro, MA 02760
(800) 554-7470
www.dcvelocity.com

Global Logistics & Supply Chain Strategies
150 Great Neck Road
Great Neck, NY 11021
(516) 829-9210, Fax (516) 829-4514
www.glscs.com

Inbound Logistics
5 Penn Plaza, 8th Floor
New York, NY 10001
(212) 629-1563, Fax (212) 629-1565
www.inboundlogistics.com

Journal of Commerce Group
33 Washington Street, 13th Floor
Newark, NJ 09102
(973) 848-7000, Fax (973) 848-7004
www.joc.com

Logistics Management
275 Washington Street
Newton, MA 02458
(617) 558-4473, Fax (617) 558-4480
www.logisticsmgmt.com

Logistics Today
1300 East Ninth Street
Cleveland, OH 44114-1503
(216) 696-7000, Fax (216) 696-2737
www.logisticstoday.com

Parcel Shipping & Distribution
2901 International Lane
Madison, WI 53704
(608) 241-8777, Fax (608) 241-8666
www.rbpub.com/parcelshipping.htm

Supply Chain Management Review
275 Washington Street
Newton, MA 02458
(888) 240-7324, Fax (617) 558-4480
www.scmr.com

Traffic World Magazine
1270 National Press Building
Washington, DC 20045
(202) 783-1101, Fax (202) 661-3383
www.trafficworld.com

Transport Topics
2200 Mill Road
Alexandria, VA 22314
(703) 838-1770, Fax (703) 548-3662
www.ttnews.com

Appendix 10-3

Trade Associations

Air Transport Associates
1301 Pennsylvania Avenue, N.W., Suite 1100
Washington, DC 20004
(202) 626-4000
www.airlines.org

Airforwarders Association, Inc.
1600 Duke Street, Suite #400
Alexandria, VA 22314
(703) 519-9846, Fax (703) 519-1716
www.airforwarders.org

American Association of Port Authorities
1010 Duke Street
Alexandria, VA 22314
(703) 684-5700, Fax (703) 684-6321
www.aapa-ports.org

American Trucking Associations
950 N. Glebe Road, Suite 210
Arlington, VA 22203-4181
(703) 838-1700
www.truckline.com

American Waterways Operators
801 North Quincy Street, Suite 200
Arlington, VA 22203
(703) 841-9300, Fax (703) 841-0389
www.americanwaterways.com

Association of American Railroads
50 F Street, N.W.
Washington, DC 20001-1564
(202) 639-2400, Fax (202) 639-2286
www.aar.org

Association of Oil Pipelines
1808 Eye Street, N.W.
Washington, DC 20006
(202) 408-7970, Fax (202) 280-1949

Express Carriers Association
P.O. Box 4307
Bethlehem, PA 18018
(866) 322-7447, Fax (866) 322-3299
www.expresscarriers.com

Intermodal Association of North America
7501 Greenbelt Center Drive, Suite #720
Greenbelt, MD 20770-3415
(301) 982-3400, Fax (301) 982-4815
www.intermodal.org

International Air Transport Association
601 Pennsylvania Avenue, N.W., Suite 300 – North Building
Washington, DC 20004
(202) 628-9292, Fax (202) 628-9448
www.iata.org

National Customs Brokers/Forwarders Association
1200 18th Street, N.W., Suite #901
Washington, DC 20036
(202) 466-0222, Fax (202) 466-0226
www.ncbfaa.org

National Private Truck Council
950 N. Glebe Road, Suite 530
Arlington, VA 22203-4183
(703) 683-1300, Fax (703) 683-1217
www.nptc.org

National Shippers Strategic Transportation Council
9382 Oak Avenue
Waconia, MN 55387
(952) 442-8850, Fax (952) 442-3941
www.nasstrac.org

Transportation Intermediaries Association
1625 North Prince Street, Suite #200
Alexandria, VA 22314
(703) 299-5700, Fax (703) 836-0123
www.tianet.org

Appendix 10-4

COMPARISON OF IN-HOUSE VS. CONTRACT CARRIER COSTS

This is a pro forma costing structure used by one company to track transportation operation expenses. This company assigns responsibility for completing the form to the controller, distribution, transportation and human resource managers. The completed information is used to compare against vendor bids.

	Previous Year Actual	YTD	YTD Annualized	Outsourcing Pro Forma	Outsourcing Better/Worse
Miles Operated ex Drayage					
Internal Cost per Mile					
Drayage Cost per Mile					
Total Cost per Mile					
For Hire Revenue					
Back Haul Revenue					
Net 3rd Party Revenue					
Inter-Div Hauling Income					
Total Truck Revenue					
Truck Wages/Benefits					
Supervision Salaries					
Clerical Wages					
Driver Wages					
Backhaul Unload Wages					
Restricted Duty Wages					
Other Wages					
Union Pension Fund					
Health & Accident Ins — Union					
Health & Accident Ins — Group					
Long-term Disability					
Quality Fund					
Other Associate Welfare					
Work Comp Admin Cost					
Work Comp Est Unpd Losses					
FICA & Unemployment Tax					
Total Truck Wages/Benefits					

Reprinted with permission from Dedicated Contract Carriage: Evaluation, Implementation, & Management, *by Lisa Harrington. Published by National Private Truck Council, Alexandria, Virginia; 1996.*

TRANSPORTATION OPERATING EXPENSES

	Previous Year Actual	YTD	YTD Annualized	Outsourcing Pro Forma	Outsourcing Better/Worse
Supplies					
Dry Ice					
Other Supplies					
Parts					
Tire					
Fuel					
Oil & Grease					
Total Supplies					
Garage Wages/Benefits					
Restricted Duty Wages					
Garage Wages					
Union Pension Fund					
Hlth & Accident Ins — Union					
Hlth & Accident Ins — Group					
Union Admin Group Ins					
Long-term Disability					
Quality Fund					
Other Associate Welfare					
Work Comp Paid Losses					
Work Comp Est Unpd Losses					
FICA & Unemployment Tax					
Total Garage Wages/Benefits					
Garage					
Garage Supplies					
Garage Parts					
Repairs Due to Accident					
Other Repairs					
Other Garage Expenses					
Total Garage Expenses					

Appendix 10-4
Page 3

	Previous Year Actual	YTD	YTD Annualized	Outsourcing Pro Forma	Outsourcing Better/Worse
Other Expenses					
Travel/Entertainment					
Training					
Miscellaneous					
Mdse Damage					
Mdse Short					
Backhaul Short/Damage					
Salvage Sales/Recoup					
Total Other Expenses					
Fixed Expenses					
Licenses					
Truck Leasing Expenses					
Less: Interest Expense on Leased Equipment					
Outbound Drayage					
Inbound Drayage					
Road Taxes					
USFT Superfund					
Truck Liability					
Vehicle Physical Damage					
Cargo Liability					
Other Insurance					
Depreciation/Amort					
InterCo Expense					
Total Fixed Expenses					
Total Truck Expenses					
Total Truck Operations					

Appendix 12-1

Example of Client Checklist
for Freight Bill Audit & Payment Services

1.   What is your annual average number of freight bills?

2.   What is your annual freight expense?

3.   Is transportation management for the company centralized or decentralized?

4.   How many shipping and receiving locations do you have?

5.   How many carriers do you use?

    a.   Top 10 carriers by dollar volume

        _____   _____

        _____   _____

        _____   _____

        _____   _____

        _____   _____

    b.   How many carriers handle 80% of your volume

    c.   What percent of volume is international?

    d.   What percent of your current invoice volume is currently processed EDI?

e.   What is the volume by mode?
        _____ TL

        _____ LTL

        _____ Air

        _____ UPS

        _____ Other

6.   Please describe your freight invoice approval process.

   a.   Inbound freight

   b.   Outbound freight

7.   Please respond concerning account coding.

   a.   What is the logic for assigning the account code?

   b.   How many codes are used?

   c.   What is the code structure and length?

   d.   How are the codes applied to invoices?

   e.   Are multiple codes assigned to an invoice? If so,
           what is the basis (weight, unit, etc.)?

8.   Do you have an accrual process?

9.   Please respond regarding your bill payment process.

   a.   Is there invoice aging to credit terms?

    b.   How many carriers bill electronically?

    c.   Are electronic bills of lading matched to outbound shipments?

    d.   Is there a receiving file for inbound shipments?

10.   Please respond regarding your scale of rates.

    a.   Do you use tariffs?

    b.   Do you use an FAK classification?

    c.   Do you use a single scale of rates or other?

    d.   Would you like a corporate tariff created?

11.   Please respond concerning periodic reports.

    a.   What are your data capture requirements?

    b.   What types of reports are required?

    c.   How often do you need reports?

    d.   What is your deadline for the receipt of reports (i.e., monthly reports due by the fifth day of the succeeding month)?

    e.   How many copies do you need?

    f.   Do you have an interest in an Internet-based report writer?

12.   Would you like any value-added services?

      a.   Loss and damage claims processing?

      b.   Carrier rate negotiations?

      c.   Shipment tracking?

      d.   Other?

13.   What is your expected implementation date?

14.   What kind of improvements do you expect after changing your freight bill payment process?

15.   Please provide any other relevant information necessary for a successful transition.

Appendix 12-2

Example of Client Checklist
for Freight Bill Audit & Payment Services
(Additional Questions for International Invoices)

1. How many invoices annually?

2. Are there both import and export invoices with this activity? If yes, what is the percentage of bills in each category? If yes, what is the percentage of dollars in each category?

3. What is the total dollars associated with these invoices annually (in U.S. funds)?

4. Are these invoices in English? If presented in other languages, please define languages and percentage of bills for each language.

5. Would these invoices be **billed** in U.S. currency or in other currencies? If currencies other than U.S., please list and provide percentage of bills for each currency.

6. Would these invoices be **paid** in U.S. dollars or other currencies? If currencies other than U.S., please list and provide percentage of bills for each currency.

7. What modes would these invoices represent? Please list percentage of invoices for all modes used.

8. Please describe and provide examples of the rate structures.

9. Are rates/contracts in English? If presented in other languages, please define languages and percentage of rates/contract in each applicable language.

10. Are rates U.S. currency-based? If not, what other currencies are used?

11. Is currency conversion required for auditing and/or payment purposes? If yes, please describe where conversions are applicable.

12. If currency conversion is required for auditing and/or payment purposes, is there a single source and date used for all conversions? If not, describe.

13. Will general ledger coding be required? If so, describe briefly the structure.

14. How many carriers? Please list whether the carrier is used for import, export or both.

15. What carriers specifically? What percentage of total shipments does each carrier handle?

16. Which of the carriers is capable of electronic invoicing?

17. What supporting documents are required for processing manual invoices (i.e., commercial invoice, entry summary, waybill, etc.)?

18. What supporting documents are required for processing EDI invoices (i.e., electronic commercial invoice, entry summary, waybill, etc.)?

19. What payment terms are associated with these invoices?

Appendix 12-3

SAMPLE
FREIGHT BILL PAYMENT SERVICE AGREEMENT

THIS SERVICE AGREEMENT ("Agreement") is made and entered into as of the ____ day of _____ 20__, by and between _____ ("Client"), a _____ corporation, and Freight Bill Payment Company ("FBPC"), a _____ corporation.

WHEREAS FBPC is in the business of handling pre-audit and payment of freight bills. _____ desires to hire FBPC to perform pre-audit, data capture, freight payment and management information services for carriers used by _____ (the "Carriers"). The parties desire to enter into this Agreement and to fully set forth their understanding of the terms, commitments and conditions of their relationship.

NOW THEREFORE, in consideration of the promises hereof and the mutual commitments and conditions hereinafter set forth and other good and valuable consideration, the receipt and sufficiency of which is hereby acknowledged, the parties hereto, intending to be legally bound, hereby agree as follows:

1. <u>Engagement</u>. _____ hereby engages FBPC and FBPC hereby agrees to perform pre-audit, data capture, freight payment and management information services for _____.

2. <u>Services to Be Provided</u>. FBPC will provide the following services:

   A. <u>Pre-Audit</u>. FBPC will audit freight bills, including but not limited to duplicate payments, rates, classifications, discounts, extensions and verification. However, _____ will be responsible for providing FBPC with updated material regarding any changes in rate agreements with certain Carriers.

   B <u>Data Capture</u>. FBPC will capture data from all freight invoices and accompanying documentation as required by _____.

C. <u>Freight Payment</u>. Payment will be performed on a weekly basis, with checks being issued to each Carrier on _____'s behalf. _____ will transfer funds to FBPC each __(day)__ and Carrier checks will be mailed the following __(day)__.

D. <u>EDI Payment</u>. FBPC shall have, and hereby confirms that it does have, the capability to receive electronic billings from such of the Carriers as may be so designated by

_____.

E. <u>Reports</u>. FBPC will compile and submit to _____ those standard weekly reports and customized monthly reports listed in Exhibit A, attached hereto.

F. <u>Internet Access</u>. FBPC will provide _____ with secure access to its data through the Internet and will provide _____ with training in the use of such system at no charge to _____.

G. <u>Software and other web services received</u>. FBPC will provide Client with SW and web system maintenance and upgrades for the entire term of this Agreement. Upon termination of this Agreement, Client hereby agrees to return all software and materials and copies thereof, relating to SW. In addition, Client acknowledges that it has no ownership rights in SW.

FBPC represents and warrants that it is the owner of SW and that it has the right and authority to license SW to Client and that there exist no outstanding claims, allegations or requests for license that SW infringes any copyright, patent, trade secret, trademark, service mark or any other intellectual property right of any third party.

FBPC will defend, indemnify and hold harmless Client, its affiliates and subsidiaries and their officers, directors, employees, representatives, agents and subcontractors from and against any and all claims, allegations and requests for a license that SW or its use infringes any US or foreign copyright, trademark, patent or any

other intellectual property right of any third party. In the event FBPC or Client is enjoined from using SW, FBPC , at its expense, shall procure for Client the right to used SW or modify SW so it is non-infringing. If it is not commercially reasonable for FBPC to procure such right or to modify
SW so it is non-infringing, either party may terminate this Agreement upon 30 days' prior written notice to the other.

3. Errors. In the event of errors by FBPC, FBPC shall file claims to recover incorrect payments at their own expense.

4. Renewal and Termination. The term of this Agreement will be for _____ (__) months from the date first entered above. Except as provided in Paragraph(s) _____, this Agreement will renew on an annual basis until cancelled. Cancellation without cause requires a minimum ___-day prior written notice by either party.

5. Fee Schedule. The fees to be paid to FBPC for the services set forth in Section ____ herein, are listed on Exhibit B attached hereto and are based on the profile by _____ and summarized in Exhibit C. Fees shall be billed and paid weekly. In the event fees are not paid as agreed, FBPC reserves the right to terminate this Agreement upon 30-days' written notice.

If after six (6) months of experience, the profile varies significantly from the profile projected in Exhibit C (+ or − 15%), FBPC reserves the right to reopen the fees for negotiation. This applies not only to total transactions, but also transactions within each category.

If no agreement is reached within 30 days of a request for a modified fee schedule, either party may terminate this Agreement upon 30 days' written notice.

6. On-Site Audit. _____ has the right to perform on-site audits at FBPC on those processes relating to the _____ account.

7. <u>Miscellaneous Provisions</u>.

A. <u>Severability</u>. If one or more of the provisions contained in the Agreement shall for any reason be held invalid, illegal or unenforceable for any reason, such invalidity, illegality or unenforceability shall not affect any other provision of this Agreement, which shall be construed as if such invalid, illegal or unenforceable provision had never been contained herein.

B. <u>Counterparts</u>. This Agreement may be executed in counterparts, each of which shall be deemed an original, but all of which together shall constitute one and the same instrument. This Agreement and all other documents to be executed in connection herewith are hereby authorized to be executed and accepted by facsimile signatures and such facsimile signatures shall be considered valid and binding as original signatures and may be relied upon by the parties hereto.

C. <u>Entire Agreement</u>. This Agreement supersedes all prior understandings, representations, negotiations and correspondence between the parties, constitutes the entire agreement between them with respect to the matters described, and shall not be modified or affected by any course of dealing, course of performance or usage of trade. It may not be changed orally but only by an agreement in writing executed by the parties hereto.

D. <u>Governing Law: Enforcement</u>. This Agreement shall be construed in accordance with the laws of the State of _____, and the rights and liabilities of the parties hereto, including any assignees, shall be determined in accordance with the laws of the State of _____. In any litigation the prevailing party shall be entitled to recover from the losing party reasonable attorneys' fees and other costs and expenses of the litigation.

E. <u>Default</u>. FBPC agrees that institution of, or consent to, any insolvency proceedings constitutes default and may result in cancellation of entire Agreement.

IN WITNESS WHEREOF, the parties have hereunto affixed their names or caused their names to be hereunto affixed by the undersigned officers who are thereunto duly authorized as of the date first above written.

_____

By: _____

Its: _____

FBPC

By: _____

Its: _____

EXHIBIT A

REPORTS TO BE FURNISHED

EXHIBIT B

FEE SCHEDULE

Implementation fee   -------- $

Installation includes all items listed in the fee schedule attached to the
_____ proposal.

Processing and Payment
      EDI Air Bills   -------- $___ per freight bill
      Manual Bills   -------- $___ per freight bill
EDI Motor Bills   -------- $___ per freight bill
Accounting Splits   -------- $___ per split
Bill of Lading Match (B/L storage) -------- $___ per BOL
Coding Freight Bills
      Computer Coded   --------
      Manually Coded   -------- $___ per freight bill
Includes:
1. Remittance advice to carriers explaining billing amendments
2. Dual data entry of all bills
3. Duplicate payment protection using pro number and bill of lading number
4. Returning freight bills in a batch order
5. Standard weekly reports
6. Individual carrier checks
7. All needed monthly reports

Internet Fees
Monthly maintenance fee   -------- $___ per month (one user)
                                      $__/month for additional
                                                passwords.

   Includes:
1. Mapping and graphing capabilities
2. Telephone support
3. Training
4. _____ database updates

Shipping Cost of Bills and Reports
      Regular U.S. Mail or UPS   --------
      All other modes   -------- At Cost

Appendix 12-3
Page 8

Rate Negotiations/Consulting -------- Available upon request
Loss & Damage Claims Processing -------- $_____ per claim
Special Programming Fees ------- Determined on a per project
basis as agreed upon by both
parties.

EXHIBIT C

ACCOUNT PROFILE

Glossary

A

Accessibility: The ability of a carrier to provide service between an origin and a destination.

Accessorial charges: A carrier's charge for accessorial services such as loading, unloading, pickup, and delivery.

Acknowledgment: A communication by a supplier to advise a purchaser that a purchase order has been received. It usually implies acceptance of the order by the supplier.

Activity Based Costing (ABC): A methodology that measures the cost and performance of cost objects, activities and resources. Cost objects consume activities and activities consume resources. Resource costs are assigned to activities based on their use of those resources, and activity costs are reassigned to cost objects (outputs) based on the cost objects proportional use of those activities. Activity-based costing incorporates causal relationships between cost objects and activities and between activities and resources.

Advanced Shipping Notice (ASN): Detailed shipment information transmitted to a customer or consignee in advance of delivery, designating the contents (individual products and quantities of each) and nature of the shipment. May also include carrier and shipment specifics including time of shipment and expected time of arrival.

Agency tariff: A publication of a rate bureau that contains rates for many carriers.

Air Transport Association of America: A U.S. airline industry association.

All-cargo carrier: An air carrier that transports cargo only.

American Society of Transportation & Logistics: A professional organization in the field of logistics.

American Trucking Association, Inc.: A motor carrier industry association that is made up of sub-conferences representing various sectors of the motor carrier industry.

American Waterway Operators: A domestic water carrier industry association representing barge operators on the inland waterways.

Amtrak: The National Railroad Passenger Corporation, a federally created corporation that operates most of the United States' intercity passenger rail service.

Any-quantity rate (AQ): The same rate applies to any size shipment tendered to a carrier; no discount rate is available for large shipments.

Application Service Provider (ASP): A company that offers access over the Internet to application (examples of applications include word processors, database programs, Web browsers, development tools, communication programs) and related services that would otherwise have to be located in their own computers. Sometimes referred to as "apps-on-tap," ASP services are expected to become an important alternative, especially for smaller companies with low budgets for information technology. The purpose is to try to reduce a company's burden by installing, managing, and maintaining software.

Audit trail: Manual or computerized tracing of the transactions affecting the contents or origin of a record.

Auditing: Determining the correct transportation charges due the carrier: auditing involves checking the accuracy of the freight bill for errors, correct rate, and weight.

B

Back order: Product ordered but out of stock and promised to ship when the product becomes available.

Backhaul: The process of a transportation vehicle returning from the original destination point to the point of origin. The 1980 Motor Carrier Act deregulated interstate commercial trucking and thereby allowed carriers to contract for the return trip. The backhaul can be with a full, partial, or empty load. An empty backhaul is called deadheading.

Balance load: This occurs when the shipper provides the carrier with round-trip loads to avoid an empty backhaul.

Bar code: A symbol consisting of a series of printed bars representing values. A system of optical character reading, scanning, and tracking of units

by reading a series of printed bars for translation into a numeric or alphanumeric identification code. A popular example is the UPC code used on retail packaging.

Bar code scanner: A device to read bar codes and communicate data to computer systems.

Barge: The cargo-carrying vehicle used primarily by inland water carriers. The basic barges have open tops, but there are covered barges for both dry and liquid cargoes.

Barrier to entry: Factors that prevent companies from entering into a particular market, such as high initial investment in equipment.

Benchmarking: The process of comparing performance against the practices of other leading companies for the purpose of improving performance. Companies also benchmark internally by tracking and comparing current performance with past performance.

Best-in-class: An organization, usually within a specific industry, recognized for excellence in a specific process area.

Best practice: A specific process or group of processes which have been recognized as the best method for conducting an action. Best practices may vary by industry or geography depending on the environment being used. Best practices methodology may be applied with respect to resources, activities, cost object, or processes.

Bill of Lading (BOL): A transportation document that is the contract of carriage containing the terms and conditions between the shipper and carrier.

Blanket rate: A rate that does not increase according to the distance the commodity is shipped.

Bonded warehouse: Warehouse approved by the Treasury Department and under bond/guarantee for observance of revenue laws. Used for storing goods until duty is paid or goods are released in some other proper manner.

Boxcar: An enclosed rail car typically 40 to 50 feet long; used for packaged freight and some bulk commodities.

Break-bulk: The separation of a single consolidated bulk load into smaller individual shipments for delivery to the ultimate consignees. This is preceded by a consolidation of orders at the time of shipment, where many individual orders which are destined for a specific geographic area are grouped into one shipment in order to reduce cost.

Broker: An intermediary between the shipper and the carrier. The broker arranges transportation for shippers and represents carriers.

Bundle of services: A grouping of services offered by a carrier that may be integrated into a total package. An example would be a carrier that offers line-haul, sorting, and segregating with local delivery to specific customers.

Business-to-Business (B2B): As opposed to business-to-consumer (B2C). Many companies are now focusing on this strategy, and their sites are aimed at businesses (think wholesale) and only

other businesses can access or buy products on the site. Internet analysts predict this will be the biggest sector on the web.

Business-to-Consumer (B2C): The hundreds of e-commerce websites that sell goods directly to consumers are considered B2C. This distinction is important when comparing websites that are B2B as the entire business model, strategy, execution, and fulfillment is different.

Business logistics: The systematic and coordinated set of activities required to provide the physical movement and storage of goods (raw materials, parts, finished goods) from vendor/supply services through company facilities to the customer (market) and the associated activities – packaging, order processing, etc. – in an efficient manner necessary to enable the organization to contribute to the explicit goals of the company.

C

Call center: A facility housing personnel who respond to customer phone queries. These personnel may provide customer service or technical support. Call center services may be in-house or outsourced. Synonym: Customer Interaction Center.

Carload: Carload rail service requiring shippers to meet minimum weight.

Carload lot: A shipment that qualifies for a reduced freight rate because it is greater than a specified minimum weight. Since carload rates usually include minimum rates per unit of volume, the higher LCL (less than carload) rate may be less expensive for a heavy but relatively small shipment.

293

Carmack Amendment: An Interstate Commerce Act amendment that delineates the liability of common carriers and the bill of lading provision.

Carrier: A firm which transports goods or people via land, sea or air.

Carrier liability: A common carrier is liable for all shipment loss, damage, and delay with the exception of that caused by act of God, act of a public enemy, act of a public authority, act of the shipper, and the goods' inherent nature.

Certificate of origin: An international business document that certifies the country of origin of the shipment.

Certificated carrier: A for-hire air carrier that is subject to economic regulation and requires an operating certification to provide service.

Civil Aeronautics Board: A federal regulatory agency that implemented economic regulatory controls over air carriers.

Claim: A charge made against a carrier for loss, damage, delay, or overcharge.

Class I carrier: A classification of regulated carriers based upon annual operating revenues – motor carriers of property: >or= $5 million; railroads: >or= $50 million; motor carriers of passengers: >or= $3 million.

Class II carrier: A classification of regulated carriers based upon annual operating revenues – motor carriers of property: $1 - $5 million; railroads: $10 - $50 million; motor carriers of passengers: <or= $3 million.

Class III carrier: A classification of regulated carriers based upon annual operating revenues – motor carriers of property: <or= $1 million; railroads: <or= $10 million.

Classification: An alphabetical listing of commodities, the class or rating into which the commodity is placed, and the minimum weight necessary for the rate discount; used in the class rate structure.

Classification yard: A railroad terminal area where rail cars are grouped together to form train units.

Class rate: A rate constructed from a classification and a uniform distance system. A class rate is available for any product between any two points.

Code: A numeric or alphanumeric representation of text for exchanging commonly used information. For example: commodity codes, carrier codes.

Collaborative Planning, Forecasting and Replenishment (CPFR): 1) A collaboration process whereby supply chain trading partners can jointly plan key supply chain activities from production and delivery of raw materials to production and delivery of final products to end customers. Collaboration encompasses business planning, sales forecasting, and all operations required to replenish raw materials and finished goods. 2) A process philosophy for facilitating collaborative communications. CPFR is considered a standard, endorsed by the Voluntary Inter-industry Commerce Standards.

Commercial zone: The area surrounding a city or town to which rates quoted for the city or tow also apply; the area is defined by the ICC.

Commodities clause: A clause that prohibits railroads from hauling commodities that they produced, mined, owned, or had an interest in.

Commodity rate: A rate for a specific commodity and its origin-destination.

Common carrier: Transportation available to the public that does not provide special treatment to any one party and is regulated as to the rates charges, the liability assumed, and the service provided. A common carrier must obtain a certificate of public convenience and necessity from the Federal Trade Commission for interstate traffic.

Common carrier duties: Common carriers are required to serve, deliver, charge reasonable rates, and not discriminate.

Confirmation: With regards to EDI, a formal notice (by message or code) from a electronic mailbox system or EDI server indicating that a message sent to a trading partner has reached its intended mailbox or been retrieved by the addressee.

Consignee: The party to whom goods are shipped and delivered. The receiver of a freight shipment.

Consignment: 1) A shipment that is handled by a common carrier. 2) The process of a supplier placing goods at a customer location without receiving payment until after the goods are used or sold.

Consignment inventory: 1) Goods or product that are paid for when they are sold by the reseller, not at the time they are shipped to the reseller. 2) Goods or products which are owned by the vendor until they are sold to the consumer.

Consignor: The party who originates a shipment of goods (shipper). The sender of a freight shipment, usually the seller.

Consolidation: Combining two or more shipments in order to realize lower transportation rates. Inbound consolidation from vendors is called make-bulk consolidation; outbound consolidation to customers is call break-bulk consolidation.

Container: 1) A "box," typically 10 to 40 feet long, which is primarily used for ocean freight shipments. For travel to and from ports, containers are loaded onto truck chassis or on railroad flatcars. 2) The packaging, such as a carton, case, box, bucket, drum, bin, bottle, bundle, or bag, that an item is packed and shipped in.

Containerization: A shipment method in which commodities are placed in containers, and after initial loading, the commodities per se are not re-handled in shipment until they are unloaded at the destination.

Container on Flatcar (COFC): A type of rail shipment where only the container or "box" is loaded on the flatcar. The chassis with the wheels and landing gear in used only to carry the container to and from the railroad.

Container rate: A rate that applies only when the shipment is placed into a container prior to tendering the shipment to the carrier. This rate recognizes that the shipment is much more easily handled by the carrier.

Continuous Improvement (CI): A structured measurement-driven process that continually reviews and improves performance.

Continuous Replenishment: Continuous Replenishment is the practice of partnering between distribution channel members that changes the traditional replenishment process from distributor-generated purchase orders, based on economic order quantities, to the replenishment of products based on actual and forecasted product demand.

Continuous Replenishment Planning (CRP): A program that triggers the manufacturing and movement of product through the supply chain when the identical product is purchased by an end user.

Contract: An agreement between two or more competent persons or companies to perform or not to perform specific acts or services or to deliver merchandise. A contract may be oral or written. A purchase order, when accepted by a supplier, becomes a contract. Acceptance may be in writing or by performance, unless the purchase order requires acceptance in writing.

Contract carrier: A carrier that does not serve the general public, but provides transportation for hire for one or a limited number of shippers under a specific contract.

Coordinated transportation: Two or more carriers of different modes transporting a shipment.

Core competency: Bundles of skills or knowledge sets that enable a firm to provide the greatest level of value to its customers in a way that is difficult for competitors to emulate and that provides for future growth. Core competencies are embodied in the skills of the workers and in the organization. They are developed through [collective] learning, communication, and commitment to work across levels and functions in the organization and with the customers and suppliers. For example, a core competency could be the capability of a firm to coordinate and harmonize diverse production skills and multiple technologies. To illustrate, advanced casting processes for making steel require the integration of machine design with sophisticated sensors to track temperature and speed, and the sensors require mathematical modeling of heat transfer. For rapid and effective development of such a process, materials scientists must work closely with machine designers, software engineers, process specialists, and operating personnel. Core competencies are not directly related to the product or market.

Cost, Insurance, Freight (CIF): A freight term indicating that the seller is responsible for cost, the marine insurance, and the freight charges on an ocean shipment of goods.

Courier service: A fast, door-to-door service for high-valued goods and documents; firms usually limit service to shipments of 50 pounds or less.

296

Council of Supply Chain Management Professionals (CSCMP): The CSCMP is a not-for-profit professional business organization consisting of individuals throughout the world who have interests and/or responsibilities in logistics and supply chain management, and the related functions that make up these professions. Its purpose is to enhance the development of the logistics and supply chain management professions by providing these individuals with educational opportunities and relevant information through a variety of programs, services, and activities.

Cross docking: A distribution system in which merchandise received at the warehouse or distribution center is not put away, but instead is readied for shipment to retail stores. Cross docking requires close synchronization of all inbound and outbound shipment movements. By eliminating the putaway, storage and selection operations, it can significantly reduce distribution costs.

Customer-driven: The end user, or customer, motivates what is produced or how it is delivered.

Customer service: Activities between the buyer and seller that enhance or facilitate the sale or use of the seller's products or services.

Customer Service Representative (CSR): The individual who provides customer support via telephone in a call center environment.

Customs broker: A firm that represents importers/exporters in dealings with customs. Normally responsible for obtaining and submitting all documents for clearing merchandise through customs, arranging inland transport, and paying all charges related to these functions.

Cycle time: The amount of time it takes to complete a business process.

D

Dashboard: A performance measurement tool used to capture a summary of the Key Performance Indicators (KPIs)/metrics of a company. Metrics dashboards/scorecards should be easy to read and usually have "red, yellow, green" indicators to flag when the company is not meeting its metrics targets. Ideally, a dashboard/scorecard should be cross-functional in nature and include both financial and non-financial measures. In addition, scorecards should be reviewed regularly – at least on a monthly basis and weekly in key functions such as manufacturing and distribution where activities are critical to the success of a company. The dashboard/scorecards philosophy can also be applied to external supply chain partners such as suppliers to ensure that supplier's objectives and practices align. Synonym: Scorecard.

Data mining: The process of studying data to search for previously unknown relationships. This knowledge is then applied to achieving specific business goals.

Data warehouse: A repository of data that has been specially prepared to support decision-making applications. Synonym: Decision-support data.

Database: Data stored in computer-readable form, usually indexed or sorted in a logical order by which users can find a particular item of data they need.

Deadhead: The return of an empty transportation container to its point of origin. See backhauling.

Dedicated contract carriage: A third-party service that dedicates equipment (vehicles) and drivers to a single customer for it exclusive use on a contractual basis.

Demand chain: Another name for the supply chain, with emphasis on customer or end user demand pulling materials and product through the chain.

Demurrage: The carrier charges and fees applied when rail freight cars and ships are retained beyond a specified loading or unloading time.

Density: A physical characteristic of a commodity measuring its mass per unit volume or pounds per cubic foot; an important factor in rate making, since density affects the utilization of a carrier's vehicle.

Density rate: A rate based upon the density and shipment weight.

Deregulation: Revisions or complete elimination of economic regulations controlling transportation. The Motor Carrier Act of 1980 and the Staggers Act of 1980 revised the economic controls over motor carriers and railroads, and the Airline Deregulation Act of 1978 eliminated economic controls over air carriers.

Detention: The carrier charges and fees applied when rail freight cars and ships

are retained beyond a specified loading or unloading time.

Direct Store Delivery (DSD): Process of shipping direct from a manufacturer's plant or distribution center to the customer's retail store, thus bypassing the customer's distribution center. Also called Direct-to-Store Delivery.

Disaster Recovery Planning: Contingency planning specifically related to recovering hardware and software (e.g., data centers, application software, operations, personnel, telecommunications) in information system outages.

Dispatching: The carrier activities involved with controlling equipment; involves arranging for fuel, drivers, crews, equipment, and terminal space.

Distribution: Outbound logistics, from the end of the production line to the end user. 1) The activities associated with the movement of material, usually finished goods or service parts, from the manufacturer to the customer. These activities encompass the functions of transportation, warehousing, inventory control, material handling, order administration, site and location analysis, industrial packaging, data processing, and the communications network necessary for effective management. It includes all activities related to physical distribution, as well as the return of goods to the manufacturer. In many cases, this movement is made through one or more levels of field warehouses. Synonym: Physical distribution. 2) The systematic division of a whole into discrete parts having distinctive characteristics.

Distribution center (DC): The warehouse facility which holds inventory from manufacturing pending distribution to the appropriate stores.

Distribution planning: The planning activities associated with transportation, warehousing, inventory levels, materials handling, order administration, site and location planning, industrial packaging, data processing, and communications networks to support distribution.

Diversion: The practice of selling goods to a competitor that the vendor assumes would be used to service that customer's store. Example: Grocery Store Chain A buys orange juice from Minute Maid. Grocery Store Chain A, because of their sales volume or because of promotion, can buy product for $12.50 per case. Grocery Store Chain B, because of a lower sales volume, buys the same orange juice for $14.50 per case. Grocery Store Chain A and Grocer Store Chain B get together and make a deal. Grocery Store Chain A resells that product to Grocery Store Chain B for $13.50 per case. Grocery Store Chain A makes $1.00 per case, and Grocery Store Chain B gets product for $1.00 less per case than it can buy from Minute Maid.

Double bottoms: A motor carrier operation involving two trailers being pulled by one tractor.

Double stack: Two containers, one on top of the other, loaded on a railroad flatcar; an intermodal service.

Drayage: Transportation of materials and freight on a local basis, but intermodal freight carriage may also be referred to as drayage.

Drop ship: To take the title of the product but not actually handle, stock, or deliver it; e.g., to have one supplier ship directly to another or to have a supplier ship directly to the buyer's customer.

Dual operation: A motor carrier that has both common and contract carrier operating authority.

Dunnage: The packing material used to protect a product from damage during transport.

E

Electronic Data Interchange (EDI): Intercompany, computer-to-computer transmission of business information in a standard format. For EDI purists, "computer-to-computer" means direct transmission from the originating application program to the receiving, or processing, application program. An EDI transmission consists only of business data, not any accompanying verbiage or free-form messages. Purists might also contend that a standard format is one that is approved by a national or international standards organization, as opposed to formats developed by industry groups or companies.

Electronic Data Interchange Association: A national body that propagates and controls the use of EDI in a given country. All EDIAs are nonprofit organizations dedicated to encouraging EDI growth. The EDIA in the United States was formerly TDCC and administered the development of standards in transportation and other industries.

EDI standards: Criteria that define the data content and format requirements for specific business transactions (e.g., purchase orders). Using standard formats allows companies to exchange transactions with multiple trading partners easily.

EDI transmission: A functional group of one or more EDI transactions that are sent to the same location, in the same transmission, and are identified by a functional group header and trailer.

Elkins Act: An amendment to the IC Act that prohibits giving rebates.

Exception rate: A deviation from the class rate; changes (exceptions) made to the classification.

Exclusive use: Carrier vehicles that are assigned to a specific shipper for its exclusive use.

Exempt carrier: A for-hire carrier that is free from economic regulation. Trucks hauling certain commodities are exempt from Interstate Commerce Commission economic regulation. By far the largest portion of exempt carriers transports agricultural commodities or seafood.

Expediting: 1) Moving shipments through regular channels at an accelerated rate. 2) To take extraordinary action because of an increase in relative priority. Synonym: Stockchase.

Export declaration: A document required by the Department of Commerce that provides information as to the nature, value, etc., of export activity.

Exports: A term used to describe products produced in one country and sold in another.

Export sales contract: The initial document in any international transaction; it details the specifics of the sales agreement between the buyer and seller.

F

Federal Aviation Administration (FAA): The federal agency charged with administering federal safety regulations governing air transportation.

Federal Maritime Commission: A regulatory agency that controls services, practices, and agreements of international water common carriers and noncontiguous domestic water carriers.

First In, First Out (FIFO): Warehouse term meaning first items stored are the first used. In accounting this term is associated with the valuing of inventory such that the latest purchases are reflected in book inventory.

Fixed costs: Costs which do not fluctuate with business volume in the short run. Fixed costs include items such as depreciation of buildings and fixtures.

Flatcar: A rail car without sides; used for hauling machinery.

For-hire carrier: A carrier that provides transportation service to the public on a fee basis.

Foreign Trade Zone (FTZ): An area or zone set aside at or near a port or airport, under the control of the U.S.

Customs Service, for holding goods duty-free pending customs clearance.

Fourth-party Logistics (4PL): Differs from third-party logistics in the following ways: 1) 4PL organization is often a separate entity established as a joint venture or long-term contract between a primary client and one or more partners; 2) 4PL organization acts as a single interface between the client and multiple logistics service providers; 3) All aspects (ideally) of the client's supply chain are managed by the 4PL organization; and 4) It is possible for a major third-party logistics provider to form a 4PL organization within its existing structure (Strategic Supply Chain Alignment; John Gattorna).

Free Alongside Ship (FAS): A term of sale indicating the seller is liable for all changes and risks until the goods sold are delivered to the port on a dock that will be used by the vessel. Title passes to the buyer when the seller has secured a clean dock or ship's receipt of goods.

Free on Board (FOB): Contractual terms between a buyer and a seller that define where title transfer takes place.

FOB Destination: Title passes at destination, and seller has total responsibility until shipment is delivered.

FOB Origin: Title passes at origin, and buyer has total responsibility over the goods while in shipment.

Freight-all-kinds (FAK): An approach to rate making whereby the ante is based only upon the shipment weight and distance; widely used in TOFC service.

Freight bill: The carrier's invoice for transportation charges applicable to a freight shipment.

Freight consolidation: The grouping of shipments to obtain reduced costs or improved utilization of the transportation function. Consolidation can occur by market area grouping, grouping according to scheduled deliveries, or using third-party pooling services such as public warehouses and freight forwarders.

Freight forwarder: An organization which provides logistics services as an intermediary between the shipper and the carrier, typically on international shipments. Freight forwarders provide the ability to respond quickly and efficiently to changing customer and consumer demands and international shipping (import/export) requirements.

Fronthaul: The first half a round-trip move from origin to destination. The opposite is "backhaul," which is the return of the equipment to its origin point.

G

Grandfather clause: A provision that enabled motor carriers engaged in lawful trucking operations before the passage of the Motor Carrier Act of 1935 to secure common carrier authority without proving public convenience and necessity; a similar provision exists for other modes.

Great Lakes Carriers: Water carriers that operate on the five Great Lakes.

H

Headhaul: The first half of a round-trip move from origin to destination. The opposite is "backhaul," which is the return of the equipment to its origin point.

Hopper cars: Rail cars that permit top loading and bottom unloading of bulk commodities; some hopper cars have permanent tops with hatches to provide protection against the elements.

Hundredweight (cwt): The pricing unit used in transportation; a hundredweight is equal to 100 pounds.

I

Image processing: Allows a company to take electronic photographs of documents. The electronic photograph then can be stored in a computer and retrieved from computer storage to replicate the document on a printer. The thousands of bytes of data composing a single document are encoded in an optical disk. Many carriers now use image processing to provide proof-of-delivery documents to a shipper. The consignee signs an electronic pad that automatically digitizes a consignee's signature for downloading into a computer. A copy of that signature then can be produced to demonstrate that a deliver took place.

Incentive rate: A rate designed to induce the shipper to ship heavier volumes per shipment.

INCOTERMS: 13 international terms of sale developed by the International Chamber of Commerce to define sellers' and buyers' responsibilities.

1. Ex works: Goods available at a named place, usually seller's docks. Buyer assumes all costs and risk.
2. Free carrier: FCA named place. Goods are cleared for export, given to carrier chosen by buyer. Buyer assumes risks from that point.
3. Free alongside ship: FAS named port and vessel. Buyer assumes responsibility.
4. Free on board: FOB named port. Goods are placed on vessel. Buyer assumes responsibility.
5. Carriage paid to: CPT named place of destination. Seller pays freight, provides export clearance. Buyer assumes risk once goods go to carrier.
6. Carriage/insurance paid to: Same as CPT plus insurance.
7. Cost and freight: CFR named port of destination. Seller pays freight. Buyer assumes risk.
8. Cost, insurance, freight: CIF named destination port. Same as CFR plus insurance.
9. Delivered at frontier: DAF named place. Goods ready for clearance but not at customs yet.
10. Delivered ex ship: DES named place of destination. Goods made available on ship but not cleared for import.
11. Delivered ex quay: DEQ named port of destination. Goods available on wharf.
12. Delivered duty unpaid: DDU named destination. Buyer pays duty, fees, etc.
13. Delivered duty paid: DDP named destination. This is maximum obligation that can be assumed by a seller.

Integrated logistics: A comprehensive, system-wide view of the entire supply chain as a single process, from raw materials supply through finished goods distribution. All functions that make up the supple chain are managed as a single entity, rather than managing individual functions separately.

Intercoastal carriers: Water carriers that transport freight between East and West Coast ports, usually by way of the Panama Canal.

Interline: Two or more motor carriers working together to haul the shipment to a destination. Carrier equipment may be interchanged from one carrier to the next, but usually the shipment is re-handled without the equipment.

Intermodal marketing company (IMC): An intermediary that sells intermodal services to shippers.

Intermodal transportation: Transporting freight by using two or more transportation modes such as by truck and rail or truck and oceangoing vessel.

International Air Transport Association: An international air carrier rate bureau for passenger and freight movements.

Interstate commerce: The transportation of persons or property between states; in the course of the movement the shipment crosses a state boundary line.

Intrastate commerce: The transportation of persons or property between points within a state. A shipment between two points within a state may be interstate if the shipment had a prior or subsequent move outside of the state and the intent of the shipper

was an interstate shipment at the time of shipment.

In-transit inventory: Material moving between two or more locations, usually separated geographically; for example, finished good being shipped from a plant to a distribution center. In-transit inventory is an easily overlooked component of total supply chain availability.

ISO 9000: A series of quality assurance standards compiled by the Geneva, Switzerland-based International Standardization Organization. In the United States, ISO is represented by the American National Standards Institute based in Washington, D.C.

ISO 14000 Series Standards: A series of generic environmental management standards under development by the International Organization of Standardization, which provide structure and systems for managing environmental compliance with legislative and regulatory requirements and affect every aspect of a company's environmental operations.

J

Joint rate: A rate over a route that involves two or more carriers to transport the shipment.

Just-in-Time (JIT): An inventory control system that controls material flow into assembly and manufacturing plants by coordinating demand and supply to the point where desired materials arrive just in time for use. An inventory reduction strategy that feeds production lines with products delivered "just in time." Developed by the auto industry, it refers to shipping goods in smaller, more frequent lots.

K

Kaizen: The Japanese term for improvement; continuing improvement involving everyone – managers and workers. In manufacturing, kaizen relates to finding and eliminating waste in machinery, labor, or production methods. Also see continuous process improvement.

Kanban: Japanese word for "visible record," loosely translated means card, billboard, or sign. Popularized by Toyota Corporation, it uses standard containers or lot sizes to deliver needed parts to assembly line "just in time" for use.

Key Performance Indicator (KPI): A measure which is of strategic importance to a company or department. For example, a supply chain flexibility metric is Supplier On-time Delivery Performance which indicates the percentage of orders that are fulfilled on or before the original requested date. Also see scorecard.

Kitting: Light assembly of components or parts into defined units. Kitting reduces the need to maintain an inventory of pre-built completed products, but increases the time and labor consumed at shipment. Also see postponement.

L

Lading: The cargo carried in a transportation vehicle.

Land bridge: The movement of containers by ship-rail-sip on Japan-to-

Europe moves; ships move containers to the U.S. Pacific Coast, rails move containers to an East Coast port, and ships deliver containers to Europe.

Lash barges: Covered barges that are loaded on board oceangoing ships for movement to foreign destinations.

Last In, First Out (LIFO): Accounting method of valuing inventory that assumes latest goods purchased are first goods used during accounting period.

Lead Logistics Partner (LLP): An organization that organizes other 3rd party logistics partners for outsourcing of logistics functions. Also see fourth party logistics.

Lead time: The total time that elapses between an order's placement and its receipt. It includes the time required for order transmittal, order processing, order preparation, and transit.

Less-than-carload (LCL): Shipment that is less than a complete rail car load (lot shipment).

Less-than-truckload (LTL) carriers: Trucking companies that consolidate and transport smaller (less-than-truckload) shipments of freight by utilizing a network of terminals and relay points.

Letter of credit: An international business document that assures the seller that payment will be made by the bank issuing the letter of credit upon fulfillment of the sales agreement.

Lighter: A flat-bottomed boat designed for cross-harbor or inland waterway freight transfer.

Line-haul shipment: A shipment that moves between cities and distances over 100 to 150 miles.

Load factor: A measure of operating efficiency used by air carriers to determine the percentage of a plane's capacity that is utilized, or the number of passengers divided by the total number of seats.

Load tendering: The practice of providing a carrier with detailed information and negotiated pricing (the tender) prior to scheduling pickup. This practice can help assure contract compliance and facilitate automated payments (self billing).

Loading allowance: A reduced rate offered to shippers and/or consignees who load and/or unload LTL or AQ shipments.

Local rate: A rate published between two points served by one carrier.

Logbook: A daily record of the hours an interstate driver spends driving, off duty, sleeping in the berth, or on duty but not driving.

Logistics Management: As defined by the Council of Supply Chain Management Professionals (CSCMP): "Logistics management is that part of supply chain management that plans, implements, and controls the efficient, effective forward and reverse flow and storage of goods, services, and related information between the point of origin and the point of consumption in order to meet customers' requirements. Logistics management activities typically include inbound and outbound transportation management, fleet management, warehousing, materials handling, order fulfillment, logistics network design, inventory management, supply/demand planning, and management of third party logistics services providers. To varying degrees, the logistics function also includes sourcing and procurement, production planning and scheduling, packaging and assembly, and customer service. It is involved in all levels of planning and execution – strategic, operational, and tactical. Logistics management is an integrating function which coordinates and optimizes all logistics activities, as well as integrates logistics activities with other functions, including marketing, sales, manufacturing, finance, and information technology."

Loss and damage: The risk to which goods are subjected during the transportation cycle. The shipment may be separated from its documentation and misdirected. Handling by the carrier as well as in-transit incidents can cause damage to or destruction of the shipment. This is a factor in mode and carrier selection as well as packaging and handling techniques. This risk factor also enters into the carrier's pricing decisions.

M

Major carrier: A for-hire certificated air carrier that has annual operating revenues of $1 billion or more: the carrier usually operates between major population centers.

Marine insurance: Insurance to protect against cargo loss and damage when shipping by water transportation.

Maritime Administration: A federal agency that promotes the merchant marine, determines ocean ship routes and services, and awards maritime subsidies.

Micro-land bridge: An intermodal movement in which the shipment is moved from a foreign country to the U.S. by water and then moved across the U.S. by railroad to an interior, non-port city, or vice versa for exports from a non-port city.

Mileage allowance: An allowance based upon distance and given by railroads to shippers using private rail cars.

Mileage rate: A rate based upon the number of miles the commodity is shipped.

Mini-land bridge: An intermodal movement in which the shipment is moved from a foreign country to the U.S. by water and then moved across the U.S. by railroad to a destination that is a port city, or vice versa for exports from a U.S. port city.

Minimum weight: The shipment weight specified by the carrier's tariff as the minimum weight required to use the TL or CL rate; the rate discount volume.

Mixed loads: The movement of both regulated and exempt commodities in the same vehicle at the same time.

N

National Industrial Traffic League: An association representing the interests of shippers and receivers in matters of transportation policy and regulation.

National Motor Freight Classification (NMFC): A tariff which contains descriptions and classifications of commodities and rules for domestic movement by motor carriers in the U.S.

O

Order cycle: The time and process involved from the placement of an order to the receipt of the shipment.

Order management: The planning, directing, monitoring, and controlling of the processes related to customer orders, manufacturing orders, and purchase orders. Regarding customer orders, order management includes order promising, order entry, order pick, pack and ship, billing, and reconciliation of the customer account. Regarding manufacturing orders, order management includes order release, routing, manufacture, monitoring, and receipt into stores or finished goods inventories. Regarding purchasing orders, order management includes order placement, monitoring, receiving, acceptance, and payment of supplier.

Order processing: Activities associated with filling customer orders.

Out of stock: The state of not having inventory at a location and available for distribution or for sell to the consumer (zero inventory).

Outbound consolidation: Consolidation of a number of small shipments for various customers into a larger load. The large load is then shipped to a location near the customers where it is broken down, and then the small shipments are distributed to the customers. This can reduce overall shipping charges where many small packet or parcel shipments are handled each day. Also see break bulk.

Outbound logistics: The process related to the movement and storage of products from the end of the production line to the end user.

Outsource: To utilize a third-party provider to perform services previously performed in-house. Examples include manufacturing of products and call center/customer support.

Over, short and damaged (OS&D): This is typically a report issued at warehouse when goods are damaged. Used to file claim with carrier.

Over-the road: A motor carrier operation that reflects long distance, intercity moves; the opposite of local operations.

Owner-operator: A trucking operation in which the owner of the truck is also the driver.

P

Pallet: The platform which cartons are stacked on and then used for shipment or movement as a group. Pallets may be made of wood or composite materials.

Panamax (ship): A ship that will fit through the Panama Canal.

Parcel shipment: Parcels include small packages like those typically handled by providers such as UPS and FedEx.

Performance measures: Indicators of the work performed and the results achieved in an activity, process, or

organizational unit. Performance measures should be both non-financial and financial. Performance measures enable periodic comparisons and benchmarking. For example, a common performance measure for a distribution center is percent of order fill rate.

Performance measurement program: A performance measurement program goes beyond just having performance metrics in place. Many companies do not realize the full benefit of their performance metrics because they often do not have all of the necessary elements in place that support their metrics. Also see performance measures, dashboard, scorecard, key performance indicator.

Physical distribution: The movement and storage functions associated with finished goods from manufacturing plants to warehouses and to customers; also used synonymously with business logistics.

Pickup and delivery (PUD): The act of collecting freight from shippers or delivering freight to consignees.

Piggyback: Terminology used to describe a truck trailer being transported on a railroad flatcar.

Pooling: A shipping term for the practice of combining shipment from multiple shippers into a truckload in order to reduce shipping charges.

Port authority: A state or local government that owns, operates, or otherwise provides wharf, dock, and other terminal investments at ports.

307

Post-Panamax (ship): A ship that will not fit through the Panama Canal.

Postponement: The delay of final activities (i.e., assembly, production, packaging, etc.) until the latest possible time. A strategy used to eliminate excess inventory in the form of finished goods which may be packaged in a variety of configurations.

Prepaid: A freight term which indicates that charges are to be paid by the shipper. Prepaid shipping charges may be added to the customer invoice, or the cost may be bundled into the pricing for the product.

Primary-business test: A test used to determine if a trucking operation is bona fide private transportation; the private trucking operation must be incidental to and in the furtherance of the primary business of the firm.

Private carrier: A carrier that provides transportation service to the firm and that owns or leases the vehicles and does not charge a fee.
Private motor carriers may haul at a fee for wholly-owned subsidiaries.

Pro number: Any progressive or serialized number applied for identification of freight bills, bills of lading, etc.

Process: A series of time-based activities that are linked to complete a specific output.

Process improvement: Designs or activities which improve quality or reduce costs, often through the elimination of waste or non-value-added tasks.

Productivity: A measure of efficiency of resource utilization; defined as the sum of the outputs divided by the sum of the inputs.

Profitability analysis: The analysis of profit derived from cost objects with the view to improve or optimize profitability. Multiple views may be analyzed, such as market segment, customer, distribution channel, product families, products, technologies, platforms, regions, manufacturing capacity, etc.

Proof of Delivery (POD): Information supplied by the carrier containing the name of the person who signed for the shipment, the time and date of delivery, and other shipment delivery-related information. POD is also sometimes used to refer to the process of printing materials just prior to shipment (Print on Demand).

Proportional rate: A rate lower than the regular rate for shipments that have prior or subsequent moves; used to overcome competitive disadvantages of combination rates.

Q

Quick Response (QR): A strategy widely adopted by general merchandise and soft lines retailers and manufacturers to reduce retail out-of-stocks, forced markdowns and operating expenses. These goals are accomplished through shipping accuracy and reduced response time. QR is a partnership strategy in which suppliers and retailers work together to respond more rapidly to the consumer by sharing point-of-sale scan data, enabling both to forecast replenishment needs.

R

Radio Frequency (RF or RFID): A form of wireless communication that lets users relay information via electromagnetic energy waves from a terminal to a base station which is linked in turn to a host computer. The terminals can be placed at a fixed station, mounted on a forklift truck, or carried in the worker's hand. The base station contains a transmitter and receiver for communication with the terminals. RF systems use either narrow-band or spread-spectrum transmissions. Narrow-band date transmissions move along a single limited radio frequency, while spread-spectrum transmissions move across several different frequencies. When combined with a bar code system for identifying inventory items, a radio frequency system can relay data instantly, thus updating inventory records in so-called "real time."

Rate basis number: The distance between two rate basis points.

Rate basis point: The major shipping point in a local area; all points in the local area are considered to be the rate basis point.

Real-time: The processing of data in a business application as it happens – as contrasted with storing data for input at a later time (batch processing).

Reasonable rate: A rate that is high enough to cover the carrier's cost but not too high to enable the carrier to realize monopolistic profits.

Reconsignment: A carrier service that permits changing the destination and/or consignee after the shipment has reached it originally-billed destination and paying the through rate from origin to final destination.

Reefer: A term used for refrigerated vehicles.

Regional carrier: A for-hire air carrier, usually certificated, that has annual operating revenues of less than $74 million; the carrier usually operates within a particular region of the country.

Regular-route carrier: A motor carrier that is authorized to provide service over designated routes.

Relay terminal: A motor carrier terminal designed to facilitate the substitution of one driver for another who has driven the maximum hours permitted.

Released-value rates: Rates based upon the value of the shipment; the maximum carrier liability for damage is less than the full value, and in return the carrier offers a lower rate.

Reliability: A carrier selection criterion that considers the variation in carrier transit time; the consistency of the transit time provided.

Request for Proposal (RFP): A document, which provides information concerning needs and requirements for a manufacturer. This document is created in order to solicit proposals from potential suppliers. For example, a computer manufacturer may use an RFP to solicit proposals from suppliers of third-party logistics services.

Reverse Auction: A type of auction where suppliers bid to sell products to a buyer (e.g., retailer). As bidding

309

continues, the prices decline (opposite of a regular auction, where buyers are bidding to buy products).

Reverse logistics: A specialized segment of logistics focusing on the movement and management of products and resources after the sale and after delivery to the customer. Includes product returns for repair and/or credit.

Routing or routing guide: 1) Process of determining how shipment will move between origin and destination. Routing information includes designation of carrier(s) involved, actual route of carrier, and estimated time enroute. 2) Right of shipper to determine carriers, routes and points for transfer shipments. 3) In manufacturing this is the document which defines a process of steps used to manufacture and/or assemble a product.

Rule of rate making: A regulatory provision directing the regulatory agencies to consider the earnings necessary for a carrier to provide adequate transportation.

S

Scan: A computer term referring to the action of scanning bar codes or RF tags.

Scorecard: A performance measurement tool used to capture a summary of the key performance indicators (KPIs)/metrics of a company. Metrics dashboards/scorecards should be easy to read and usually have "red, yellow, green" indicators to flag when the company is not meeting its targets for its metrics. Ideally, a dashboard/scorecard should be cross-functional in nature and include both financial and non-financial measures. In addition, scorecards

should be reviewed regularly – at least on a monthly basis and weekly in key functions such as manufacturing and distribution where activities are critical to the success of a company. The dashboard/scorecards philosophy can also be applied to external supply chain partners such as suppliers to ensure that suppliers' objectives and practices align. Synonym: dashboard.

Ship agent: A liner company or tramp ship operator representative who facilitates ship arrival, clearance, loading and unloading, and fee payment while at a specific port.

Ship broker: A firm that serves as a go-between for the tramp ship owner and the chartering consignor or consignee.

Shipper: The party that tenders goods for transportation.

Shipper's agent: A firm that acts primarily to match up small shipments, especially single-traffic piggyback loads to permit use of twin-trailer piggyback rates.

Shipper's association: A nonprofit, cooperative consolidator and distributor of shipments owned or shipped by member firms; acts in much the same as for-profit freight forwarders.

Shipping: The function that performs tasks for the outgoing shipment of parts, components, and products. It includes packaging, marking, weighing, and loading for shipment.

Shipping lane: A predetermined, mapped route on the ocean that commercial vessels tend to follow between ports. This helps ships avoid hazardous areas. In general transportation, the logical route between the point of shipment and the point of delivery used to analyze the volume of shipment between two points.

Shipping manifest: A document that lists the pieces in a shipment. A manifest usually covers an entire load regardless of whether the load is to be delivered to a single destination or many destinations. Manifests usually list the items. Piece count, total weight, and the destination name and address for each destination in the load.

Short shipment: Piece of freight missing from shipment as stipulated by documents on hand.

Shrinkage: Reductions of actual quantities of items in stock, in process, or in transit. The loss may be caused by scrap, theft, deterioration, evaporation, etc.

Single sourcing: When an organization deliberately chooses to use one supplier to provide a product or service, even though there are other suppliers available.

Six-Sigma Quality: A term used generally to indicate that a process is well controlled; i.e., tolerance limits are ± Six Sigma (3.4 defects per million events) from the centerline in a control chart. The term is usually associated with Motorola, which named one of its key operational initiatives Six-Sigma Quality.

Sleeper team: The use of two drivers to operate a truck equipped with a sleeper berth; while one driver sleeps in the berth to accumulate the mandatory off-duty time, the other driver operates the vehicle.

Slip seat operation: A term used to describe a motor carrier relay terminal operation where one driver is substituted for another who has accumulated the maximum driving time hours.

Special-commodities carrier: A common carrier trucking company that has authority to haul a special commodity; there are 16 special commodities, such as household goods, petroleum products, and hazardous materials.

Split delivery: A method by which a larger quantity is ordered on a purchase order to secure a lower price, but delivery is divided into smaller quantities and spread out over several dates to control inventory investment, save storage space, etc.

Spot: To move a trailer or boxcar into place for loading or unloading.

Spur track: A railroad track that connects a company's plant or warehouse with the railroad's track; the cost of the spur track and its maintenance is borne by the user.

Steamship conferences: Collective rate-making bodies for liner water carriers.

Strategic alliance: Business relationship in which two or more independent organizations cooperate and willingly modify their business objectives and practices to help achieve long-term goals and objectives.

Strategic sourcing: The process of determining long-term supply requirements, finding sources to fulfill those needs, selecting suppliers to provide the services, negotiating the purchase agreements and managing the suppliers' performance. Focuses on developing the most effective relationships with the right suppliers, to ensure that the right price is paid and that lifetime product costs are minimized. It also assesses whether services or processes would provide better value if they were outsourced to specialist organizations.

Supply chain: 1) Starting with unprocessed raw materials and ending with the final customer using the finished goods, the supply chain links many companies together. 2) The material and informational interchanges in the logistical process stretching from acquisition of raw materials to delivery of finished products to the end user. All vendors, service providers and customers are links in the supply chain.

Supply Chain Management (SCM): As defined by the Council of Supply Chain Management Professionals (CSCMP): "Supply Chain Management encompasses the planning and management of all activities involved in sourcing and procurement, conversion, and all logistics management activities. Importantly, it also includes coordination and collaboration with channel partners, which can be suppliers, intermediaries, third-party service providers, and customers. In essence, supply chain management integrates supply and demand management within and across companies. Supply Chain Management is an integrating function with primary responsibility for linking major business

functions and business processes within and across companies into a cohesive and high-performing business model. It includes all of the logistics management activities noted above, as well as manufacturing operations, and it drives coordination of processes and activities with and across marketing, sales, product design, finance and information technology."

Surcharge: An add-on charge to the applicable charges; motor carriers have a fuel surcharge, and railroads can apply a surcharge to any joint rate that does not yield 110% of variable cost.

Switch engine: A railroad engine that is used to move rail cars short distances within a terminal and plant.

Switching company: A railroad that moves rail cars short distances; switching companies connect two mainline railroads to facilitate through movement of shipments.

SWOT analysis: An analysis of the strengths, weaknesses, opportunities, and threats of and to an organization. SWOT analysis is useful in developing strategy.

T

Tandem: A truck that has two drive axles or a trailer that has two axles.

Tank cars: Rail cars that are designed to haul bulk liquids or gas commodities.

Tapering rate: A rate that increases with distance but not in direct proportion to the distance the commodity is shipped.

Tare weight: The weight of a substance, obtained by deducting the weight of the empty container from the gross weight of the full container.

Tariff: A tax assessed by a government on goods entering or leaving a country. The term is also used in transportation in reference to the fees and rules applied by a carrier for its services.

Tender: The document which describes a business transaction to be performed.

Terminal delivery allowance: A reduced rate offered in return for the shipper or consignee tendering or picking up the freight at the carrier's terminal.

Third-party logistics (3PL): Outsourcing all or much of a company's logistics operations to a specialized company.

Third-party logistics provider: A firm which provides multiple logistics services for use by customers. Preferably, these services are integrated or "bundled" together by the provider. These firms facilitate the movement of parts and materials from suppliers to manufacturers and finished products from manufacturers to distributors and retailers. Among the services which they provide are transportation, warehousing, cross docking, inventor management, packaging, and freight forwarding.

Ton-mile: A measure of output for freight transportation; it reflects the weight of the shipment and the distance it is hauled; a multiplication of tons hauled and distance traveled.

Tracing: The practice of relating resources, activities and cost objects using the drivers underlying their cost causal relationships. The purpose of tracing is to observe and understand how costs are arising in the normal course of business operations. Synonym: assignment.

Tracking and tracing: Monitoring and recording shipment movements from origin to destination.

Traffic management: The management and controlling of transportation modes, carriers and services.

Trailer on a Flatcar (TOFC): A specialized form of containerization in which motor and rail transport coordinate. Synonym: piggyback.

Tramp: An international water carrier that has no fixed route or published schedule; a tramp ship is chartered for a particular voyage or a given time period.

Transaction: A single completed transmission; i.e., transmission of an invoice over an EDI network. Analogous to usage of the term in data processing, in which a transaction can be an inquiry or a range of updates and trading transactions. The definition is important for EDI service operators, who must interpret invoices and other documents.

Transit time: The total time that elapses between a shipment's pickup and deliver.

Transportation: The act of moving goods or people from an origin to a required destination. It also includes the creation of time and place utilities.

Transportation Management System (TMS): A computer system designed to provide optimized transportation

313

management in various modes along with associated activities, including managing shipping units, labor planning and building, shipment scheduling through inbound, outbound, intra-company shipments, documentation management (especially when international shipping is involved), and third-party logistics management.

Transportation mode: The method of transportation: land, sea, or air shipment.

Truckload carriers (TL): Trucking companies, which move full truckloads of freight directly from the point of origin to destination.

Truckload lot: A truck shipment that qualifies for a lower freight rate because it meets a minimum weight and/or volume.

Twenty-foot Equivalent Unit (TEU): Standard unit for counting containers of various capacities and for describing the capacities of container ships or terminals. One 20-foot ISO container equals 1 TEU. One 40-foot ISO container equals 2 TEU.

U

Uniform Product Code (UPC): A standard product numbers and bar coding system used by the retail industry. UPC codes are administered by the Uniform Cod Council; they identify the manufacturer as well as the item, and are included on virtually all retail packaging.

Unit train: An entire, uninterrupted locomotive, cars, and caboose movement between an origin and destination.

User charges: Costs or fees that the user of a service or facility must pay to the party furnishing this service or facility. An example would be the landing fee an airline pays to an airport when one of its aircraft lands or takes off.

V

Value-added: Increased or improved value, worth, functionality or usefulness.

Value chain: A series of activities which, when combined, define a business process; the series of activities from manufacturers to the retail stores that define the industry supply chain.

Value-of-service pricing: Pricing according to the value of the product being transported; third-degree price discrimination; demand-oriented pricing; charging what the traffic will bear.

Variable cost: A cost that fluctuates with the volume or activity level of business.

Vendor: The manufacturer or distributor of an item or product line.

W

Weight break: The shipment volume at which the LTL charges equal the TL charges at the minimum weight.

Y

Yard Management System (YMS): A system which is designed to facilitate and organize the coming, going, and staging of trucks and trucks with trailers in the parking "yard" that serves a warehouse, distribution, or manufacturing facility.

Z

Zone price: The constant price of a product at all geographic locations within the zone.

Zone skipping: For shipments via the U.S. Postal Service, depositing mail at a facility one or more zones closer to the destination. This option would benefit customers operating in close proximity to a zone border or shipping sufficient volumes to offset additional transportation costs.

Numbers

24-hour Manifest Rule (24-hour Rule): U.S. Customs rule requiring carriers to submit a cargo declaration 24 hours before cargo is laden aboard a vessel at a foreign port.

Index